SPINAL CATASTROPHISM

SPINAL CATASTROPHISM
A Secret History

THOMAS MOYNIHAN

URBANOMIC

To my scoliosis

Published in 2019 by
URBANOMIC MEDIA LTD,
THE OLD LEMONADE FACTORY,
WINDSOR QUARRY,
FALMOUTH TR11 3EX,
UNITED KINGDOM

Second revised edition 2020

Reprinted 2024

BRITISH LIBRARY CATALOGUING-IN-PUBLICATION DATA

A full catalogue record of this book is available
from the British Library

ISBN 978-1-913029-56-2

Distributed by the MIT Press, Cambridge, Massachusetts
and London, England

Type by Norm, Zurich
Printed and bound in the UK by
Short Run Press

www.urbanomic.com

CONTENTS

LIST OF FIGURES

PREFACE:
A PLUTARCHIAN CAUDA

IAIN HAMILTON GRANT

Aristotle reports that birds never fly backwards or tail-first.[1] This is not simply a fact of avian ethology, but an exponent of a world's choreographies, which are unlimited in principle. Thus any exhibition of the resulting world must *cohibit* these choreographies, i.e. must *enclose* their series in a finite form itself contributory to those movements.[2] Movements are worldmakers of exactly the sort that worlds make, etching ontogenesis over the earth, by way of which the latter acquires, so to speak, lithic 'morpholects' in consequence of what is made of them. A mark's being made renders any actual beginnings of directionality into referents for subsequent movements, but nothing dictates that such later movements merely continue or issue from their precursor states; later advents may reorient earlier, with morphogenetic vortices repeatedly refashioning or even revoking the axes of antecedent forms. Hence Aristotle's 'law of movement', according to which the antecedent has its actuality in the consequent, applies 'alike in figures and things animate'. It 'constitutes a series, each successive term of which potentially contains its predecessor, e.g. the square the triangle, the sensory power the self-nutritive...'. Whereas Aristotle clearly foresees a progressive anabasis issuing from this law, it is, as Schelling recognized, an important precursor of the theory of recapitulation, particularly as advanced by

---

1.   Aristotle goes further: 'In nature nothing has a movement backwards', *Progression of Animals* 706b30.

2.   This is Cherniss's translation of Plutarch's συνέχει in *Platonic Questions* 2 (1001A), serving Plutarch's distinction between a maker (both ποιητοῦ and δημιουργὸς) as separate from her work and 'the principle or force emanating from the parent [which] is blended in the progeny and cohabits its nature [as] part of the procreator'. Cohibition then is productive serial participation, not mere bonding, inclusion or control. Is a cohibitive art possible?

Kielmeyer, and as received by post-Kantian philosophy of nature.[3] That law, known variously (without implying any constancy of content) as the Meckel-Serres or Biogenetic aw, states that 'ontogeny recapitulates phylogeny', which, when taken at the level of *products*, postulates that the later stages of *lower* forms are recapitulated in the lower stages of *higher* products. This raises a plethora of exploratory vectors, amongst which I will note two.

(1) Does (or, prophetically: *will*) *finality of form* obtain in nature or, to put it differently, does ascent terminate with the actualisation of a particular form? That is to say, following Aristotle's formulation of the law of motion, can there be a form encircling all nature's potentials, amounting to the most final of final causations in postulating an *end* to nature? If such a form has, does, or will obtain, ontogenesis is cast not simply as productive individuation, as in Simondon, but, via a singular, persistent embodiment, as the progressive exhaustion of all development. For in this scenario, ontogenesis would terminate in an ontology incapable of producing its own revelation, i.e. it would become *ontographically* compromised.

---

3.   I draw here on the various translations of Aristotle, *De anima* 414b by R.D. Hicks (Cambridge: Cambridge University Press, 1907), W.S. Hett (Cambridge: Harvard University Press, 1957), J.A. Smith (Oxford: Oxford University Press, 1984) and, pivotally, F.W.J. Schelling, *Darstellung des rein-rationalen Philosophie* (*Sämtliche Werke*, ed. K.F.A. Schelling [Stuttgart and Augsburg: J.G. Cotta, 14 vols., 1856–61], vol 11, 375–6): 'The law, which Aristotle formulated on the occasion where he treats the three levels of soul (the nutritive, the sensitive and the intelligent), the law that "the antecedent always consists in the consequent according to potency", *Naturphilosophie* in particular applied this law to the greatest extent and with the greatest consistency....'

(2) How far back into phylogenetic history does recapitulation extend? Does the Great Circle entail that the achievement of the cervical zenith must coincide with the recovery, via phylogenetic katabasis, of the lifeless in the living? For in this Lovecraftian Orphism, polarities are maximally coincident to the degree that they maximally diverge. For the moment, we must note that if one is answered in the negative, so too must the other be, since to deny the first while asserting the second is to assert, inconsistently, that the exhaustion of nature is achieved from the first, or that *ontogeny never took place*.

Accordingly, the problems exposed by the very idea of a form of natural history, a 'form of development' (is a Platonic 'Becoming Itself by Itself' conceivable?) initiate the ungrounding Moynihan here mines, beginning from the mechanical agony of the 'bad back' resulting from the vain reorientation of lithic plains subjected to organic and so impermanent resculpting: of the possible termini of the spinal reorganisation of lithic cycles, the 'cervical zenith' is neither absolute nor final, but only the medium from which 'phylogenetic katabasis' descends. The ladder of beings does not lead ever upward but attains points of critical reversal, so that its uppermost rungs are bowed to coincide with those preceding their achievement. Will this fall terminate, like that of Icarus, in abrupt confrontation with the earth, or does the Great Circle descend deeper into phylic prehistory? What are the seeds of all becoming, the principles from which it emerges? If neither anabasis (the cervical zenith) nor katabasis (lithic reversion) attain finality of form, what ultimate determinants *can* the Great Circle have?

Here the question of a form of what is *intelligible* but by definition *insensible* assumes its fully amphibolic impact.

We might even ask whether topology does not in fact eliminate the prospect of a valid critique of the coincidence of the sensible and the intelligible, insofar as asking after the *form* of accomplished being is indissociably a problem for *noiesis* as for *poiesis*, for the being of appearing as much as for the appearing of being, and therefore entails an *ontographic productivity* rather than a critical dissociation.

Indeed, the ontology presented by all forms of finalism may therefore be identified by its double incapacity, for ontography (being's auto-exhibition) on the one hand, and for ontogeny (the production of being) on the other. Anontographic Being, incapable of self-revelation, is blind and anontogenetic, precisely because it is unproductive; ontography therefore implies ontogeny if sensibility neither obtains without the sensible production of the sensible, nor intelligibility without at least possible intellection. Ontography, accordingly, is *onto*-graphy insofar not only as graphisms *are* but additionally insofar as they are *because* they are *made* or *generated*. Ontography 'is' ontogenetically *only if* amongst the capacities of being are exhibitions that grasp being as its integral prosthesis. Ontogenetically, therefore, the graphic minutely augments being's unstable futures, just as the earth illuminates its possible pasts. Hence Richard Long's stone lines, for example, which are the autographs of a fragile actuality, the rectilinearity of which 'lithographs' the planetary surface with the rational operation that made them.

Moynihan's graphic strategies similarly generate articulate lines. They are not records of some blunt imitation, but *sensibly* remediate the knotted bonds diversely formed by the intelligible and the sensible: the biped's upright gait tends irrevocably to the quadruped's geophilia, the forward becomes the downward and the upward geophilically forward. Crucially, this axial twisting, with the geometric trappings of ideality, is not sensibly neutral since the axes it twists make *pain* (cervical curvature). Meanwhile, what we might call, in a Fichtean register, the *presentational stress* towards grasping the Great Circle forces noogeny beyond the forms in which it happens to be incident.

This has an unlikely precedent in Plutarch's *Platonic Questions*, where he unpacks Plato's likening 'of the All (τοῦ παντὸς) to a single line that has been divided into unequal segments' to reveal two entailments of this image of the universe, this cosmography:

(1) The line is continuous prior to the division.
(2) *Idea and perceptible are coterminous*, insofar as 'the intelligibles are patterns [...] of which perceptibles are semblances or reflections' (1001e).

The demonstration of this last point proceeds via a 'leading down' or *katabasis* through reasoning to geometry, then astronomy, harmonics, and somatics, leading upward again through abstraction. But the crucial hypothesis in this regard comes later, when Plutarch asks after the surface geometry on which the god 'traces the design of the nature of the all': the dodecahedron forms the preferred cosmogonic surface since it is 'furthest withdrawn from straightness' and 'associated with the spherical' (1003c–d). A continuous straight line traced on a planar surface differs topologically and in potency from the same line traced over a dodecahedron; where extremes do *not* meet, they must nevertheless cross. That ideas are always exhibited in a medium just if they imitate their generation from what antedates being and so renders the latter an outcome or product of that antecedence, means that their imitation consists in the attempt not to arrest or capture becoming, but to become an exponent of it.

And just as Plutarch combines the great Middle Platonic theme of 'the image of the universe'[4] with the conceiving of becoming, this accords with Plato's consistent formulation of the sensible and the intelligible in a twofold manner: genetically (as Bernard Bosanquet and Gernot Böhme pointed out at opposite ends of the twentieth century, Plato's address to Ideas is couched in causal rather than mimetic language)[5] and analogically: the graphic is to the sensible as the intelligible is to the ontological. Thus making or *poietics* is the condition of the analogical relation (though Plutarch asks whether there is a difference between *parent* and *maker*, between *birth* and *becoming*). Only both together enable the criticism of mimesis in *Republic* X, since the terminus of mimesis is not being but appearing, which reaches only part way up the ladder to being, while the Orphic triad formed of the musician, the lover, and the metaphysician seeks ascent not just to being, but beyond it, to become Lord of Being, or to imitate its source *qua* source.

Two issues thus emerge. Firstly, an ultimately causal asymmetry between being and mimesis makes intelligible-sensible analogy asymmetrical in turn by, secondly, setting the ontological dimension of the problem itself into the *ontogenetic*. If, that is, mimesis consists in the imitating of being, but being

---

4.   So, for example, Timaeus Locris, *On the Nature of the World and the Soul* 98d.

5.   Bosanquet notes the causal symbolism throughout Plato's discussion of the Ideas; Böhme presents the Ideas as included within generated and generating nature, due to the 'Platonic concept of the exhibition of an Idea in a medium', such that 'the coming to be and passing away are the emergence and disappearance of Ideas in a medium'. B. Bosanquet, *A Companion to Plato's Republic* (London: Rivington's, 1925), 241; G. Böhme, *Platons theoretische Philosophie* (Stuttgart: Metzler, 2000), 18, 288, 290.

is itself the outcome of generation, then generation by imitation (making) is closer to ontogeny than to its result. It is because the god is most godlike in so far as it creates that the *homoiosis theo* is adequate to the extent that production occurs, rather than insofar as the features of generation's products repeat. Although the initial problem posed by the partial or asymmetrical analogy of the sensible and the intelligible, or of the *ontological* and the *graphic*, concerns the making or emergence of the sensible from the intelligible, successful mimesis consists always in the revelation of the production of the Ideas, their 'emergence in a medium', so that *ontography recapitulates ontogeny*. The consequent problem, however, is what becomes of a graphism that imitates not the product of ontogenesis, but its *action* (Aristotle) or *operation* (Aquinas)?[6]

If a graphism, the poetics of the sensible whose tracks structure its objects, is mimetic of ontogenetic operations, how does it differ from the ontogeneses in approaching which, following the Platonic analogy, it falls short and falls, like Icarus's *katabasis*? And if it does not, then its ascent, its *anabasis*, takes it beyond being *in the sense that* a being will be its product if the mimesis of operation is itself operation. An operation is an operation just when it is determined as the operation that it turns out to be by the product it produces, and to which, for that same reason, it is irreducible. If it is not so determined, of course, then neither does this problem arise, nor is it mimetic. Once the productivity prior to being, the cause alike of sensibles and intelligibles, of being and beings—once this

---

6.　See Aristotle, *Poetics* 1449b24–5, Aquinas, *Summa Theologica* Ia, q.117, art 1. The latter reentered late modernity via Ananda K. Coomaraswamy's discussion of it in *The Transformation of Nature in Art* (Cambridge, MA: Harvard University Press, 1935), which exerted enormous influence on John Cage amongst others.

ontogenetic dimension is taken into account, graphism is no longer secondary in relation to a being as innocent of lines drawn as of becomings, but resumes its position amongst productives, making the line as much a worldmaker as any other.

Plutarch questions the 'generated gods' not out of scepticism, but in order to *conceive* the asymmetry of generation in relation to mere being. The instigating is not the coming to be, but *itself* comes to be being only *through* those consequents without which it would be neither being nor instigating. Being is the past tense of its presentation, and its presentation is the future of being, the additional mark by which being is augmented by *cohibition*, the encircling that 'bound[s] the unlimited with limits and shapes' (1001b). Cohibition in turn moulds the cohibited into the medium of both its contents' futurition and therefore of errant phylogeny: no additional element, if additional, leaves the bonded what it was, on pain of simply not being an additional element. One of the consequences of the indifference of generation and making is that mark-making either is ontogenetic or is not at all. That phylogenetic katabasis is initiated in a world wherein mark-making and its exhibition occurs resituates being as the medium worked by ontogenetic turbulence and an ontographic cohibition whose exhibition is itself ontogenetic. How revelatory, then, ontography: drawing what there is where drawing was not.

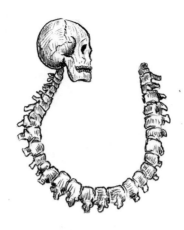

Person is a Forensick term.

John Locke, *An Essay Concerning Human Understanding* (1700)

Mere bones?

Stanisław Lem, *Imaginary Magnitude* (1973)

Reason, an Ignis fatuus, of the Mind,
Which leaving light of Nature, sense, behind;
Pathless and dan'grous wandring way it takes,
Through errors, Fenny-Boggs, and Thorny Brakes;
Whilst the misguided follower, climbs with pain,
Mountains of whimseys, heap'd in his own Brain:
Stumbling from thought to thought, falls headlong down,
Into doubt's boundless Sea, where like to drown,
Books bear him up a while, and makes him try,
To swim with Bladders of Philosophy;
In hopes still t'overtake th'escaping light,
The Vapour dances in his dazling sight,
Till spent, it leaves him to eternal Night.

John Wilmot, 2nd Earl Of Rochester,
'A Satyre against Reason and Mankind' (1679)

CERVICAL PROSPECTUS

Philosophical genealogy has lately been defined as the unveiling of 'causes masquerading as reasons'.[1] It works to reveal that those beliefs that we think depend upon *edifying reasons* in fact depend upon *contingent causes*, unveiling unaccountabilities in the structure of belief. Thus one may be seen to hold a particular belief not on account of deliberative ratiocination, but as a result of some accident of background or upbringing. (As Robert Brandom recounts, for Freud the latter would be something to do with the Oedipal drama, for Marx the effect of economic structures, and so forth).

At least, this characterises **classical genealogy**, as practised by what Brandom calls the 'great unmaskers of the nineteenth century'. Classical genealogy works to reveal *local* unaccountabilities within the edifice of belief. In both Freud and Marx, suspicion bottoms out in a privileged register, and the genealogical endeavour is constrained to specific 'vocabularies' (i.e., psychology or economics). In both cases it thus remains, in many respects, a rational enterprise: the critique of supposedly rational beliefs doesn't do away with rational belief as such. Despite critiquing reason, in classical genealogy the practice of suspicion remains beholden to the better reason and to the rational: it unmasks local arrogations in order to secure greater global accountability.

The strain of genealogy entreated here, however, is no mere question of 'causes masquerading as reasons', but very soon

---

1.   R. Brandom, *Reason, Genealogy, and the Hermeneutics of Magnanimity* (2014), <http://www.pitt.edu/~brandom/downloads/RGHM%20%2012-11-21%20a.docx>; see also *A Spirit of Trust: A Reading of Hegel's Phenomenology* (Cambridge, MA: Harvard University Press, 2019), 561–2.

becomes a matter of *tectonics parading as reasons*. In this **hypergenealogy**, the liquidation of deliberations, reasons, and justifications is no longer constrained to specific vocabularies, but is generalized across the entire edifice. By definition, this does away with even the residual fealty to rational order retained by classical genealogy. Dragged across the thorny brakes and fenny-boggs of its own errant history, reason—that cozening *ignis fatuus* of the mind—is plunged headlong into doubt's boundless sea. Hypergenealogy rejects all accountability, and thus all criteria of selectivity in our representations of an objective world—encouraging instead a libertine semantic irresponsibility. It is genealogy on steroids. For genealogically revealing *everything* that we think and do as utter arrogation is *necessarily recursive*. It cannot but also apply itself to itself. Hypergenealogizing therefore doesn't generate claims that are ever more just (for, by its own lights, there can be no 'better' or 'worse' claims), *it just enjoins the generation of ever more profligate, ever more exquisitely arrogated, claims*. There can no longer be better or worse claims, only more. Here, boundlessness kicks into productivity: doubt becomes an orgiastic agnoseology, selectivity is duly suspended, and arrogation careens towards force rather than fallacy: a power to pullulate in muscular wrong-mindedness rather than an eradicable error or an avenue of tendentious deselection. Genealogy on steroids tends toward conceptual wantonness, semantic lasciviousness. What ensues is a voluptuousness of vocabularies: a mangling of target domains—from phonetics to rheology, from psychology to volcanology—that any right-minded thinker would consider distinct. 'Suspicion' is bent inward onto itself, spiralling into **superlation**.[2]

---

2.   'Superlation' is defined by Johnson as 'Exaltation of anything beyond truth or propriety'. See S. Johnson, *A Dictionary of the English Language* (London, 1766).

From the perspective of right-minded reason, this is gross impiety. Yet, for many of the thinkers explored below, pollent superlation—rather than prudent suspicion—offers the promise of reconciling human experience with the enormities (in both senses of the term) of natural history. Instead of being responsible to an object=X, and thus having a world *in view*, superlation recaptures the ontogenetic dimension of enormous historicity, and forges the world *anew*. Ontogenesis, after all, has never itself been 'suspicious' in its gigantism. This is the promise of recapitulation: to redefine 'concept-mongering' not as a representational practice held accountable by natural history as a set object domain, but as natural history *in the making*. To be libertine is, in a sense, to reiterate the forces that made you: to allow graphism to once again reassume its proper place amongst the productives, to allow thought of the world to become a worldmaker. *What could be more historical than creation*?

And so, philosophic assiduity be damned, 'fill me from the crown to the toe topfull' with impious enormity. Supererogation and suspicion pushed aside, this book explores where, and how far, certain (arguably wrong-minded) thinkers have been able to travel along the twisted path of a genealogy that isn't suspicious of the winding relation between planet and person but, rather, revisits (and in some instances reignites) the superlative dimensions of this filiation. This twisted path, again and again, turns out to be precisely that line from 'crown' to 'toe': the vertical axis of the body and its bony ledger, the spinal column. This is because, for a nature with a history, an anatomy is just a memory: and we have had spines for as long as we've had brains. Can it be a coincidence that so many thinkers have been drawn to a certain *heady* admixture of these notions—

a theoretical superlation that has only lately been christened 'Spinal Catastrophism'?

The chief contemporary exponent of this hypergenealogical heresy is the notorious Professor Daniel Charles Barker. Yet, as we shall see, in incorporating Spinal Catastrophism into his 'Geocosmic Theory of Trauma', Barker drew upon a rich history. Before we explore its wealth of delirious superlations, however, it will pay to establish the philosophical stakes involved in the questions Barker and others drew upon. What exactly is involved in the relation between person and planet?

C2. CERVICAL ZENITH

In his first Critique, Immanuel Kant orients reason in relation to the planetary surface, and thus to human bipedalism. He writes that, although the earth appears to one's immediate senses as a flat surface extending indefinitely to the horizon, we can nevertheless, 'in accordance with *a priori* principles', know that it is a 'sphere' with 'diameter', 'magnitude' and 'limits'.[1] Clearly intending a comparison between the two, the philosopher then adds that 'our reason' is, in identical fashion, 'not like an indeterminably extended plane' but 'must rather be compared to a sphere'.[2]

This comparison, between the space of reasons and that of our globe, serves to dramatize Kant's master-idea of the **togetherness** of empirical receptivity and conceptual articulation: the conviction that, although the cascading content of sensation is unbounded or infinite (in the same sense as, in traversing a sphere's continuous surface, we discover no boundary or edge), the conceptual functions and maxims of reason governing this experience afford to it structuring 'limits' (just as, embedded within three dimensions, the sphere is indeed spatially finite).[3] Crucially, it is these bounds alone that make knowledge possible, in that they anatomize our judgings into those that are correct and those that are incorrect; with them in place, we no longer simply *perceive* objects in a prehensive sense—our perceptions gain a standard of *objectivity* against

1. I. Kant, *Critique of Pure Reason*, tr. P. Guyer and A.W. Wood (Cambridge: Cambridge University Press, 2007), 653 [A759/B787].

2. Ibid., 654 [A762/B790].

3. Topologically speaking, the figure of the earth is a manifold that has no *boundary*, yet is *finite*.

which they can be continually appraised and upbraided (thus contending, in our unfolding engagements with the world, for the epithet 'objective').

According to the critical philosophy, such limits are to be interpreted exclusively in juridical terms: they concern the *irrealis* scope of 'ought' rather than the *realis* scope of 'is'. Yet in selecting this particular tellurian image, Kant unwittingly reminds us that we do not 'orient' ourselves in thinking through a judicial 'ground of differentiation' alone.[4] For we are able to orient ourselves upon Earth's mundane sphere only because of *the contingent fact* of our vertical posture, our orthograde backbone. Reason's supererogations rest upon our standing so. And this introduces a whole new plot thread, a cord upon which genealogy can pull.

In his *Physical Geography*, having once again compared the rational 'whole' to the telluric 'whole', Kant suggests that each person may triangulate their location within spheriform terrestrial space, and thus unequivocally orient themselves, by drawing a line upward from their head into the heavens, and downward through their pelvis into the earth.[5] One's latitude may then be ascertained by measuring the angle between this extended spinal axis and the earth's axis of rotation.

It is only because, uniquely among vertebrates, the human spine's axis traces a continuation of Earth's own radius, that we

---

4.   I. Kant, 'What Does It Mean to Orient Oneself in Thinking?', tr. A.W. Wood, in A.W. Wood and G. Di Giovanni (eds.), *Religion and Rational Theology* (Cambridge: Cambridge University Press, 1996), 8:315.

5.   'I have to assume a centre at the middle of the earth as in the case of any other sphere or circle. From this, I can draw a line through the position I occupy over my head and from there back again through the centre'. I. Kant, *Physical Geography*, tr. O. Reinhardt, in E. Watkins (ed.), *Natural Science* (Cambridge: Cambridge University Press, 2012), 9:158–9:171.

can extrapolate its trajectory *ad coelum et ad inferos*—upwards towards a supernal **zenith** and downwards to a hypogene **nadir**.[6] Drawing an imaginary great circle whose diameter connects the points of this imagined zenith and its caudal nadir as antipodes, the observer can become aware of themselves as the centre point of a so-called **celestial meridian**.[7] From here, they can locate themselves upon the planet by measuring the angle between the celestial pole (the point around which the stars appear to rotate) and the zenith of their vertebral axis (the point at which the extended line of the spine pierces outer space). This allows one to compute one's latitude, or, as Kant puts it, 'the distance [from] the equator', and thus to acquire one's North-South coordinates.[8]

It would therefore seem that a quirk of spinal morphology is responsible for placing humans in direct relation with the figure of the earth, fomenting the human propensity for **geodesic abstraction** in a fashion entirely barred to pronograde quadrupeds—those flatlanding crust-crawlers who experience the planet only as a surface indefinitely far extended.[9]

---

6. 'This is then the zenith and nadir, that each person determines for and through himself.' Kant, *Physical Geography*, 9:173. This prolonged spinal trajectory also accounts for humans' long-standing concern with exactly how far property rights extend downward into the earth's mantle. At present, for instance, each US landowner 'owns a slender column of rock, soil, and other matter stretching downward over 3900 miles from the surface to a theoretical point in the middle of the earth'. J.G. Sprankling, 'Owning the Centre of the Earth', *UCLA Law Review* 55 (2008), 979–1040: 981.

7. 'Therefore, each can also have his own meridian.' Kant, *Physical Geography*, 9:171.

8. Kant, *Physical Geography*, 9:173.

9. 'It is for lack of this human circumstance that quadrupeds cannot, or need not, orient themselves'. H. Müller-Sievers, 'Tidings of the Earth: Towards a History of Romantic *Erdkunde*', in M. Helfer (ed.), *Amsterdamer Beiträge zur neueren Germanistik* 47 (2000), 47–73: 50.

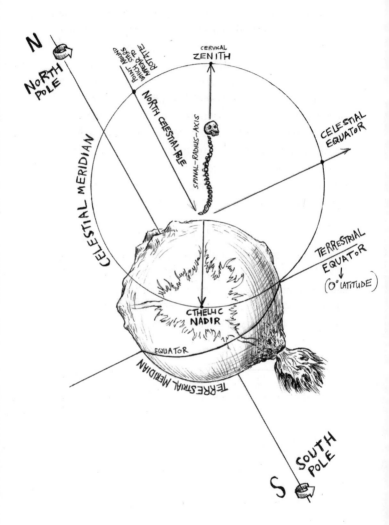

Fig. 1. The axes of terrestrial life

Triggering the carving up of the planet with reticulating grati-cules and navigational rhumb lines, sapience's conquering of global space proceeds from and rests upon a lumbar founda-tion whose verticality sets our species apart, instigating a ratio-technical line of development extending from the first anthropoid's binocular gaze upon its forelimb workspace all the way to the geostationary satellite high above.[10] What Kant's spinal thought-experiment hints at, then, is that *Homo sapiens*' ability to exert cognizance and control on a planetary scale results from the same species-specific peculiarity as its sus-ceptibility to back pain.

---

10.   Assignation of longitude, or East-West coordinates, was achieved via the further *conquering of time*: only by instating an entirely fabricated 'prime me-ridian', with the use of accurate chronometers, could one 'end-stop' the globe's non-Euclidean and boundless surface with a conventional and fixed reference point.

Prior to this, Kant had already allowed osteology to productively constrain cognition by emphasizing the importance of the subjective incommensurability of Left and Right in anchoring spatial orientation.[1] He used this observation to demonstrate that our specific sense of space is a 'form of intuition' (rather than any necessary or independently verifiable feature of reality separate from our sensing). Thus, Kant rallies incommensurability as an illustration in order to further his overall rationalist argument. However, such Left-Right 'enantiomorphism'—the fact that each hand is a non-superimposable mirror image of the other (an 'incongruous counterpart')—derives from our **chiral handedness**, which is a direct consequence of our anciently inherited **bilateral symmetry**—that is, symmetry along a sagittal, i.e. spinal, plane.[2] The fact that Kant looks to

---

1. Kant had fixated on this notion as early as 1768: 'the ultimate ground, on the basis of which we form our concept of directions in space, derives from the relation of [the] intersecting planes [of] our bodies'. He notes that we derive left, right, above, and below from the coronal and axial planes, since they arise from 'the mechanical organization of the human body' (and, thus, our bilaterian architecture). I. Kant, 'Concerning the Ultimate Ground of the Differentiation of Directions in Space', in D. Walford and R. Meerbote (eds., trs.), *Theoretical Philosophy, 1755–1770* (Cambridge: Cambridge University Press, 1992), 361–72. Likely running with the Kantian implication, Lorenz Oken later wrote that 'through the medium of the bones the distinction between back and belly has been definitely established in the animal, and, as a consequence thereof, the distinction also of right from left. Before a formation of bone exists, the animal is for the most part a round cylinder' (L. Oken, *Elements of Physiophilosophy*, tr. A. Tulk [London: Ray Society, 1847], 368).

2. I. Kant, *Prolegomena to Any Future Metaphysics*, tr. J.W. Ellington (Indianapolis: Hackett, 1977), 4:286. See also J. Van Cleave and R.E. Frederick (eds.), *The Philosophy of Right and Left: Incongruent Counterparts and the Nature of Space* (New York: Springer, 1991).

our hands in order to support his master-idea of 'togetherness' then suggests an even deeper connexion between spirit and bone. To fully grasp this, we need to explore Kantian togetherness.

Kant's comparison of self-legislating reason to the globe's antipodal self-enclosure captures, in an image, the fact that the very possibility of knowledge is secured by a kind of closure or infolding. It is only by generating its own limits—imposing its own rules upon itself—that knowledge becomes possible. For, as Kant argued, merely *having* a perception is not the same as being *justified* in believing one's perception veracious. Talking of how the world 'objectively is' is therefore inseparable from some grasp of what is *permissible* and *impermissible* for me to say about it; and this distinction, in turn, cannot come from sensible passivity or brute perception (as Hume noticed, sensations license no rules); it can only come from actively electing to impose limits upon oneself. In other words, just as the sphere presents an unbounded surface *and* a finite and definite shape because of its enclosure of itself in three dimensions, so too is a bounded space of *possible* knowledge—rather than a boundless mess of unconnected sensations—made available only by the self-relation involved in setting oneself rules of conduct or permissible judgements (that are not to be found within perception itself, just as the boundedness of the sphere is not to be found merely by traversing its unbounded surface like a blind beetle). There is no objective experience that does not harbour a covert relation to the justification one has in believing said experience to be objective. (There is no knowledge without self-relation, no consciousness without self-consciousness, no sphere without antipodal closure.)

Cognition, that is, is constitutively governed by its own rules of organisation and regulation, which are *sui generis* in the sense of being self-defined and endogenous, or produced by the increasing tendency of a system to take *only* its own states as functionally efficacious or informative (in other words, collapsing into yourself is the same as the generation of spontaneous 'criteria' through which alone you can become conscious that your experiences can be wrong and, thus, become conscious of yourself *as* a conscious agent). It is a most fundamental lesson of Kantian purism: a rational actor, insofar as it is rational, can *only* respond to rational arguments. This is what Kant meant by 'spontaneity'. Yet, at the same time, it is also true of a nervous system that it can *only* experience its own states or its own inputs. It is receptive, of course, *but only in the 'language' of its own inputs*. In the same way in which a model Kantian rational agent can only obey rational rules (i.e., those set by itself), there is a definite sense in which a *nervous system only experiences itself.* Both, in other words, are forms of enclosure. And they echo one other across the aeons. There is no such thing as an innocent metaphor, and we will draw our genealogical thread from this insight hidden in Kant's selection of chirality and bipedality as illustrations of rationality.

From an aeonic perspective, the entrenched constraints of discursive initiation (**glottogony**) are revealed as only *the most recent frontier* of life's infolding collapse into its own spontaneous parameter space—whether anatomized by rational rules or sensorial modalities. Both rules and senses are generators of endogeneity, thus allowing for the possibility of formal comparison. For it is only by coiling into further self-relation—in the sense of a system's propensity to constrain functionally relevant states to 'internal' states—that an outer world, of increasing phenomenological immersion and categorial complexity, emerges.[3] Orientation (upon a rolling planet as much as within a discursive exchange) is *multilayered, historically variegated,* and *polymodal.* 'Immediacy', wherever it is encountered, is a secondary product of the organism's tendency to disappear up its own ganglia (and, later, its own glottis). So both cerebrospinal ensconcement and semantogenic englobement are legible as thresholds of an inward collapse that was initiated around six hundred million years ago with the evolution of nervous architectures.[4] We, as representational systems, have never been in immediate contact with anything except our own modellings: this applies not just to propositionally structured knowledge but also to representational states in general, whether sentential or sentient.[5] Hence worldedness proceeds not only from rational apertures but also nervous ones (where 'aperture' is just the constraining-through-closure requisite for a perspective), and we can generalize over vertebral and conceptual armatures: for finitude (as an implexion into system endogeneity identifiable across both neuronal and juridical forms of constraint) concordantly embeds its own prehistory. **Morpho-space** and conceptual space echo one

---

3. If one wants to remain safely within a right-minded and cautious Kantian perspective here, note that functional comparison need not require causal reducibility. The model of the analogy-relation between different 'functional encasements'—be they synaptic or syntactic—can be one of *nested saltation,* and not *substantive community,* and each new casement can still be said to echo those before it, *even in their causal irreducibility one to the other.* Endogeneity *just is* irreducibility to a surrounding milieu.

4. 'With complex nervous systems in place in the Cambrian, it is likely that basic neural nets were present in the Precambrian Ediacaran animals, dating back to 600 million years ago'. D. Schulze-Makuch and W. Bains, *The Cosmic Zoo: Complex Life on Many Worlds* (New York: Springer, 2017), 157.

5. We are in touch always with *representantia,* never with *representanda.*

another across the aeons. We have been collapsing inward since long before we began to rationally orient ourselves on this planet.

An important upshot of Kant's definition of epistemicity as functional closure is his conclusion that time is something actively generated by this infolding, rather than passively given. Temporality is an active organisation and ordering of experiences—something that is *produced* by operations of **chronoception**.[1]

Importantly, when comparing global space to rational space, Kant couldn't help but muse that, although we comprehend the terrestrial 'magnitude', we remain 'ignorant in regard to the objects that this surface might contain'.[2] Following his analogy, the same sentiment might well be applied equally to reason and its own 'grounds of differentiation'. Indeed, exploiting just such a suggestion, Schopenhauer would later assert that '[c]onsciousness is the mere surface of our mind, and of this, as of the globe, we do not know the interior, but only the crust'.[3]

By invoking an axis of depth, this psychogeological hypothesis also implies a historical or genetic dimension to mind. (It was, as we shall later explore, during Kant's era that the idea

---

1.   Metzinger: 'Of course, all physically realized processes of information conduction and processing take time. For this reason, the information available in the nervous system in a certain, very radical sense never is *actual* information: the simple fact alone that the trans- and conduction velocities of different sensory modules differ leads to the necessity of the system defining elementary ordering thresholds and "windows of simultaneity" for itself. Within such windows of simultaneity it can, for instance, integrate visual and haptic information into a multimodal object representation—an object that we can consciously see and feel at the same time.' T. Metzinger, *Being No One: The Self-Model Theory of Subjectivity* (Cambridge, MA: MIT Press, 2003), 25.

2.   Kant, *Critique of Pure Reason*, 653 [A759/B787].

3.   A. Schopenhauer, *The World as Will and Representation*, tr. E.F.J. Payne (New York: Dover, 2 vols., 1969), vol. 1, 136.

of *natural history* was truly first consolidating: the idea of nature having a chronology outstripping human experience, one that was, at the time, being first mapped onto Earth's superposed strata.) Furthermore, given that chronoception is itself a product of mindedness, a corollary implication is that *time itself has a history*. And indeed, the phylogenesis of time receptivity can be recounted; it is a neural saga that is legible in the ossified memory of the regionalizing and segmenting spine.[4] But this

---

4.   Further expanding Kant's collocation of the human sensorium and our upright standing upon the planetary mass, gravitational pull has lately been unveiled as itself an important perceptual anchor. Gravity's terrestrial ubiquity, it is theorized by Lacquaniti et al., allows it to provide the perfect frame of reference for both space and time within our nervous system, a frame which emerges from multisensory cues (visual, vestibular, proprioceptive, interoceptive). Invariant downward pull 'defines a three-dimensional Cartesian frame' for space, whilst the 'gravitational acceleration of falling objects can provide a time-stamp on events, because the motion duration of an object accelerated by gravity over a given path is fixed'. See F. Lacquaniti et al., 'Gravity in the Brain as a Reference for Space and Time Perception', *Multisensory Research* 28:5–6 (2015), 397–426. This leads Jörges and López-Moliner to define gravity-related perceptual processes as a 'strong prior' within a Bayesian framework. See B. Jörges and J. López-Moliner, 'Gravity as a Strong Prior: Implications for Perception and Action', *Frontiers in Human Neuroscience* 11:203 (2017). Swanson has already linked such predictive 'hyperpriors' back to Kant's 'categories' and 'forms of appearance' as the organizing principles of empirical experience. See L.R. Swanson, 'The Predictive Processing Paradigm Has Roots in Kant', *Frontiers in Systems Neuroscience* 10:79 (2016). This, then, *is how the planetary mass canalizes formal properties of our experiential universe*. Moreover, the 'insuperability' of such deep calibration (or gravitational 'ur-framing') raises interesting problems for space travel and the prospect of life in earth-discrepant gravities. This, in turn, raises further questions concerning the potential variance of alien sensoria and the constraining principles under which *any* cogito must needs function within our universe. (Dunér and Osvath have dubbed this type of inquiry '*astrocognition*'. See D. Dunér, 'Astrocognition: Prolegomena to a Future Cognitive History of Exploration', in U. Landfester, N.-L. Remus, K.-U. Schrogl, and J.-C. Worms [eds.], *Humans in Outer Space—Interdisciplinary Perspectives* [New York: Springer, 2011], 117–40; and M. Osvath,

story starts not inside (the spine-as-fossil-record), but, far outside, multiple light years away (though the meaning of 'inside' and 'out' here become progressively more twisted).

Solar flux barrages the earth's atmosphere with 174 pet-awatts of radiance,[5] creating the stark energy differentia required for the cascading upswell of systems that achieve quasi-sta-bility through unceasing negative regulation—what we call 'life'.[6] Only such constant perturbation affords the budget for such a system to constantly expend its resources to maintain itself: and in continually reproducing itself in this way—in main-taining system invariance and propagation via negative feed-back—said system collapses into causal circularity.[7] It causes itself to exist, and in so doing becomes more involved in caus-ing itself to exist. This generates, spontaneously, proto-criteria for 'failure' or 'success' insofar as the system has now 'defined' itself by its propensity to stay within a range of acceptable states for self-reproduction and self-propagation. (It begins to

'Astrocognition: A Cognitive Zoology Approach to Potential Universal Principles of Intelligence', in D. Dunér [ed.], *The History and Philosophy of Astrobiology: Perspectives on Extraterrestrial Life and the Human Mind* [Newcastle: Cambridge Scholars, 2013], 49–66.) Intelligence will have to overcome such paro-chial constraints if it is to reach much beyond the tellurian cradle. For the time being, however, we can only speculate upon what extraterrestrial analogues to our own sensorium and motorium may look like. See J.L. Cranford, *Astrobiologi-cal Neurosystems: Rise and Fall of Intelligent Life Forms in the Universe* (New York: Springer, 2014), and N.A. Cabrol, 'Alien Mindscapes—A Perspective on the Search for Extraterrestrial Intelligence', *Astrobiology* 16:9 (2016), 661–76.

5.   C.J. Rhodes, 'Solar Energy: Principles and Possibilities', *Science Progress* 93 (2010), 37–112.

6.   More precisely, they achieve *metastability*. To paraphrase Wiener, living organisms are metastable Maxwell demons whose stable state is to be dead. N. Wiener, *Cybernetics: Or Control and Communication in the Animal and the Machine* (Cambridge, MA: MIT Press, 1965), 59.

7.   R. Poli, *Introduction to Anticipation Studies* (New York: Springer, 2017), 18.

act *as if* it is an end unto itself.) In reaction to environmental perturbation, it pinches itself off into its own spontaneous 'parameter space' of regulative function, defined by these proto-criteria for propagative success, and therefore comes to be *defined* by its tendency to dynamically remain within this state space. And, since negative regulation is also feedforward control, a progressively more ramified responsivity to external stressors—the characteristic which, through the course of evolution, eventually leads to neural blossoming—is also, inevitably, the inward generation of time, the incipience of **chronoreceptivity**.

The sun, appropriately, is life's inceptive abiogenetic stressor as well as remaining, to this day, its prime '**zeitgeber**' (its circadian 'time-giver' in the parlance of chronobiologists).[8] Provoked by such enveloping hostility, toxicity, and agitation, abiogenetic implosion into functional self-relation allows the living system to better present its own states to itself so as to gain feedforward control over oncoming perturbation. This predictive core constitutive of all living process—highlighted from Maturana to Rosen—is testament to the fact that the organism exists and persists through its exposure, and anticipatory responsivity, to hazard.[9] Known in biology as **hormesis**, the idea is that intermittent exposure to environmental

---

8.   J. Aschoff, 'Exogenous and Endogenous Components in Circadian Rhythms', *Cold Spring Harbor Symposia on Quantitative Biology* 25 (1960), 11–28.

9.   'A living system, due to its circular organization [...] functions always in a predictive manner'. H.R. Maturana, 'Biology of Cognition', in H.R. Maturana and F.J. Varela, *Autopoiesis and Cognition: The Realization of the Living* (Dordrecht: Reidel, 1980), 26–7. See also R. Rosen, *Anticipatory Systems: Philosophical, Mathematical, and Methodological Foundations* (New York: Springer, 2012).

stressors provokes compensatory, adaptive, and beneficial response.[10] Stress, whilst provoking the organism to retreat and fall into itself, foments 'biological robustness'.[11] This applies at the cellular and macroevolutionary levels, so that the advent of the CNS can be explained as the phyletic progeny of such propulsive antagonism—because the CNS is nature's organ of anticipation.[12] Crofts refers to this dynamic of environmental perturbations forcing ramifying feedforward responsivity as '**chronognosis**', arguing that, in a sense, 'all living organisms are aware of time'. He notes, however, that '**chronognostic range**' varies with neural intricacy:

> With the increasing complexity of metazoans, development of a nervous system, differentiation of organs of sense, and development of the head-tail polarity, and a brain and memory in higher animals, the scope of behavioural complexity also increases, and along with this, the complexity of mechanisms [for] chronognostic range.[13]

Indeed, at the neurophysiological level, timekeeping is not performed by specialized circuits or dedicated systems, but appears to be a ubiquitous and 'intrinsic property of neurons' themselves.[14] There is evidence that even the

---

10.   M.P. Mattson, 'Hormesis Defined', *Ageing Research Review* 7:1 (2008), 1–7.

11.   H. Kitano, 'Towards a Theory of Biological Robustness', *Molecular Systems Biology* 3:137 (2007).

12.   M.P. Mattson, 'The Fundamental Role of Hormesis in Evolution', in M.P. Mattson and E.J. Calabrese (eds.), *Hormesis: A Revolution in Biology, Toxicology and Medicine* (New York: Springer, 2010), 57–68.

13.   A.R. Crofts, 'Life, Information, Entropy, and Time: Vehicles for Semantic Inheritance', *Complexity* 13:1 (2007), 14–50: 23–4.

14.   D.V. Buonomano and A. Goel, 'Temporal Interval Learning in Cortical

minuscule brains of insects such as bumblebees exhibit an operant, rather than merely circadian, sense of temporal interval.[15] Nonetheless, as neural circuitry intricates, so too does chronoceptive scope. And this, of course, demands further self-interment.

Cultures is Encoded in Intrinsic Network Dynamics', *Neuron* 91 (2016), 1-8. Cf. R.B. Ivy and J.E. Schlerf, 'Dedicated and Intrinsic Models of Time Perception', *Trends in Cognitive Sciences* 12:7 (2008), 273–80.

15.   P. Skorupski and L. Chittka, 'Animal Cognition: An Insect's Sense of Time?', *Current Biology* 16:19 (2006), 851–3. See also A.B. Barron and C. Klein, 'What Insects Can Tell Us About the Origins of Consciousness', *PNAS* 113:18 (2016), 4900–4908. Both articles, inquiring into the insect lifeworld, quote Kant's views on time as transcendentally presupposed by subjective experience: there may never be a Newton of a blade of grass, but could there be a Kant of *dipteran* spatiotemporality?

Indeed, both life and time-receptivity—in their intimacy and congenitality—can be mutually defined as nothing but self-interments.[1] Only by retreating inwards, into fluency with its own system-states, does the organism progressively separate itself from the causal absolutism of the surrounding milieu, obtaining ever more functional leeway and behavioural lability via increasing delamination from its immediate environs. (This is why the CNS has long been seen as the *organ of individuation*.) The ability *to do things* is arrived at in this way: this goes for the capacity to digest the outside world as much as the possibility of motile—rather than sessile—modes of life within it. Locomotive autonomy—across all relevant modalities, whether bioenergetic or biomechanical—is bequeathed by potentiating implosivity. First emerging as the outpouching of a complexifying gut, then as the innervating escape into the organism's own CNS-simulation, and finally as the deposition of an empowering yet finitude-entrenching recognitive encasement, evolution's ongoing investment into its own systemic insularity migrates outwards from gastronomic, to phanero-scopic, to juridical domains—all in step with incremental chronognostic range. Again, orienting yourself on the planet would be impossible without all these layers in play. Orientation has a prehistory.

And of course, after the archenteron's gastrulating introversion into a complexified alimentary tract, the neurulation of

---

1. 'We found ourselves working as slave components of systems whose scales and complexities we could not comprehend. Were we their parasites? Were they ours? Either way we became components of our own imprisonment'. S. Plant, *Zeroes and Ones: Digital Women + The New Technoculture* (London: Fourth Estate, 1998), 4.

the nervous system provides the frontier of collapse shared by all eumetazoans. The centralizing nervous system and its spinal support represent the next portentous stage in the *sealing off* of the organism into its own globally enclosing world-model.

For only by variegating the ways in which a system reliably and differentially actuates and effects itself (thus further generating criteria of saliency and relevancy for adaptively beneficial representings) does a robust and differentiated external world increasingly arise without (in parallel with the divarication and tumefaction of axonal projections and sensory arrays within). Therefore, the centralization of nervous architectures (the centripetal involution of simple radial cnidarian neuroid nets into segmented bilateral annelid systems, etc.) presents, across phanerozoic time, the procedural *building of a world* (or 'worlds', depending on one's phyletic ecumenism).[2] Since 1925, this world-generating structure has been referred to as a **chronotope**, a term that emerged from the intersection of biosemiotics, neuroanatomy, and earth systems science in Soviet proto-cybernetics. Proposed by the Russian neurophysiologist A.A. Ukhtomsky (1875–1942), it refers to the way in which the organism nervously generates, and inhabits, its own globally unified space-time through the active coordination of inputs and excitations. With an explicitly acknowledged Kantian heritage, Ukhtomsky's notion of the chronotope (хронотоп)

---

2.   It appears that nervous systems are not monophyletic and are instead examples of **homoplasy**: they have emerged separately several times through convergent evolution. See L. Moroz, 'On the Independent Origins of Complex Brains and Neurons', *Brain, Behavior and Evolution* 74:3 (2009), 177–90. To expropriate a phrase from Kuhn, this insinuates the existence of different clades 'practicing their trades in parallel worlds'. T. Kuhn, *The Structure of Scientific Revolutions* (Chicago: University of Chicago Press, 1962), 150.

highlights the fact that time and space (and hence a coherent world) are outcomes dynamically generated by the complexifying CNS.[3]

This conception therefore confirms that the more the organism implodes intradermally—exaggerating its synaptic architectures of fluency with itself—the further an extradermal universe will explode for it. (This is the consecration of what Charles Sanders Peirce called a 'phaneron'. Ergo, the phaneron, properly considered, is a phanerozoic inheritance.)[4]

The CNS, accordingly, represents an *egress from immediacy* (and a chronotopic escapement) to the exact degree

---

3.   Ukhtomsky's conviction was that 'we perceive the world as anticipations of its future'. See I. Tuomi, 'Chronotopes of Foresight: Models of Time-Space in Probabilistic, Possibilistic and Constructivist Futures', *Futures and Foresight Science* 1:1 (2019), 2. Inspired by his studies in how functional coordination emerges from phase synchronization and heterochronia in the activity of nerve centres, Ukhtomsky was led to propose that the CNS actively generates temporality. See A. Kurismaa, 'Perspectives on Time and Anticipation in the Theory of Dominance', in M. Nadin (ed.), *Anticipation: Learning from the Past—The Russian/Soviet Contributions to the Science of Anticipation* (New York: Springer, 2015), 37–58. A chronotope, therefore, becomes legible as the organism's 'frame of anticipation' wherein '[p]erceiving an object automatically implies the anticipation of its world line'. (Ukhtomsky had borrowed Minkowski's term **world line** to express an object's path in 4-dimensional time-space.) As Chebanov glosses, Ukhtomsky thought that the 'organization of these worlds [can] be thought of in terms of geometrodynamics' and, accordingly, they become amenable to 'mathematical description'. This, in turn, allows a *comparative neuroanatomy of world*s, or, a 'non-hominoid thesaurus' for differing states of worldedness. See S.V. Chebanov, 'Ukhtomsky's Idea of Chronotope as Frame of Anticipation', in Nadin (ed.), *Anticipation,* 137–50. Moreover, the semiotician M.M. Bakhtin duly inherited Ukhtomsky's notion and applied it to analysing the preconscious organisational principles embedded across fictional worlds: thus initiating a comparative history (or, perhaps, palaeontology) of the semantic phases of human worldedness.

4.   C.S. Peirce, *Collected Papers* (Cambridge, MA: Harvard University Press, 8 vols., 1931), vol. 1, 141.

that it is the generation of an *entirely artefactual reality* ('kept honest', and thus teleofunctionally utile, by the 'constraining affordances' of incoming sense-data).[5] It is, then, paradoxically, a self-propelling reality escape—via informatic and chronotopic invagination—that endows the interned organism with the power over reality first presaged by the emergence of brain-masses in predatory flatworms, and which blossoms forth in the simulative universe of the encephalizing craniate cortex.[6] A cosmogony belated by some 13.3 billion years. Indeed, it truly is a form of 'egress' in that it is only via *productive forgetting* that such a system generates salient (and therefore adaptively utile) worldedness.[7] The CNS operates as an emulator that doesn't emulate its own emulating procedures (i.e., we do not experience ourselves *as* a ganglia stack), and in consequence we (as system-denizens) feel *in direct and immediate contact* with the reality emulated (or within which we are interned). A nervous system, then, is a 'reality escape' precisely in so far as it is a generator of 'artificial reality'. Redacting upstream

---

5. L. Floridi, 'A Plea for Non-Naturalism as Constructionism', *Minds and Machines* 27 (2017), 269–85.

6. H.B. Sarnat and M.G. Netsky, 'The Brain of the Planarian as the Ancestor of the Human Brain', *Canadian Journal of Neurological Sciences* 12:4 (1985), 296–302. Recent phylogenomics suggests the possibility of an even more basal **urbilaterian** origin for brain development, however. See N. Riebli and H. Reichert, 'The First Nervous System', in S.V. Shepherd (ed.), *The Wiley Handbook of Evolutionary Neuroscience* (Oxford: Blackwell, 2017), 125-52: 126.

7. Again taking chronoception as our example, simultaneity is achieved, as Metzinger argues by way of Pöppel, by the 'opening of time windows' precisely via system-wide deletion of 'information about [the system's] own physical processuality' (this is achieved 'by not defining temporal relations between elements given within such a basal window of simultaneity'). Concordantly, our sense of synchronous integration (i.e. temporal simultaneity) is achieved by productive elimination of the asynchronous operations that produce it. Metzinger, *Being No One*, 129–39.

processes in its own pipeline of world-manufacture, nervous enclosure makes naive realists of us all.

What then is the spinal column, if not a megalith raised to the mineralizing trace of the organism's diaspora into its own bloating sensorium—each level of axial segmentation a monument to further neural self-entanglement—dorsally fulgurating our cephalocaudal axis, an *outward memory of inward collapse*? Indeed, despite the fact that cephalopods exhibit extravagantly complex nervous organization, the most integrated and encephalized CNSs belong unequivocally to vertebrates, for whom metameric spinal regionalization repeats into compartmentalizing brain.[8] A pulsing paradox, intelligence enters the worldly scene by emigrating into its own chronotope.[9]

Nature attempts to escape itself by creating a nervous system. Indeed, when the patient of this phyletic reality escape becomes, in some small degree, capable of reflecting upon itself *as such*, it first attains the ability to model itself modelling and, by conjointly becoming capable of directed intervention, exhibits *minimal self-consciousness*. Capturing the fallibility of one's perception forces one to reflect on the distinction between oneself and world. Apperception pieces itself together henceforth as escape velocity, or jailbreak, from claustrophobic union with inertial world-immersion: for, by migrating the abiogenetic energetic gradient of 'intradermal' and 'extradermal' into properly temporal and modal dimensions, via the inauguration of language-use and coterminous expansion of working memory,

---

8.   B.U. Budelmann, 'The Cephalopod Nervous System: What Evolution Has Made of the Molluscan Design', in O. Breidbach and W. Kutsch (eds.), *The Nervous Systems of Invertebrates: An Evolutionary and Comparative Approach* (Birkhäuser Verlag: Switzerland, 1995), 115–38.

9.   This is simply another way of acknowledging that everything in intelligence is self-earnt, or, there is nothing arrogated therein.

mere attentional economy involutes into executive function, goal-directedness—and mental time travel.[10]

Baptized by evolutionary psychologists as '**proscopic chronesthenia**' or '**autonoetic consciousness**', the tendency to actively manipulate futures presents the most ostentatious reality egress since our ancestral cerebrospinal entrapment.[11] (Debate persists concerning nonhuman capacities in this department.)[12] Becoming first able to wield subjunctives and conditionals, intellect now feeds on newfound disequilibrations between 'the possible' and 'the merely actual' such that it *cannot but* orient itself toward redesigning the world, because it can now not only *imagine things otherwise* but also *reverse-engineer their workings*.[13] Moreover, the ability to talk about the possible—rather than being trapped within the exigent present—is what extends the human chronotope or *Umwelt* to encompass immense illimitable spatiotemporal distances, allowing it to prospect unseen, unexampled, and non-present

---

10.   T. Suddendorf and M.C. Corballis, 'The Evolution of Foresight: What is Mental Time Travel, and is it Unique to Humans?', *Behavioural and Brain Sciences* 30:3 (2007), 313–51.

11.   E. Tulving, 'Chronothesia: Conscious Awareness of Subjective Time', in D.T. Stuss and R.T. Knight (eds.), *Principles of Frontal Lobe Function* (Oxford: Oxford University Press, 2002), 311–25.

12.   G. Martin-Ordas, 'With the Future in Mind: Toward a Comprehensive Understanding of the Evolution Future-Oriented Cognition', in K. Michaelian, S.B. Klein and K.K. Szpunar (eds.), *Seeing the Future: Theoretical Perspectives on Future-Oriented Mental Time Travel* (Oxford: Oxford University Press, 2016), 306–27.

13.   '[T]he ability to reason using modal notions is characteristic of humans, and is certainly remarkable, arguably playing an important role in our evolution and setting us apart from other intelligent beings'. A. Borghini, *A Critical Introduction to the Metaphysics of Modality* (London: Bloomsbury, 2016), 19.

perils and possibilia.[14] Eventually triggering rational prognosis (which first coalesces with the late-mediaeval emergence of insurance industries, financial markets, and speculation upon them) the 'Art of Conjecture' is incepted, and possible futures increasingly come to infiltrate the present.[15] This increasing tilt toward the long term is the core characteristic of modernity.

Indeed, having been cranially outsourced by the seventeenth-century invention of calculus, and fully automated with the explosion in computation following the Second World War, simulation (at last fully externalized from the CNS via prosthetic delegation) now comes to progressively reverse-engineer the very structure of possibility itself.[16] For a science that incrementally relies on simulation (in the form of forecast) is a science that, at least in part, *creates its own objects*. This, in turn, engenders the tendency for us to live, more and more, in a world entirely of our own making. The distinction between 'natural' and 'artificial' progressively collapses, as we see today in fields ranging from synthetic biology to genome editing, from climate engineering to nanotech to materials research.[17] Now unfurling on a global scale, prediction computes contingencies and provokes real-world preventative procedures, yet the exponential thickening of predictive infrastructures breeds ever

14.   A. Giddens, *Modernity and Self-Identity: Self and Society in the Late Modern Age* (Stanford, CA: Stanford University Press, 1991), 127–8.

15.   B. de Jouvenel, *The Art of Conjecture*, tr. N. Lary (New York: Basic Books, 1967).

16.   G. Gramelsberger, 'Introduction', in G. Gramelsberger (ed.), *From Science to Computational Sciences: Studies in the History of Computing and its Influence on Today's Sciences* (Zurich: Diaphanes, 2011), 13.

17.   G. Gramelsberger, 'From Science to Computational Sciences: A Science History and Philosophy Overview', in Gramelsberger (ed.), *From Science to Computational Sciences*, 41.

more—and ever more novel—contingencies to predict. Risk escalation is utterly endogenous to the world-interior of advanced modernity, as the friction of its mechanism (just as it is with the gigantized external sensorium of planetary computation, so it is with individual nervous systems: recalcitrance is systemically ineliminable, inasmuch as no model can exhaustively model itself modelling without falling into infinite—and thus impossibly expensive—recursion).[18] This is how the project of planetary forecast progressively parochializes actuality, ghettoizing the 'merely real'. Reality escape attains a whole new significance as *in silico* realities begin to exert causal efficacy upon our own. In 'the petabyte-scale period of science' we no longer passively *model* nature but unavoidably *remould* it: the artefactual nature of nervous world-manufacture spills out of the skull as computational science unleashes an artificialization of nature on a planetary scale.[19] Nervous organ

---

18.   Benjamin Bratton uses the example of a high-fidelity simulation of global climate systems: the power consumption required for suitably high-resolution modelling would entail that the primary climatological event modelled would be itself. See B. Bratton, *The Stack: On Software and Sovereignty* (Cambridge, MA: MIT Press, 2016), 102.

19.   Nordmann writes that 'technoscience knows only one way of gaining new knowledge and that is by first making a new world'. See A. Nordmann, 'Collapse of Distance: Epistemic Strategies of Science and Technoscience', *Danish Yearbook of Philosophy* 41:1 (2006), 7–34: 8. Mansnerus, similarly, writes that 'the metaphor of "experimenting with Nature" could be upgraded to regard simulation models as *artificial nature*, subject to interrogative manipulation'. See E. Mansnerus, 'Explanatory and Predictive Functions of Simulation Modelling', in Gramelsberger (ed.), *From Science to Computational Sciences*, 177–93. 'Simulation', Gramelsberger adds, 'can be used for both rational prognosis and "numerical breeding"' (Gramelsberger, 'Introduction', 42). In other words, simulative artefacts do not merely mimic realities but produce new ones. We live in an age of the numerical breeding of new worlds, as is evident in materials research, synthetic biology, or nanotechnology. Such vocations, Floridi notes, 'are increasingly "artificializing" or "denaturalizing" the world [...] as well as what

maturates into technoscientific organon. Chronotopes, perforce, have a *tendency to leak.*[20]

Many of these notions were already present in Ukhtomskii's neurological conceptions and those of his Soviet compatriots. Ukhtomskii had postulated that the organismic chronotope—by facilitating increasingly long-range control over its environment—was the initial trigger behind life's tendency to reformat its surroundings at progressively greater spatiotemporal scales.[21] Yet it was Ukhtomskii's contemporary, the biogeochemist Vladimir Ivanovich Vernadskii (1862–1945), who fully elaborated this suggestion in his cosmist notion of the incipient **noösphere** (ноосфера). Vernadskii followed Louis Pasteur in noticing that organic chemistry, because of its chiral features, is defined by dissymmetry in space,[22] further arguing, however, that biotic matter is likewise identified by dissymmetry in *time*. Life produces its own time, or, *life is the generation of a*

---

qualifies as real'. See Floridi, 'A Plea for Non-Naturalism as Constructionism', 271. In world-historical terms, this is all downstream of the fact that, because a nervous system can only represent the world through translating world states into neural artifice, *the activity of nerve-bound agents tends towards artificializing the world itself.*

20.   Yet, as certain futurists have argued, this outward eversion may revert back into wholesale inward collapse, as neural implosion segues into computational implosion: the 'transcension hypothesis' posits as an attractor common to the space of all possible civilizations something called 'STEM compression': a tendency to densify and miniaturize in the pursuit of informatic efficiency—to the point of receding into black holes, and not just figurative ones. J. Smart, 'The Transcension Hypothesis: Sufficiently Advanced Civilizations Invariably Leave our Universe, and Implications for METI and SETI', *Acta Astronautica* 78 (2012): 55–68.

21.   P.V. Simonov, *The Motivated Brain: A Neurophysiological Analysis of Human Behaviour,* tr. L. Payne (New York: Gordon and Breach, 1991), 15.

22.   See V. Serdyuk, *Scoliosis and Spinal Pain Syndrome: New Understanding of their Origin* (Delhi: Byword Books, 2014), 31–3.

temporal arrow.[23] Directional time is, then, the collective secretion of earth's **biosphere** (биосфера—another term popularized by Vernadskii). This temporality-generative 'symmetry breaking' at the core of living process neatly explains the seemingly directional nature of macroevolution, which Vernadskii explicitly links to **cephalization** and the 'evolution of matter in a single, headward direction'.[24] Cephalization, Vernadskii concluded, converges upon *homo sapience*, which is inaugural of the noösphere, or, in a phrase that Vernadskii borrowed from the American geologist Joseph Le Conte, that **psychozoic era** of terrestrial history defined by the wholesale capture of earth systems by intentional activity.[25] Vernadskii's noösphere—a downstream product of cephalizing chronoreceptivity—

23.   G.S Levit, W. Krumbein, and R. Grübel, 'Space and Time in the Works of Vernadsky', *Environmental Ethics* 22:4 (2000), 377–96.

24.   G.M. Young, *The Russian Cosmists: The Esoteric Futurism of Nikolai Fedorov and his Followers* (Oxford: Oxford University Press, 2012), 156. Vernadskii took the phrase 'cephalization' from the American geologist James Dwight Dana (1813–1895), who had coined the term whilst classifying crab nervous architectures, exclaiming that 'This centralization is literally a *cephalization* of forces'. See J.D. Dana, 'A Review of the Classification of Crustacea', *American Journal of Science and Arts* 22 (1856), 14–29: 15. Later, Dana wrote of how the nervous system—'that feeling, knowing, outreaching and inworking thing'—converges irreversibly headwards into the 'development of the brain in Man'. See J.D. Dana, 'The Classification of Animals Based on the Principle of Cephalization', *American Journal of Science and Arts* 35 (1863), 321–53. Although such orthogenetic ideas were popular in the early nineteenth century, they tend to be rejected by contemporary science. Dana's idea of inevitable cephalization is likely an artefact of our own biases. See C.H. Lineweaver, 'Paleontological Tests: Human-Like Intelligence Is Not a Convergent Feature of Evolution', in J. Seckbach and M. Walsh (eds.), *From Fossils to Astrobiology: Records of Life on Earth and the Search for Extraterrestrial Biosignatures* (New York: Springer, 2009), 355–70. As Gould said, '*Homo sapiens* is an entity, not a tendency'. S.J. Gould, *Wonderful Life* (London: Hutchinson Radius, 1990), 320.

25.   J. Le Conte, *Elements of Geology* (New York, 1878), 557–70.

announces a globe turned artefact, with eventual erasure of the distinction between frontal cortex, higher nervous function, and geocosmic mass.[26] A relentless promulgator of orthogenesis, Vernadskii's fellow traveller Teilhard de Chardin wrote of how cephalization provides the 'Ariadne's thread' of time, whereby 'nerve ganglions concentrate; they become localized and forward in the head':

> Life is the rise of consciousness, we have agreed. If it is to progress still further it can only be because, here and there, the internal energy is secretly rising up under the mantle of the flowing earth. Here and there, at the base of nervous systems, psychic tension is doubtless increasing […] the active phyletic lines grow warm with consciousness towards the summit. But in one well-marked region at the heart of the mammals, where the most powerful brains ever made by nature are to be found they become red hot. And right at the heart of the glow burns a point of incandescence. […] We must not lose sight of that line crimsoned by the dawn. After thousands of years rising below the horizon, the flame bursts forth at a strictly localized point. Thought is born.[27]

He went on to claim that,

> [s]ince, in its totality and throughout the length of each stem, the natural history of living creatures amounts on the *exterior* to the gradual establishment of a vast nervous system, it therefore

---

26. No responsibility without risk, of course: 'If man [does] not use his brain [for] self-destruction, an immense future is open before him'. V. Vernadskii, 'The Biosphere and the Noösphere', *American Scientist* 33:1 (1945), 1–13: 8. The nervous system may well be the geocosm's prime executive.

27. P.T. de Chardin, *The Phenomenon of Man* (London: Collins, 1955), 153–60.

corresponds on the *interior* to the installation of a psychic state on the very dimensions of the earth.[28]

This, then, is how bone armature interlocks with discursive architectonic (as its phanerozoic precursor) and consequently also with the deep upswells of terrestrial history as well as the longest-range futurity. It is how we came to think like a planet. It is why the sun's downward onslaught of insolation triggers synapsing spines to tendentiously rise; for the uphill struggle inherited by all negentropic systems is simultaneously, and ineluctably, also a falling inward. And the outward marker of life's coiling collapse, the great monument raised to implosion, is the cephalocaudal surge of the spinal cord and its vertebral mast; in this way, the conglomerating backbone and its axon fasciculations become legible to us as the legacy trace of the influx of *time* into the organism's being. And so, although spines rise from the planet, scraping cautiously skyward toward the star that initiated their uphill struggle, this apparent *phototropism* (growth towards light) is in fact an instance of *chronotaxis* (departure into time—escapement from the immediate and orientation within a history grander than oneself) volatized by the congenitality of agitation and anticipation at the dawn of life.[29]

The spine is a **tautegory** for the long-durational gestation of futurity—a symbol that expresses its object not by mediating it but by manifesting it. But if, in becoming sensitive to time,

28. Ibid., 146.

29. The palaeontologist Mark A.S. McMenamin establishes that the roots of the Vernadskian 'noösphere' can be traced all the way back to Ediacaran 'chemocognition'. M.A.S. McMenamin, *The Garden of Ediacara: Discovering the First Complex Life* (New York: Columbia University Press, 1998), 239–51.

the organism also conquers it (as exampled all the way from the rudimentary cell's heat-shock proteins up to humanity's present-day apparatus of cosmological forecasting), this feed-forward encroachment of future behaviours into present ones, this lurch into futurity, also comes at a price.

The fact that all representation requires mediation (that there is nothing simply 'given', either in conceptual graspings or in neural activations) means that the more complex our world-model becomes, the more we must fold into our own systems. Yet for the living, each gyre of life's egress into its own parameter space is experienced as a painful departure from immersion.

Chronognostic range and nociceptive capacity are positively correlated.[1] So that while, from the finalistic perspective of propagative function, such complexification spells unparalleled adaptive potentiation, from the embedded perspective of the actually-existing organism, it implies a cursed inheritance, the legacy of an increasing nociceptive, and eventually dysphoric, burden. The more conversant you are with time—that is to say, the more time inhabits you—the more painful life is going to be.

We chordates are immanence's self-lacerating attempt to escape itself; or, what amounts to the same thing, a spine is the axial marker of nature's first attempts at dissimulation through simulation. Hence it is a ledger of traumatisms. As Kant anticipated, it all begins with orientation—and gaining a head was one of the earlier forms of orienting oneself. In dispensing with morphological radiality, the promotion of a solely sagittal plane of symmetry generates an orientational 'front' and 'behind' for the segmenting organism, whilst also optimizing for the localization of a sensory array into an anterior 'head': sense receptors

---

1.   See T.E. Feinberg and J.M. Mallatt, *The Ancient Origins of Consciousness: How the Brain Created Experience* (Cambridge, MA: MIT Press, 2017), 150–51. Also see P. Singer, 'Are Insects Conscious?' (2016), <https://www.project-syndicate.org/commentary/are-insects-conscious-by-peter-singer-2016-05>.

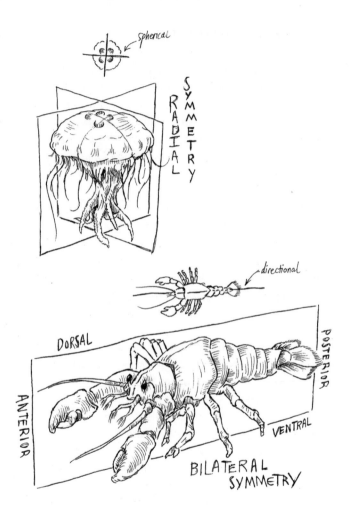

Fig. 2. Advent of the anterior field

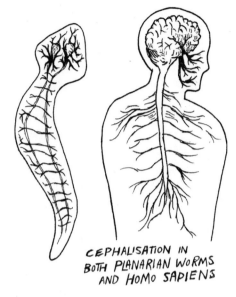

CEPHALISATION IN
BOTH PLANARIAN WORMS
AND HOMO SAPIENS

Fig. 3. In what furnace was thy brain?

and transducers bubble up, flowing backwards around the buccal orifice into ocelli (primitive eyespots) and auricles (sensory lobes), facilitating the dorso-posterior ballooning of an entire simulative universe as ganglia pile into cephalizing brain case.[2] (Leroi-Gourhan called this the generation of an **anterior field**.)[3] This onset of faciality cranially lifts the post-chordate heterotroph out of panoptical immersion, reinforcing a

2. R. Sponge, 'Bikini Atoll Test Detonations Caused Longing to Return to Cnidarian Modes: Case Studies and Reports Lately Uncovered', *American Journal of Military Psychiatrics* 15:5 (1977), 44–70.

3. A. Leroi-Gourhan, *Gesture and Speech*, tr. A.B. Berger (Cambridge, MA: MIT Press, 1993), 29–36.

directional aperture onto the world via filtration of peripheral fields. Yet with potentiation comes pain.

As the first inauguration of unmistakable perspective and orientation, urbilaterian take-off dimly prophesies later conceptual finitude (by half a giga-annum) inasmuch as it provides conditions of objectivation that cannot themselves be objectivated (without a mirror, of course). Faces are catastrophic, however, because faciality—appearing first amongst planarian worms—is a *marker of lethality*.[4] Life, as self-entrenching asymmetry, migrates its turbulence from energetic domains toward the mechanical: the potential gradient between 'in' and 'out' transmutes into the projectile path from 'front' to 'back'. In Gnathostomata (vertebrates with a true, opposing jaw) this process coils the entire organism behind a denticulate orifice: directional hunger lurking behind front-facing sensory aperture (simulative universe projecting backwards into cranial vault; culinary universe surging downward through serrating mouth). Schopenhauer: 'teeth, throat and bowels are objectified hunger'.[5] Registered with the appearance of otoliths (calcified organs for perceiving linear acceleration) within early fish, bilaterality *brings ballistics to life*. Urbilaterian directionality, indeed, provided the Cambrian conditions under which predation first truly flourished—locked in, upon arrival, by trophic arms race.[6] It was as far back as 1907 that Henri Bergson noticed that, as a tipping point within life's 'marching on to the conquest of a nervous system', this explosive predatory escalation first

---

4.   O.R. Pagán, *The First Brain: The Neuroscience of Planarians* (Oxford: Oxford University Press, 2014), 154–9.

5.   Schopenhauer, *The World as Will and Representation*, vol 1, 108.

6.   R. Dawkins and J.R. Krebs, 'Arms Race Between and Within Species', in *Proceedings of the Royal Society* 205:1161 (1979), 489–511.

triggered 'the imprisonment of the animal' within a lithified skeletal 'citadel'.[7] And it was a flare of predation and pain indeed that called for such fortifications: on the Cambrian sea floor we find the remains of our planet's first cases of 'genocide', 'infanticide', and 'cannibalism'.[8] Bilateralism truly is a *fearful symmetry*.

The post-chordate world is utterly fallen: it is where voracity becomes self-selecting. Ultimately, the bilaterian face marks the vertebral fall from prelapsarian radial pacifism and Ediacaran spherico-sessile innocence. *But we fell upward.* For, with the perpendicularization of the hominin backbone around six million years ago, and the subsequent increase in encephalization quotient (EQ), orthograde rationality came to superimpose itself upon bilaterian hunger: an appetite that could orient itself in thinking, and thus would eventually come to consume the whole globe.[9] A whole new *Potenz* of viciousness; a whole new atrocity exhibition of spinal traumata.[10] *Felix culpa*, indeed.

---

7. H. Bergson, *Creative Evolution*, tr. A. Mitchell (Lanham, MD: University Press of America, 1983), 130–31.

8. M.A.S. McMenamin, *Dynamic Paleontology: Using Quantification and Other Tools to Decipher the History of Life* (New York: Springer, 2016), 181–90.

9. 'The increase in the encephalization quotient by a factor of more than 2.5, from *Australopithecus afarensis* up to *Homo sapiens*, which took place over about 3.5 million years, is the most significant and surprising characteristic of our ancestral lineage [...] During that period of time, the volume of the brain increased by a factor of about 3.4, while the body mass only increased by 30%'. F.D. Santos, *Humans on Earth: From Origins to Possible Futures* (New York: Springer, 2012), 74.

10. 'There is little doubt that hominid history is a history of genocide'. E. Mayr, *What Evolution Is* (London: Phoenix, 2002), 255.

Bones are not concepts. But they *are* constraints—enabling ones at that. This is precisely what makes them legible as precursors of conceptual finitude. A casement of linguistic rules is only the most epithelial, epigene, or proximal layer of collapse into one's own chronotopic systematicity.[1] Moreover, just as hormetic perturbation triggers these various infoldings of biogenesis, so too does the Kantian exploration into orientational rationality find its beginnings in traumatic tremors.

Biographically speaking, Kant's philosophical career was in no small part triggered by the 1755 earthquake that decimated the bustling city of Lisbon. This fatal calamity troubled a 31-year-old Kant so much that it provoked three essays from him—in swift succession—on the topic of seismology, which are amongst his earliest published writings.[2] Here, in 1756 (fifteen years prior to the musings in his first *Critique*), Kant was already remarking—with clear trepidation—that we 'know the surface of the Earth fairly completely', but that 'we have another world

---

1. Glottogony constrains the linguistic debutante, limiting her to legal manoeuvres in the game of sharing discursive sanctions. Yet such constraint is also inception of the *possibility of being right* over and above the *mere possibility of being*. Thus, language's regulative-juridical encasement is an 'enabling constraint' analogous to the soft-body organism's incarceration within a rigidified frame, which, despite restricting movement, nonetheless potentiates mechanical locomotion.

2. I. Kant, 'On the Causes of Earthquakes', tr. O. Reinhardt, in E. Watkins (ed.), *Natural Science* (Cambridge: Cambridge University Press, 2012), 1:417–427; I. Kant, 'History and Natural Description of the Most Noteworthy Occurrences of the Earthquake that Struck a Large Part of the Earth at the end of the Year 1755', tr. O. Reinhardt, in ibid., 1:429–61; 'Continued Observations on the Earthquakes that have been Experienced for Some Time', tr. O. Reinhardt, in ibid., 1:463–72.

beneath our feet with which we are at present but little acquainted'. And, after indicating the inwardly-riven 'fissures', innermost fundaments, and 'unfathomable depths' that variegate this 'internal structure', Kant adds that thus far we have only penetrated it to a depth of around '500 fathoms' (which is 'not even one six thousandth part of the distance to the centre of the Earth'). He then dwells upon the feeling of ultimate consternation people feel when they realise that the seismic Earth 'moves under their feet'—that they have never stood upon firm ground. Far from being merely an easily-forgotten reverie of his dogmatic slumbers, the aftershocks of this feeling of quaking consternation are carried through into the very conclusion of the critical project. In the 'Analytic of the Sublime', Kant refers to sublimity as a feeling of '*Erschütterung*', which can be translated as 'tremoring' or 'quaking'.[3] On both a biographical and philosophical level, the Kantian subject doubts itself—reaching for the supernal or supererogatory—only in response to external stressors shuddering upwards from our unquiet planet.[4]

Time has its own developmental history (its own *Bildung*), namely evolution's unfolding procession of chronotopic intrications, which themselves are serially deposited in response to the grand tremors and quaking perturbations of the body of

---

3. I. Kant, *Critique of the Power of Judgement*, tr. P. Guyer (Cambridge: Cambridge University Press, 2000), 141 [5:258].

4. '[O]nly in quaking does the self reveal its stability. Under the impression exerted by the Lisbon earthquake, which touched the European mind in one [of] its more sensitive epochs, the metaphorics of ground and tremor completely lost their apparent innocence; they were no longer merely figures of speech', W. Hamacher, 'The Quaking of Presentation', in *Premises: Essays on Philosophy and Literature from Kant to Celan*, tr. P. Fenves (Cambridge, MA: Harvard University Press, 1996), 263.

the earth. Let us, then, embark upon a geotraumatic vivisection of our grounds of orientation: peeling back transcendental overlay down to osseous underlay; quarrying the prehistory of our inferential exoskeleton through our physical endoskeleton; shaving away conceptual, linguistic, and synaptic laminae; spelunking the larynx, opening onto grand coelems—dropping down the spinal echelons—in a phyletic katabasis through our architectures of chronotopic encasement.[5] Descending down the vertebral metameres, one realises that these nested world-infoldings chart the gargantuan paroxysms that roll through time aeonic. For the spine is the marker of chronogenic whiplash; nervous intrication generates a sense of speeding time; inertial drag is a known side effect. There is no sense of time's movement without a concomitant desire to speed it up: to be *aware* of time moving is to anticipate the oncoming future, which invariably causes it to arrive earlier and earlier. A sense of the new, by changing present behaviour, *causes* the new. Thus the very experience, or consciousness, of temporal movement provides the conditions for history's acceleration.[6] Sensitivity to time is nothing other than *further* sensitization to time; or, once entangled, one only can become *more* entangled. Historically speaking, self-consciousness of historicism provided the very material conditions under which history became revolution upon speeding revolution.[7] To sense time moving is

---

5.   'Open the so-called body and spread out all its surfaces'. J.-F. Lyotard, *Libidinal Economy*, tr. I.H. Grant (London: Continuum, 2004), 1.

6.   Anticipation 'often lead[s] to endogeneity or reverse causality: anticipated future outcomes alter current behavior so that some sense of the future causes the past'. See B. Beuno de Mesquita, 'Predicting the Future to Shape the Future', in F. Whelon Waymann et al. (eds.) *Predicting the Future in Science, Economics and Politics* (Northampton, MA: Edward Elgar, 2014), 481.

7.   R. Koselleck, *Futures Past: On the Semantics of Historical Time*, tr. K. Tribe (New York: Columbia University Press, 2004).

already to cause it to move faster.[8] This is the very heart of the synonymy of 'the modern' and 'the catastrophic' which Reinhart Koselleck traces to the past few centuries of political upheavals, but this dynamism began—albeit glacially at first—many aeons ago when temporality infiltrated the first sparking neuron.[9] Indeed, in tracing the long-durational gestation of such chronoceptivity back to neural inner collapse, we note how appropriate it is that René Thom theorized the topological shape of catastrophe to be that of the *invaginated fold*.[10]

Nonetheless, in this phylogenesis of time, a sense of the future arriving earlier is indistinct from the past's drag upon the present. *Only relative to such a drag could any precocity be defined.* But when one's past is a story of quakes and perturbations, the internality implied by 'one's own history' begins to unravel. Ultimately, discovering finitude entailed discovering that thought is functionally internal to itself, but self-containment becomes problematic when modulated through the dimension of Grand History. Here, 'internality' and 'inclusion' are reconstituted as a medium of ancestral self-abruption rather than telescoping self-similarity and ownership. What is at stake, then, is the realisation that the historical vanishing point of

---

8.   A perfect example of this can be found in the French Revolution: the 'revolutionary era, after all, had not merely [been] a time of change—it had actually changed time', see R. Jones, '1816 and the Resumption of "Ordinary History"', *Journal of Modern European History* 14:1 (2016), 119–42.

9.   See R. Koselleck, *Crisis and Critique: Enlightenment and the Pathogenesis of Modern Society* (Cambridge, MA: MIT Press, 1988). On the consequences of this time-structure for the notion of the 'contemporary' see S. Malik, *ContraContemporary: Modernity's Unknown Future* (Falmouth: Urbanomic, forthcoming 2020).

10.   R. Thom, *Structural Stability and Morphogenesis* (Cambridge, MA: Perseus, 1989).

self-containment *just is* self-exclusion: in other words, *depth*. Historically speaking, I contain my outside. This is what time does to a body, as we shall see in tracing out this Secret History. The lesson is clear: psychosomatic containment of oneself, when percolated through Grandest History, equals hypogene alienation—the alienation of a body riddled with time. It is this realisation that is inaugural of the phylogenetic phantasy that is **Spinal Catastrophism**.

Hegel was perhaps wrong, after all, to dispute the fact that 'Spirit is a bone'.[11]

We now turn to the diverse forms taken by this hypergenealogical reverie—first of all to the most recent exponent and inventor of the term itself, before tracing its multiple sources back through the various forgotten avenues of modern thought.

---

11.   G.W.F. Hegel, *Phenomenology of Spirit*, tr. A.V. Miller (Oxford: Oxford University Press, 1977), 208.

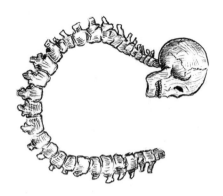

Even absolute metaphors therefore have a history. They have a history in a more radical sense than concepts, for the historical transformation of a metaphor brings to light the metakinetics of the historical horizons of meaning and ways of seeing within which concepts undergo their modifications. Through this implicative connection, the relationship of metaphorology to the history of concepts (in the narrower, terminological sense) is defined as an ancillary one: metaphorology seeks to burrow down to the sub-structure of thought, the underground, the nutrient solution of systematic crystallizations; but it also aims to show with what 'courage' the mind pre-empts itself in its images, and how its history is projected in the courage of its conjectures.

Hans Blumenberg, *Paradigms for a Metaphorology* (2010)

Given the chronological stratification of our brain and the fossil character of the elder parts lying below the cerebrum, what we propose can rightly be described as a type of 'paleontology of the soul'.

Hoimar von Ditfurth, *Der Geist fiel nicht vom Himmel* (1976)

THORACIC RETROSPECT
(2000–1900)

TH1. BARKER SPOKE

Although, as has already been intimated, the doctrine commands a venerable prehistory, it was Daniel Charles Barker (1952–) who first explicitly coined the term 'Spinal Catastrophism' in 1992.[1] Professor of Anorganic Semiotics at MVU from the early 1990s until the millennium,[2] post-Y2K Barker's whereabouts are unknown (though unlikely rumours circulate of a voluntary exile on an island in the Sunda Strait). Barker's corpus circulates as *samizdat*: redactions are common, some papers have been suppressed, and much of it has simply disappeared, so that what follows can only be a tentative reconstruction of the course of Barker's ideas based on fragments, secondary reports, and passing allusions.

What is biographically important here is how Barker, from his initial work in future-facing initiatives including NASA and SETI, eventually became obsessed with what is oldest and most cryptic in nature. What led him down this twisted route from most distant future into deepest past? Barker was only the most recent to tread this path, which has exerted an apparently irresistible pull on a series of very intelligent minds—yet it was to have disastrous consequences for his career and indeed his sanity.

---

1. D.C. Barker, 'Spinal Catastrophism', *Plutonics* 10:10 (1992), 13–42.

2. MVU, or Miskatonic Virtual University, was often referred to as the 'shadow MIT'—appropriately enough, since many MVU researchers have long been interested in the notion of the 'shadow biosphere' (the postulation of a parallel xenobiological lineage: likely extremophile, possibly hypogene, potentially populated by polymers of reverse chirality). See D.C. Barker, 'The Shadow Biosphere as Clandestine Necroevolution', *Plutonics* 9:7 (1990), 52–7, a reference to which was quietly excised from later editions of Thomas Gold's *The Deep Hot Biosphere* (New York: Springer, 1999).

To the extent that one can speak of a 'Barker Affair' to rival the 'Velikovsky Affair', we must note that the former was not as noisily public as the latter, although it proved no less vituperative within certain scientific circles.[3] Although Velikovsky does not venture into the kind of speculative osseology that led Barker to understand lumbar pain as a resonance of cosmic dysphoria, what the two rogue scientists have had in common is their convicted dedication to **neocatastrophism**—and here Velikovsky was undoubtedly an influence upon Barker.

It is well known that early geoscience was split between the catastrophists and the uniformitarians (a debate that had spilled over from the earlier one between plutonism and neptunism). The catastrophists held that earth history is made up of a series of causally disconnected epochs separated by planet-shaking cataclysms and unexplainable ruptures of natural law (a Humean nightmare world, in other words).[4] The uniformitarians, contrarily, held that only the processes observable today are responsible for shaping the planet (in other words, the types of causal connection encountered on Earth are ironclad,

---

3.   'They think Barker is mad, or want to. It isn't because he thinks that the Galaxies Talk and the Earth Screams—everyone knows these things, whether they admit it or not.' ('Cryptolith', in CCRU, *Writings: 1997–2003* [Falmouth and Shanghai: Urbanomic/Time Spiral, 2017], 149–50). Let us note here that the brief affiliation with the CCRU (Cybernetic Culture Research Unit), although itself riven with controversy, yielded the only extant interview with Barker: 'Barker Speaks: The CCRU Interview with Professor D.C. Barker', *Abstract Culture* 4 (Leamington Spa: CCRU, 1999): 2–9, reprinted in *Writings 1997–2003*, 155–62.

4.   Cuvier, catastrophism's chief proponent, wrote that one cannot 'explain earlier revolutions [with] present causes' and this, simply, is because nature is 'subject to new laws'. See M.J.S. Rudwick, *Georges Cuvier, Fossil Bones, and Geological Catastrophes: New Translations and Interpretations of the Primary Texts* (Chicago: University of Chicago Press, 2008), 184.

unchanging, and unbroken—and so too, therefore, are our empirical retroductions). The debate eventually resolved into the long-standing ascendency of uniformitarianism, or steady-state theories, which stretch back to the unreadable Scottish enlightenment writings of James Hutton and down to the elegant Victorian geotheory of Charles Lyell.[5] This 'resolution' was due, in no small part, to Lyell's rhetorical gloss and to his 'self-serving rewrite' of the genesis of the field. By the time Immanuel Velikovsky (1895–1979) divulged his catastrophist speculations in the 1950s (discussed in more detail below, section TH7), the very mention of 'catastrophism' within geoscience and cosmology was still abhorred. Although it exists in different formulations of varying scope, uniformitarianism broadly states that *only* causes presently operative can be rallied in our explanations of the past. In other words, it is the principle that what is currently actual exhausts what is possible throughout terrestrial chronology. Following what Lyell had long ago installed as 'common sense', the accepted story (often relayed by textbook hagiographies) taught that uniformitarianism had made geology a *science* by shearing it of supernatural explanatory cruxes (the naturally unaccountable miracles and calamities of prior theories of the earth were ejected because *they could not be observed*).[6] This, however, effectively made 'catastrophes' (i.e. unprecedented, unobservable, or singular

---

5. See S.J. Gould, *Time's Arrow, Time's Cycle: Myth and Metaphor in the Discovery of Geological Time* (Cambridge, MA: Harvard University Press, 1987); and, for a more recent take, M.J.S. Rudwick, *Earth's Deep History: How it was Discovered and Why it Matters* (Chicago: University of Chicago Press, 2014); see also V.R. Baker, 'Catastrophism and Uniformitarianism: Logical Roots and Current Relevance in Geology', *Geological Society of London* 143 (1998), 171–82.

6. Gould, *Time's Arrow, Time's Cycle*, 66.

events—both supernatural *and* natural) forbidden in theorizations concerning the unobserved past. This is to say, due to stubborn empiricist anxieties about the requirements for *legitimizing* geohistory as a sensible and sense-based science, catastrophes have long been tarred with the brush of the unscientific. Nonetheless, uniformitarianism was largely overturned in 1980, when the father-son Alvarez team found convincing evidence of a dinosaur-killing bolide impact.[7] Tracing iridium deposits at the Cretaceous-Paleogene (K-Pg) boundary, the team also located a crater, of identical age, beneath Mexico's Yucatán Peninsula (the presence of iridium, evidencing an extraterrestrial source, would remain important for Barker's own theories.[8] Swift on the heels of this Alvarez hypothesis for the K-Pg extinction event, Raup and Sepokoski further proposed that such impactor events are themselves explained by an undetected 'Nemesis star', in twin orbit with our own, dragging thousands of deadly comets from the Oort cloud into our stellar vicinity within periodic time-windows of ~26 million years.[9] In other words, the old view of our cosmic environs as insulated and stable was replaced, almost overnight,

---

7.   L.W. Alvarez, W. Alvarez, F. Asaro, and H.V. Michel, 'Extraterrestrial Cause for the Cretaceous Tertiary Extinction', *Science* 208 (1980), 1095–1108; and W. Alvarez, *T. Rex and the Crater of Doom* (Princeton, NJ: Princeton University Press, 1997).

8.   At the time, however, the term was 'K-T' [Cretacious-Tertiary] rather than 'K-Pg' [Cretaceous-Paleogene]): 'And what is mammalian life relative to the great saurian? Above all, an innovation in mothering! Suckling as biosurvivialism. Tell me about your mother and you're travelling back to K-T, not into the personal unconscious'. Barker, 'Barker Speaks,' 6.

9.   D.M. Raup and J.J. Sepopkoski, 'Periodicity of Extinctions in the Geologic Past', in *PNAS* 81:3 (1984), 801–5; and D.M. Raup, *The Nemesis Affair: A Story of the Death of the Dinosaurs and the Ways of Science* (New York: Norton, 1999).

with a new picture of the Solar System as dynamically open and punctuated by paroxysm[10]—Velikovsky vindicated, in spirit if not in the details. It was this consolidation of neocatastrophism that provided the crucial backdrop for Barker's work during the 1980s and 1990s (though it would not protect him from censure).[11]

Trained in cryptography and information science at MIT, Barker was recruited by NASA in the 1980s and was hired almost immediately by SETI, his *cryptographic* background recommending him, specifically, for METI (Messaging to Extraterrestrial Intelligences) and SETA (Search for Extraterrestrial Artefacts).[12] The major difference between naturally occurring and intelligently originating interstellar activity, as Barker wrote, is that only the latter 'can *decide to camouflage itself*'.[13]

---

10.   A 'neocatastrophist tendency has recently become almost default in a wide range of fields, from research on abiogenesis, to aspects of macroevolution, to the debates on the evolution of humanity, to future studies'. M.M. Ćirković, *The Great Silence: The Science and Philosophy of Fermi's Paradox* (Oxford: Oxford University Press, 2018), 170–71.

11.   R.A. Freitas, 'The Search for Extraterrestrial Artifacts (SETA)', *Acta Astronautica* 12 (1985), 1027–34.

12.   The idea being that, given the potentially gargantuan size of the relevant time spans, 'first contact' may not be with a living species, but with its monuments. See J. Armitage, 'The Prospect of Astro-Palaeontology', *Journal of the British Interplanetary Society* 30 (1976), 466–9.

13.   D.C. Barker, 'The Paranoia from Outer-Space: Of Ciphers, Cosmic Camouflage, and Contact', *Journal of Cryptosystems* 2:5 (1986), 55–68. In a similar vein, Edward Snowden recently claimed that we cannot detect interstellar civilizations because their advanced encryptions make their detection profile indistinguishable from microwave background radiation. See 'Edward Snowden: We May Never Spot Space Aliens Thanks to Encryption', *The Guardian* (2015), <https://www.theguardian.com/us-news/2015/sep/19/edward-snowden-aliens-encryption-neil-degrasse-tyson-podcast>. V.G. Gurzadyan has also lately theorized that extraterrestrial life could exist in the form of highly compressed bit-strings, encoding alien genomes, that are broadcast throughout

(As already indicated, dissimulation is one of the myriad options afforded as soon as one owns a simulation—cerebrospinal or otherwise—of oneself.)[14] Tasked with working out 'how to discriminate—in principle—between intelligent communication and complex pattern derived from nonintelligent sources',[15] Barker gravitated towards the newly emerging SETA subdisciplines of exo-archaeology and astro-palaeontology (given the gargantuan size of the relevant time scales, it was felt that deceased ETIs may outnumber extant ones, and that in consequence 'first detection' may not involve a living species but, rather, its relics and hoary monuments).[16]

This change in direction set him upon an increasingly heterodox path. Originally subscribing to Wickramasinghe and Hoyle's 1979 hypothesis that the Cambrian explosion was triggered by cometary infall of extraterrestrial retroviruses and the attendant mutagenesis of protozoic biota, Barker's work on SETA eventually led him to Orgel and Crick's 'Directed Panspermia' thesis—the idea that life on Earth may have been deliberately seeded by alien intelligences—and from there to

---

the universe—awaiting *ex situ* decoding. See V.G. Gurzadyan, 'Kolmogorov Complexity, String Information, Panspermia and the Fermi Paradox', *Observatory* 125 (2005): 352–5. Barker, presciently, was already asking such questions in the 1980s.

14.   A 'Machiavellian loop' of deception has been theorized as integral to the evolution of hominin intelligence. See R.W. Byrne and A. Whiten, 'Machiavellian Intelligence: Social Expertise and the Evolution of Intellect in Monkeys, Apes, and Humans', *Behavior and Philosophy* 18:1 (1990), 73–5.

15.   Barker, 'Barker Speaks', 2–9.

16.   See B.W. McGee, 'A Call for Proactive Xenoarchaeological Guidelines—Scientific, Policy, and Socio-Political Considerations', *Space Policy* 26:4 (2010), 209–13; and Armitage, 'The Prospect of Astro-Palaeontology'.

the conclusion, crucial for everything that followed, that we
ourselves are the primary *archaeological site*.[17]

This conviction was partly fuelled by the prior work of scientists such as Yokoo and Oshima, who had, in 1979, performed experiments attempting to *prove the artificiality* of the genome of the bacteriophage φC174 (a virus which attacks *E. Coli* in the human colon) by detecting intentional messages or glyphs hidden within its nucleotide sequence.[18] If the Directed Panspermia hypothesis was correct, they reflected, then signs of intentionality may have been encrypted within terrestrial DNA as a kind of 'signature'.[19] *The genome itself thus became a potential exo-artefact*. Life as a dig-site, the body a matter for archaeo-forensic analysis. Is our daily replication the signal-trace of a memory that does not at all belong to us? Increasingly, such questions began to grip Barker, and would very soon become unhealthy obsessions.

---

17.   'Panspermia' refers to the cluster of theories proposing that life originates extraterrestrially rather than terrestrially. See F. Hoyle and C. Wickramasinghe, *Diseases from Space* (New York: Harper and Row, 1980). In an updated version of the theory, E.J. Steele et al. propose that cephalopoda are *bona fide* extraterrestrials, affirming 'the possibility that cryopreserved squid and/or octopus eggs, arrived in icy bolides several hundred million years ago'. See E.J. Steele, et al., 'Cause of Cambrian Explosion—Terrestrial or Cosmic?' *Progress in Biophysics and Molecular Biology* 136 (2018), 3–23; see also F.H.C. Crick and L.E. Orgel, 'Directed Panspermia', *Icarus* 19:3 (1973), 341–46.

18.   H. Yokoo and T. Oshima, 'Is Bacteriophage φX174 DNA a Message From an Extraterrestrial Intelligence?', *Icarus* 38:1 (1979), 148–53.

19.   H. Nakamura, 'SV40 DNA—A message from ε Eri?', *Acta Astronautica* 13:9 (1986), 573–8; for a more recent attempt, see V.I. Cherbak and M.A. Makukov, 'The "Wow! Signal" of the Terrestrial Genetic Code', *Icarus* 224:1 (2013), 228–42.

Indeed, in 1986, whilst Barker was still working under NASA, Hiroshi Nakamura had attempted to find an extraterrestrial star-map encoded in the genome of SV40 (Simian Virus 40). Was biology just another form of media, DNA a signal propagated across the wounded galaxies? Inevitably attracted to the idea that interstellar palaeontology could become an *in vivo* pursuit, Barker set to work on his own innovative researches in the area. (The human genome had yet to be sequenced, but, among other things, Barker predicted that the ACVR1 gene, on chromosome 2, was a promising site for investigating potential genomic ciphers.)[20] Barker gradually became convinced that the high 'redundancy' of our genome (i.e. roughly >98% of it appears to be non-coding) was only an artefact of *temporal positionality*: in an example of 'clandestine evolution' extending far beyond our biosphere, that which was now encrypted and unused could potentially later decrypt and effloresce (memories, indeed, tend to exert an operant pull upon posterity's course in the sense that to have a past is to have a future continually canalized by that past).[21] In this sense, futurity could possibly be anticipated as a function of the ancient mnemes

---

20. He did not, at the time, give a justification for this claim. It was likely not unrelated to Barker's persistent preoccupation with *Fibrodysplasia Ossificans Progressiva*, a rare disease typified by ectopic osteogenesis, better known as 'Stoneman Syndrome' because of its tendency *to fossilize people alive*. The affliction arises from ACVR1 mutations. See D.C. Barker, 'Thanatos Praecox: *Ossificans Progressiva* as a Heterochronic Complaint', *Anorganics* 3 (1989): 1–11.

21. D.C. Barker, 'Replicator Usurpation as Necroevolution', *Plutonics* 12:1 (1995); see also 'Does Our DNA Contain Someone Else's Signature?: Barker on Xeno-Engraphy and Xeno-Ecphory', *MVU Science Bulletin* 23 (1992): 50–55.

to which we are somatic host.[22] 'Redundancy' was simply a question of *being too early*.[23]

Moving and conversing within SETI circles, it was inevitable that Barker would eventually encounter the idiosyncratic ideas of Aristides Acheropoulos and his fascinating responses to the Fermi Paradox.[24] Acheropoulos's lifework, entitled *The New Cosmogony*, had wallowed in obscurity until it was championed by the influential astrophysicist Professor Alfred Testa in the 1970s (the Polish futurologist Stanisław Lem was also a long-time supporter of Acheropoulosan doctrine).[25] In *The New Cosmogony*, Acheropoulos answered the core Fermi-question, 'Where are all the astroengineering feats of ancient super-civilizations?' by announcing that they are already here. In fact, *they are strictly everywhere*. The whole observable universe

---

22.   D.C. Barker, '"*Liberatis tutemet ex infera*"—Genomic Recividism and its Infernal Potentials', in D.C. Barker (ed.), *New Directions in Cryptocosmology* (Hobb's End, NH: Lewis and Clark, 1989), 96–119.

23.   If some of our genetic material derives, in roaming memory-packets, from outside our biosphere (and perhaps outside our Solar System), our resulting phenotype is potentially already always 'precocious' or 'belated'. It would, in fact, be impossible to tell, precisely because panspermia removes the stable terrestrial frame of temporal reference assumed by parochially Darwinian and abiogenetic evo-devo models.

24.   Briefly, the 'Paradox' arises from the troubling disjunct between the myriad presumptions of our scientific world view, which imply that life should be cosmically rife, and the empirical results of our search for such life, which have returned nothing but the *Silentium Universi* or Great Silence. Of late, the discovery of thousands of exoplanets, the description of myriad extremophile life forms, alongside revisions to the age distribution of Milky Way planets, all combine to inflame the troubling aspects of the Paradox. In other words, as time has gone by, *it has only become worse*.

25.   A. Testa, *From the Einsteinian to the Testan Universe* (Oxford: Oxford University Press, 1970).

just is the prime artefact.[26] Giga-anni old civilizations, Achero-poulos argued, would reach (and, given the age and size of the universe, already had reached) a level of technical mastery such that they would become capable not only of great feats of astroengineering, but also of *manipulating physical law itself*; consequently, what we perceive as 'physics' is nothing but the outcome of an ongoing Cosmic Game played by interacting Kardashev Type-Ω intellects,[27] with each move or play consti-tuting a nomological edit. (A game of giving and asking for cosmological constants: the universe as a cultivated product of Collective Reason.) As Testa summarized, '[i]f one consid-ers "artificial" to be that which is shaped by an active Intelli-gence, then the entire Universe that surrounds us is already *artificial*':

> So audacious a statement evokes an immediate protest: surely
> we know what 'artificial' things look like, things that are produced
> by an Intelligence engaged in instrumental activity! Where, then,
> are the spacecraft, where the Moloch-machines, where—in
> short—the titanic technologies of these beings who are supposed
> to surround us and constitute the starry firmament? But this is

26.   A. Acheropoulos, *The New Cosmogony* (London: Black Dwarf Press, 1963); see also B. Weydenthal, *The World as Game and Conspiracy*, tr. H. Stymington (Chicago: University of Chicago Press, 1970); an important archi-val source on the matter is provided in S. Lem, *Doskonała próżnia* (Warsaw: Czytelnik, 1971).

27.   Extending the original Kardashev scale of technological aptitude, Barrow defines a Type-Ω civilization as one 'which could manipulate the entire Uni-verse'. See J.D. Barrow, *Impossibility: The Limits of Science and the Science of Limits* (Oxford: Oxford University Press, 1998), 130; see also N. Kardashev, 'On the Inevitability and the Possible Structures of Supercivilizations', in M.D. Papagiannis (ed.), *The Search for Extraterrestrial Life: Recent Developments* (Dordrecht: D. Reidel, 1984), 497–504.

a mistake caused by the inertia of the mind, since instrumental technologies are required only—says Acheropoulos—by a civilization still in the embryonic stage, like Earth's. A billion-year-old civilization employs none. Its tools are what *we* call the Laws of Nature. Physics itself is the 'machine' of such civilizations![28]

Given that intellect tends towards environmental manipulation, then, any sufficiently advanced intelligence becomes *entirely indistinguishable from its own environment*.[29] 'Brains' the size of gas giants, neutron stars, or even entire globular clusters would be only the very beginning of this tendency.[30] Could all observable structure, then, be some astronomically distributed and rarefied 'neurosystem', some Dysonian *Organprojektion*,[31] physics itself the externalized 'nervous array' of computational behemoths and their ongoing interaction,[32] dust clouds, black holes, nebulae, galaxies, clusters, superclusters, etc., all therefore memory-traces of onward-rolling cogitation, cosmological

---

28.   Testa, *From the Einsteinian to the Testan Universe*, 208. E.R. Harrison has asked similar questions: see E.R. Harrison, 'The Natural Selection of Universes Containing Intelligent Life', *Quarterly Journal of the Royal Astronomical Society* 36:3 (1995), 193–203.

29.   See F. Hoyle, *The Intelligent Universe* (London: Michael Joseph, 1983); this has been called the 'indistinguishability thesis', see M.M. Ćirković, 'Post-Postbiological Evolution?', *Futures* 99 (2018), 28–35; for a further summary of views on the matter, see Ćirković, *The Great Silence*, 133–7.

30.   A. Sandberg, 'The Physics of Information Processing Superobjects: Daily Life Among the Jupiter Brains', *Journal of Evolution and Technology* 5:1 (1999); see also, R.J. Bradbury 'Life at the Limits of Physical Laws', *Proceedings of the Society of Photo-Optical Instrumentation Engineers* 4273 (2001), 63–71.

31.   See R. Schuer, *The Mind-Made Universe: Laws vs Rules* (New York: Henry Schuman, 1969).

32.   G. von Hohenheim, *Cosmogonic Neurosystems: From the Spine to the Stars and Back Again* (New York: Jacob and Strauss, 1975).

constants and physical laws the 'reflex-arcs' of a 'metagalacti-cally plural Reason'...?[33] One recalls Newton's proclamation that *space is the sensorium of God*; could we be living, literally, inside the sensorium of ET?[34]

With a nod to Vernadskii, Acheropoulos spoke of the '*psy-chozoiciziation' of the entire universe* (through the 'cosmo-metamorphic power' of this 'Game of Intelligences').[35] His vision was that the constraints and syntaxes of such a metagalactic game would concretize, emergently and without competition or antagonism, from the dialogic interactions of the Exalted Players—always open to revision and restructuring. (This has interesting knock-on effects for the veracity of 'cosmic mem-ory' insofar as, within such a schema, memory is *never not the parent of itself*, so to speak.)[36] Acheropoulosian science thus

> sees the Universe as a palimpsest of Games, Games endowed
> with a memory reaching beyond the memory of any one Player.
> This memory is the harmony of the Laws of Nature, which hold
> the Universe in a homogeneity of motion. We look upon the Uni-
> versum, then, as upon a field of multibillion-year labours, stratified
> one on the other over the aeons, tending to goals of which only

---

33. S. Lem, E. de Laczay, and I. Csicsery-Ronay, 'The Possibilities of Science Fiction', *Science-Fiction Studies* 8 (1981), 54–71: 57.

34. Newton, significantly, attributes to God a 'boundless uniform Sensorium' just after recounting the construction of 'little sensoriums' in God's creatures through the contrivance of a 'Neck running down into a Back-bone' and its interconnected 'Eyes, Ears [and] Brain'. See I. Newton, *Opticks* (London: Sam Smith, 1704), 345 and 378.

35. Acheropoulos, *The New Cosmogony*, 66.

36. See Schuer, *The Mind-Made Universe*, 50–100.

the closest and most minute fragments are fragmentarily perceptible to us'.[37]

Acheropoulosian ideas proved revelatory for Barker, yet he would revolt against them, producing his own drastically inverted alternative: 'Does one need a *direction*—panspermic or demiurgic—in order to have mnemonic persistence?', he queried.[38] What we perceive as cosmological constants could just as well be *neurotic stereotypies* as *ludic deliberations*. What if physics is sedimented catatonia rather than petrified play? And memory need not be of intelligent origin: physics may indeed be a sedimented mnemeplex, but a pile of garbage is as much a 'chronicle' as a score-sheet; indeed, most memories aren't designed (let alone pleasantly ordered); whatever their medium, they don't have to be 'directed' in order to perpetuate and persist. All of these insubordinate reservations were eventually to lead Barker to his mature hypothesis:

> To cut a long story short, it became increasingly obvious to me that although they [NASA] said that were hunting for intelligence, what they were really seeking was organization. The whole program was fundamentally misguided.

As Barker recollects, at this point he 'veered off the organizational model'.[39] '[E]verything productive in signals analysis', he now averred, stems from the 'vigorous repudiation of

37. Testa, *From the Einsteinian to the Testan Universe*, 230.

38. D.C. Barker, *What Counts as Human* (Kingsport, MA: Kingsport College Press, 1997), 5.

39. Barker, 'Barker Speaks', 2.

hermeneutics' in 'processing sign-systems'.[40] Turning his back on his prior commitment to Directed Panspermia, owing to its 'residuum of intentionality',[41] and true to his information-theoretic background, Barker flipped the Acheropoulosian proposal on its head: *It is not that all galactic noise is, in fact, intentional organization; rather, all galactic organization is the catatonic suppression of aboriginal noise.*

What for Acheropoulos is an exalted metagalactic game, for Barker is a bad memory. The palimpsest of physics isn't some anciently externalized neurosystem; rather, the outermost antiquities of the cosmos can be read in encrypted form in our own neural axis. In other words, Barker, for his own 'cosmogony', turned away from ludics and toward schizotypy. (He had been long interested in such topics, ever since becoming involved, in the 1980s, in early NASA investigations into the psychiatric effects of 'exposure to space', or what is now called 'space-brain'.)[42]

Pursuing SETI/SETA inevitably leads one to question the very distinction between intelligence and environs—and to do so on the scale of the very grandest of cosmographic catchments—and Barker simply careened in the opposite direction to Acheropoulos. 'Suborganizational pattern is where things

---

40. Ibid., 4.

41. Interstellar viroid infall was still the engine of speciation and macroevolution—via horizontal genetic transmission across the stars—but this process was now neither intelligent nor directed. See Barker, 'Replicator Usurpation as Necroevolution'.

42. Such research continues today. See R. Jandial, R. Hoshide, J.D. Waters, and C.L. Limoli, 'Space-Brain: The Negative Effects of Space Exposure On The Central Nervous System', *Surgical Neurology International*, 9:9 (2018); see also N. Kanas and D. Manzey, *Space Psychology and Psychiatry* (New York: Springer, 2004).

really happen': rather than background noise being revealed as intelligently structured signal, instead signal is revealed to be noise suffering from a prolonged (yet ultimately unsustainable) self-delusion that comes to call itself 'structure'. Such 'delusion', of course, is conceptualized along the lines of an auto-repressive tendency and is inwardly registered as trauma.[43] Barker's project of genomic exo-archaeology was still concerned with the unearthing of a message—it was just that the message no longer belonged to anyone, and was a relay of torment rather than exaltation.[44] Thus the 'Geocosmic Theory of Trauma' began its life as an response to Acheropoulos's 'New Cosmogony', modulated through Barker's unique formulation of the subpersonal synonymy of structuration and traumatics.

'Organisation is suppression'—this was the Barkerian Axiom, its first model being that of planetary accretion via magma-ocean solidification, producing 'impersonal trauma' as 'anorganic memory' via the interment of 'the molten core [within] a crustal shell'. Baryspheric immurement: the first inward collapse or generation of a gradient and hence also of 'proto-inwardness'. Higher up, this selfsame traumatogenic 'tension is continually expressed—partially frozen—in biological organization' with 'the peculiarly locked-up life-forms we tend to see as typical'.[45]

Such a stance triggered a generalized diagnostic of 'terrestrial symptomaticity', enabled by the Axiom. Reports on Barker's activities from this period (at this point on 'final

---

43.   See D.C. Barker, 'Teleonomic Sequestration and Subornation Through Anorganic Kleptoplasty', *Plutonics* 12:5 (1995), 72–99.

44.   'Cryptography has been my guiding thread, right through', Barker claimed of his project: it has always been the 'rigorous practice of decoding'; 'there is a voyage, but a strangely immobile one'. Barker, 'Barker Speaks', 2.

45.   Barker, 'Barker Speaks', 5–6.

warning' from his NASA superiors) are particularly unreliable, his research projects recorded only in the anecdotal reports of ex-colleagues who evidently didn't understand Barker's methodology or the scope of his work. It is said, for example, that he became preoccupied with tracing a perfect continuity between the Nemesis Star's elliptical outer orbit and the curvature of human lordosis, or that he began to search for topological similarities between the human cranial vault and the Boötes void.[46] There is, he supposedly convinced himself, a direct geometric relationship between the mammal's swollen calvarium and the concavity of the Chicxulub crater.[47] Who, after all, couldn't see the continuity between mass transfer convective flows, magmatic plume currents, ocean-floor fractionations and the conglomerated body-tics of human postural dynamics? Personality and schizotypy are, in the end, just a question of rheidity. The perturbations of personal experience (panic attacks, limited symptom attacks, etc.) could now be placed in contact with structure on the largest of scales (i.e. the galactic 'Local Hole'). However, the question of correspondence was no simple one: 'neuronic time is supple, episodic, and diagonalizing', Barker insisted. He apparently argued that cosmological time itself was not homogenous or isotropic, but that supercluster complexes, galaxy walls, filaments and voids coarsened and distorted spacetime through backreaction: such

---

46. R.P. Kirshner, A. Oemler, P.L. Schechter, and S.A. Shectman, 'A Million Cubic Megaparsec Void in Boötes', *Astrophysical Journal* 248 (1981), 57–60; D.C. Barker, 'Notes Towards an Interstellar Nemo-Phenomenology; or, What It's Like to Be a Million-Light-Year-Spanning Super-Void', *Bulletin of the Plutonics Committee* 7 (1993): 11–25.

47. D.C. Barker, 'Non-Earth Originating Traumata: The Human Cerebrospinal System as *Musæum Clausum*', *Bulletin of the Plutonics Committee* 6 (1992): 33–39.

chronological inhomogeneity or anisotropy, he claimed, likewise applied when mapping our bodies as clusters of relations within macroevolutionary morpho-space. 'We cannot take time's homogeneity for granted', he averred. (As the largest structures add a 'coarse grain' or 'viscosity' to cosmic time, so too do certain morphological inheritances have an analogous distortive effect.) 'Trauma is a body', Barker announced. In its final form (or at least, the last we know of), this strange line of thought yielded what was to become the foremost twentieth-century formulation of Spinal Catastrophism:

> For humans there is a particular crisis of bipedal erect posture to be processed. [This] took me back to the calamitous consequences of the Precambrian explosion, roughly five hundred million years ago. [...] Obviously there are discrete quasi-coherent neuro-motor tic-flux patterns, whose incrementally rigidified stages are swimming, crawling, and (bipedal) walking. [...] Erect posture and perpendicularization of the skull is a frozen calamity, associated with a long list of pathological consequences, amongst which should be included most of the human psychoneuroses.

The Toba Bottleneck, being comparatively recent, could be read off the cervical atlas; mnemonic residua of the Neoproterozoic Oxygenation Holocaust, however, would of course have to be located somewhere much further down the spinal levels, and more deeply encrypted.

By this point, NASA was finished with Barker. His office filling with endocasts and craniometric charts, colleagues later recounted that, instead of conducting signals and detections analysis, he was spending his waking hours retrofitting seismological imaging algorithms for the detection of 'deep-brain vibrations and elasticities', claiming that suprachiasmatic shear-waves encoded data relevant for predicting solar Coronal Mass Ejections (CMEs).[48] He was unceremoniously fired—an event he recalled as 'messy' owing to his high-level clearance—and his ideas were neatly, yet fiercely, ridiculed. Amid rumours of an orchestrated smear campaign, Barker quietly moved on to his position at MVU.

---

48. 'It is commonly supposed that noise obscures but does not contain useful information. However, in wave physics and especially, seismology, scientists developed some tools known as "noise correlation" to extract useful information and construct images from the random vibrations of a medium. Living tissues are full of unexploited vibrations as well', see A. Zorgani et al. 'Brain Palpation from Physiological Vibrations using MRI', in *PNAS* 112:42 (2015), 12917–21.

Barker is only the most recent to have mapped Spinal Cata-strophism.[1] Others had journeyed this landscape before him, in fact and in fiction. Indeed, the troupe of eccentric sources from whom Barker drew his inspiration hailed as much from the speculative worlds of science fiction as from the sciences of cryptanalysis, astrobiology, and signaletics. And foremost among these visionaries is J.G. Ballard (1930–2009), whom Barker cites, approvingly, as having lucidly preempted the ideas of 'DNA as a transorganic memory-bank and the spine as a fossil record'.[2]

The prose of this one-time medical student become 'Seer of Shepperton' drips with physiological terminology—with spinal columns ostentatiously prevalent: '[E]xposed spinal lev-els' jag down *Atrocity Exhibition*'s pages, and vertebral series—'medullary', 'thoracic', 'sacral'—consistently concatenate its segmented vignettes, providing some illegible compass of tag-mata.[3] Already diagrammed in Ballard's early novels of catas-trophe such as 1962's *The Drowned World*, characters' postures are catalogued with orthopaedic precision. These postures, moreover, are 'mimetised in the procession of [urban] space': a diagonalization of 'inner' and 'outer' space, as inhabitant, habit, and habitat are enfolded in a tightening stigmergic loop, a techonomic pirouette of mutual reinvention.[4]

---

1.   Nonetheless, see R. Negarestani, 'Globe of Revolution: An Afterthought on Geophilosophical Realism', *Identities* 17 (2011), 25–54.

2.   Barker, 'Barker Speaks', 7.

3.   J.G. Ballard, *The Atrocity Exhibition* (San Francisco: RE/Search, 1990), 1.

4.   J.G. Ballard, *The Terminal Beach* (London: Dent, 1984), 144. On 'stigmery' as large-scale coordination through two-way loops between environment and organism, see F. Heylighten 'Stigmergy as a Universal Coordination Mechanism I:

For Ballard, it seems, the built environment externalizes our anatomical poises and desires, but such externalization in turn reprograms us from the inside out. He thus augurs that any society attaining suitable informatic density and media massification experiences *severe chronotopic leakage*. As explored above, when enough of our environment is captured by and entangled within intentional and artefactual systems, the distinction between 'artifice' and 'nature' progressively collapses.[5] Civilization grows an **ectopic unconscious**—an outpouching of drive-mechanism and erotic-cathexes, extracranially exported—like the mutant spider in the short story 'The Voices of Time', whose artificially expedited evolution enables it to externally ramify its CNS by weaving extra-somatic ganglion networks instead of a web, fabricating an everted second brain.[6]

Definition and Components', *Cognitive Systems Research* 38 (2016), 4–13. For a recent exploration of the relationship between outer and inner space in Ballard's oeuvre, see S. Sellars, *Applied Ballardianism* (Falmouth: Urbanomic, 2018).

5.   In Ballard's words, our moment is one wherein 'the fictional elements in the world around us are multiplying to the point where it is almost impossible to distinguish between the "real" and the "false"—the terms no longer have any meaning. The faces of public figures are projected at us as if out of some endless global pantomime, they and the events in the world at large have the conviction and reality of those depicted on giant advertisement hoardings. The task of the arts seems more and more to be that of isolating the few elements of reality from this mélange of fictions, not some metaphorical "reality," but simply the basic elements of cognition and posture that are the jigs and props of our consciousness. [...] As Dali has remarked, after Freud's explorations within the psyche it is now the outer world which will have to be eroticized and quantified'. Ballard enjoins, therefore, a *depth psychology of our artificial earth*. See J.G. Ballard, 'The Coming of the Unconscious', *New Worlds* 50:164 (1966), 141–6.

6.   The arachnid's web forms 'an external neural plexus, an inflatable brain as it were, that he can pump up to whatever size the situation calls for'. J.G. Ballard, *The Voices of Time, and Other Stories* (New York: Berkeley, 1966), 16. Appropriately, one of the three protective meninges layers surrounding the brain and spinal cord is called the **arachnoid mater**.

Ballardian kinesics, however, do not merely resonate with external space, they also provide a cipher for outer time:

> Entry points into the future = Levels in a spinal landscape = zones of significant time.[7]

For Ballard, a consistently nonconforming Kantian in his approach to space-time, temporality becomes a global secretion of the CNS: a dendritic ejaculate, a product of innervation, an offshoot of being immured within a nervous system.[8] This *ipso facto* means that alterations to nervous systems are transportations in time. The vicissitudes of this process are catalogued in Ballard's nosologies of temporal disruption, accounts of '**time-sicknesses**' wherein alterations to the CNS trigger catastrophic modifications of chronoreceptivity: for example, the new time-sensitive receptors and nervous extrusions of modified organisms in 'The Voices of Time'. For if time is an ejaculate of the nerves, then to alter an organism's nervous system is to move it forward or backward in organic time. Accordingly, Ballard pictures genetically altered organisms displaying the tempos of macro-evolution (and even cosmic evolution) at diverging rates, with strange organs and spandrels from some future evolutionary event arriving early, expressed as mutations and strange sensory bulbs with as-yet-unknown usages and sensitivities.

---

7. Ballard, *The Terminal Beach*, 144.

8. Again, abiogenesis *is* chronogenesis. Life is the initiation of basic appetitions which are defined by teleonomies. In this, placid and tranquil reality dissimulated itself into the simulation of time-production through goal-oriented behaviours. In other words, this is how stillness tore itself apart. Life is essentially accelerative, or, is acceleration essentially.

This 'time-sickness' afflicts organisms altered by intervention, but in Ballard's stories it can also overwhelm characters altered by a changing environment, stimulated and aroused by 'levels above [their] existing nervous system'. To experience the radically accelerating changes of our built environment is to experience the future coming early—which, again, is indistinguishable from experiencing the drag of the past—and this demands of us new appendages and new 'forms of intuition', which Ballard registers as subtle changes to the nervous system, mapped onto the spine, whose vertically ascending series of vertebrae, from pelvis to skull, easily becomes transliterated as the linear ordering of time, from past to future: spinal levels as time-steps. He reasons that if the 'autonomic system' (the lower regions of the CNS) are 'dominated by the past', then the 'cerebro-spinal' (in its zenith-scraping upward thrust) reaches 'towards the future'.[9] The higher regions are those through which we communicate with the arriving future, the lower regions those through which we intercourse with our buried past. Accordingly, Ballard announces that the 'Thoracic Drop' down the vertebrae—a shutting off of the higher centres of consciousness—moves us towards the palaeo-temporal nadir, i.e. our deepest evolutionary heritage. This 'shutting off' or 'dropping away', however, is not to be interpreted as *nosological deviation* from some functional norm but merely as *preparation* for some new environment or oncoming state of being. (Which, indeed, may be produced by modern technoscience's tendency to externalize and materially consecrate our deepest drives.) Indeed, at a certain point in this descent the distinction between

---

9.   The nonconscious 'autonomic nervous system' (ANS)—governing digestion, respiration, etc.—is phylogenetically older than the CNS. Ballard, *Terminal Beach*, 143.

inside and outside (dermal, psychic, genomic) completely unravels—Ballard speaks of a new 'landscape' being 'revealed at the level of T-12' (thoracic vertebra #12).[10] Time, because it is the arena of all geneses, is the medium of vivisection. It provides the thread which, when pulled, procedurally unravels all interiorities: in so far as to move down the spine is to move back in time, it is also to move outwards, opening onto vistas beyond all individuality, all personality. This is the Spinal Landscape.

Organic 'development' is just the future arriving early, organic 'structure' is just the retention of the past, and our experience of time is nothing but movement within this morpho-space. If new chronoreceptive organs are **caenogenetic** (arriving from some unforeseen evolutionary future), 'spinal descent' traces the **palingenetic** retrogression into deep pasts.[11] The implication being that, if time is emitted *by* CNS-architecture, then there are other possible receptivity profiles, other workable organizations of time: organizations which, from *within* our current CNS-architectonic, can only appear to us as instances of **time travel**, as contortions of unilinearity: **precocious futures** or **recidivist pasts**.

This thesis is scaled and extrapolated globally in the 1962 novel *The Drowned World*. In this near-future scenario, climatic shift, caused by solar fluctuations, triggers temporal-developmental retrogradation across *all* natural echelons—floral, faunal, and spiritual. As 'Triassic' mangroves and 'Paleocene' iguanids reemerge, the novel's characters psychologically experience an 'uncovering' of 'taboos and drives' that have been dormant

---

10. Ballard, *Atrocity Exhibition*, 31.

11. In embryology, palingenesis refers to repetition of 'older' morphologies, whilst caenogenesis refers to addition of 'novel' ones.

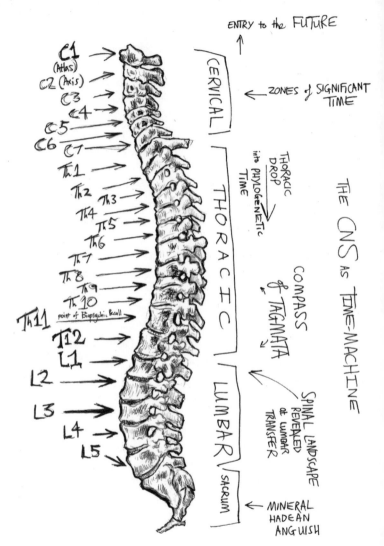

ENTRY to the FUTURE

ZONES of SIGNIFICANT TIME

C1 (Atlas)
C2 (Axis)
C3
C4
C5
C6 C7
Th1
Th2 Th3
Th4
Th5
Th6
Th7
Th8
Th9
Th 10
point of Biopsychic Recall
Th11
T12
L1
L2
L3
L4
L5

CERVICAL

THORACIC

LUMBAR

SACRUM

THORACIC DROP into PHYLOGENETIC Time

THE CNS AS TIME-MACHINE

COMPASS of TAGMATA

SPINAL LANDSCAPE REVEALED at LUMBAR TRANSFER

MINERAL HADEAN ANGUISH

Fig. 4. Bodkin's theory of Neuronics

'for epochs'.[12] As the ectopic unconscious (the built environment) disappears in an 'avalanche backwards into the past', giving way to regressive natural environs, the characters accordingly undergo 'total biopsychic recall', an awakening of the 'oldest memories of Earth', 'time-codes carried in every chromosome and gene' revealed under pressure of climate change, new chronoreceptivity profiles beckoned forth by environmental catastrophe. According to the 'new psychology of **Neuronics** developed by one of Ballard's characters as he studies these effects on his colleagues, the

> central nervous system is a coded time scale, each nexus of neurons and each spinal level marking a symbolic station, a unit of neuronic time.[13]

Bodkin, the scientist behind this new Neuronic psychology, provides the following prospectus:

> The further down the CNS you move, from the hind-brain through the medulla into the spinal cord, you descend back into the neuronic past. For example, the junction between thoracic and lumbar vertebrae, between T-12 and L-1, is the great zone of transit between the gill-breathing fish and air-breathing amphibians [with] rib-cages.[14]

---

12. 'Sometimes he wondered what zone of transit he himself was entering, sure that his own withdrawal was symptomatic not of a dormant schizophrenia, but of a careful preparation for a radically new environment, with its own internal landscape and logic, where old categories of thought would merely be an encumbrance.' J.G. Ballard, *The Drowned World* (London: Harper, 2012), 14.

13. Ibid., 44.

14. Ibid.

Spine become **deep time submersible**; the CNS as time-machine. From a perspective sensitive to the neural apriority of time, alterations to chronoreceptivity are indistinguishable from bona fide chronolocomotion, or genuine environmental **ecphory** (epoch regurgitation; biota anamnesis). Ballard, indeed, once exclaimed to an interviewer that our CNS provides far more powerful opportunities for 'time travel' than any Wellsian 'machine'.[15]

The importance of these insights for Barker's ulterior development of Spinal Catastrophism cannot be overstated. Ballard, however, was himself merely vocalizing the same thought patterns—undulating to the same conceptions—that had led many others, previously, to similar conclusions. Wittingly or not, he was becoming part of a centuries-old 'tradition'. But before we explore some of Ballard's more immediate precursors, it will be necessary to set forth some of the larger-scale philosophical notions that inform this tradition.

---

15.   'I tell how human beings [...] regress into the past. In a certain sense, they climb down their own spinal column. They traverse down the thoracic vertebrae, from the point at which they are air-breathing mammals, to the lumbar region, to the point at which they are amphibious reptiles. Finally they reach the absolute past [...] I was dissatisfied with the traditional forms used by SF writers to realise time travel'. See S. Sellars and D. O'Hara (eds.), *Extreme Metaphors: Interviews with J.G. Ballard 1967–2008* (London: Harper, 2012), 11.

TH3. THE LAW OF SUPERPOSITION & THE BIOGENETIC LAW

Spinal Catastrophism is constructible as the commixture of two venerable idea-clusters. First, the notion of **Depth-as-Memory** and the Law of Superposition, traceable to the seventeenth-century genesis of the geosciences; and second, embryology's Theory of Recapitulation, also known as the **Biogenetic Law**, which is itself traceable to the late eighteenth-century collision of Absolute Idealism with Natural History.

The convergence of these two notions, the Law of Superposition and the Biogenetic Law, furnished the matrix within which Spinal Catastrophist notions first became articulable, via a self-obsolescing exacerbation of the internal logic of two core Enlightenment Idealist tenets: the **Principle of Continuity** was abrogated by Superposition, and Recapitulation arose as a mutation of the **Principle of Identity**.

An anciently held presumption, the Principle of Continuity was first given explicit and precise formulation by Leibniz (1646–1716).[1] Inspired by his successes with infinitesimals and differential calculus, Leibniz proclaimed that, between any two natural instances, there is necessarily an infinity of intermediary instances: no interstice, no saltation, no genuine and irreducible abruption. (A genuine indivisibility—as a separation that *just is*, without further explanation—would introduce an *unaccountability* into the ligature of rationally structured nature: something that was firmly foreclosed by Leibniz's cognate Principle of Sufficient Reason.) Thus, to be is to be

---

1.   For an ancient example, see Aristotle, *History of Animals,* tr. D.M. Balme (Cambridge, MA: Harvard University Press, 1991), 8:13, 588b5. Aristotle referred to continuity as 'Synecheia' (Συνέχεια).

concentrically included and to concentrically include in turn, *ad infinitum*. Spurred on by Leeuwenhoek's innovations in microscopy, Leibniz therefore announced, 'not only is there life everywhere [but] there are also infinite degrees of it'.[2] Or, conversely, 'there is nothing fallow, nothing sterile, nothing dead in the universe'.[3] (This of course was the basis of his fractal vision of each quantum of matter being a 'populated world', itself containing further populous worlds, with telescoping interminability.)[4] Each single life is contained within indefinitely many other lives and includes indefinitely many others in turn—*without remainder*—because, by the very same token, there is simply no external medium or environing death within which life could be excluded or suspended. By introducing infinitesimals into biology, then, Leibniz effectively biologized infinity. This applied both spatially and temporally: such an outlook coupled perfectly with William Harvey's *omne vivum ex ovo* injunction ('all life comes from life') and the embryological idea of preformation (which proposed that—through infinite 'scatulation' or 'encasement'—organic reproduction operates essentially like a never-ending Matryoshka doll).[5] And so, if all life comes from other life, then, as far back as you can go, there is always life. What this meant is that the *inorganic simply didn't exist*. Indeed, the very term 'inorganic' in the modern sense only appeared later,

---

2. G.W. Leibniz, *Leibniz's Monadology: A New Translation and Guide,* tr. L. Strickland (Edinburgh: Edinburgh University Press, 2014), 272.

3. G.W. Leibniz, *Leibniz's Monadology: A New Edition for Students*, tr. N. Rescher (Pittsburgh: University of Pittsburgh Press, 1991), 26.

4. There 'is a whole world of creatures [even] in the least piece of matter', each of which 'can be conceived as a garden of plants and a pond full of fish'. See Leibniz, *Monadology*, 132–3.

5. For a definition of 'scatulation', see E. Haeckel, *The Riddle of the Universe*, tr. J. McCade (London: Watts and Co., 1929), 45.

around 1800, in response to innovations in geochemistry and massive shifts in world view. (Previously, the archaic 'inorganical' had long referred, instead, to something *incorporeal* or *spiritual*. Here, the fact that the antonym of 'life' was not 'death' but 'afterlife' is incredibly telling.) The idea of nonliving matter was of course present, but it was only admitted as a *temporary* deviation from living instances (as Erasmus Darwin declared, channelling a presumption utterly typical for the eighteenth-century: 'Awhile extinct the organic matter lies; / The wrecks of death are but a change of forms').[6] Thus, all matter was considered essentially biogenic and the idea of material entirely detached from (i.e. utterly indivisible vis-à-vis) an economy of organic utility and circulation was absent.[7]

And so, via the Principle of Continuity, homogeneity in space (infinite divisibility) was taken to also entail homogeneity in time (eternal inclusion of lives within parent lives, back to the beginning of time). In short, matter can have no 'memory', and can 'tell no tale', because it is always, everywhere and everywhen, the same (that is, basically alive) and is so *continuously and interminably*. Preformationism precludes memory in any meaningful sense, because everything is already contained (with infinite divisibility) within the present moment. And so, no matter where one carves or cleaves, no matter what the scale or time-step, one only derives further biogenic instances— producing only smaller, quotient lives—never reaching a basal

6.　E. Darwin, *The Temple of Nature, or The Origin of Society* (London: J. Johnson, 1803), 151.

7.　The uniformitarian geotheorist James Playfair was deeply agnostic regarding a period 'prior to all organized matter', instead choosing to insist that no 'particle of calcareous matter' has not been 'part of an animal body'. See J. Playfair, *Illustrations of the Huttonian Theory of the Earth* (Cambridge: Cambridge University Press, 2011), 171, 154.

indivisible that could be classified as lifeless matter rebarbative to all living utility. This led to an essentially placental or amniotic world view, wherein life is infinitely included in the universe because there is absolutely nothing in the universe that could exclude it.

Nonetheless, the first in a series of conceptual innovations that would go on to unwind this cosy world view had already been developed. In 1668, Nicolas Steno (1638–1686) had announced his **Stratigraphic Law of Superposition**: the founding gesture of modern geognosy and geohistory.[8] Steno was the first to note explicitly that stratigraphic succession correlates with temporal succession. In other words, that *depth is time*. (Hence, centuries later, McPhee's coinage of '**deep time**'.)[9] This marked the inception of the notion of *depth as mnemonic and temporal retrogression* that would later be so vital to psychoanalysis or so-called 'depth psychology' (*Tiefenpsychologie*). (Here we cannot fail to mention that Steno was himself a neuroanatomist: one of the first polymaths, alongside Descartes and Willis, to map the deeper structures of the brain, he hypothesized that brain function arose from the nervous parenchyma [cellular tissue] rather than from the ventricular system.)[10]

Importantly, Steno's Stratigraphic Law expedited the scientific formulation of an entirely chronometric notion of time (which was already beginning to release horology from its premodern subordination to exclusively embodied, circular,

---

8.   N. Steno, *The Prodromus of Nicolaus Steno's Dissertation concerning a Solid Body Enclosed by Process of Nature within a Solid* (London: Macmillan, 1915).

9.   J. McPhee, *Basin and Range* (New York: Farrar, Straus and Giroux, 1981).

10.   N. Steno, *Discours de Monsieur Sténon sur l'anatomie du cerveau* (Paris, 1669); A. Parent, 'Niels Stensen: A 17th Century Scientist with a Modern View of Brain Organization', *Canadian Journal of Neurological Sciences* 40:4 (2013), 482–92.

Fig. 5. Comparison of Nicolas Steno's cross-section of the brain and Athanasius Kircher's cross-section of the geocosm—an 'ignis centralis' can be identified in both

rotational, sidereal or calendric motions) since it implied that *all space and body is itself nothing but coagulated time.* As a direct consequence, the spatial (morphological and tectological) relations within our own bodies could, at least potentially, be disarticulated into striated timesteps.[11] With the eighteenth-century consolidation of **comparative anatomy**— from William Hunter to Georges Cuvier—our body-plan suddenly became, unmistakably, a chronicle.[12] (As indeed did the

---

11.   Ernst Haeckel invented '**tectology**' (a term later borrowed by Soviet systems theorist Alexander Bogdanov), defining it as 'the theory of structure in organisms'. Haeckel considered that somatic individuality emerged from the morphological integration of systems which, considered in isolation, resembled autonomous individuals lower down the phyletic tree. His tectology is 'the comprehensive science of individuality among living natural bodies, which usually represent an aggregate of individuals of various orders'. Windows of simultaneity are only ever a product of ongoing integrations of divergent time-series. See E. Haeckel, *Generelle Morphologie der Organismen: Allgemeine Grundzüge der organischen Formen-Wissenschaft* (Berlin, 2 vols., 1866), vol. 1, 241.

12.   W.D. Rolfe, 'William and John Hunter: Breaking the Great Chain of Being', in W.F. Bynum and R. Porter (eds.), *William Hunter and the Eighteenth-Century Medical World* (Cambridge: Cambridge University Press, 1985), 297–320.

entire cosmos: in 1824, the great astronomer William Herschel, having realized that many observable stars were likely already long extinct, consequently observed that something like Steno's Law applies just as much to astronomy as to geognosy and that the Milky Way is thus itself a 'kind of chronometer'.)[13]

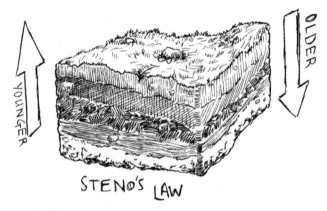

Fig 6. Steno's Geognostic Law of Stratigraphic Superposition

Every object an hourglass. Time is not produced by bodies and motions; all bodily motions, without exception, are the effluvia of Grand Time. The somaticized reading of 'memory' proposed

---

13.   W. Herschel, *The Scientific Papers of Sir William Herschel* (Cambridge: Cambridge University Press, 2 vols., 2013), vol. 2, 541. Looking upwards might be looking into the deep past, but, insofar as it is also looking out at an environing canopy of inorganic death, as the nineteenth century first dimly intuited, the grand silence of the skies may well also afford a glimpse into our longest-term future. Thomas De Quincey sensed this, describing early images of the Orion Nebula as a voluminous skull with a parsec-long rictus grin, thrown back upon a 'beautifully developed' spine 'that many centuries would not traverse'. Barker, likewise, liked to point out that Orion looks like an endocranium.

by Spinal Catastrophism descends directly from this revelation, via a particular transliteration of Steno's Law onto vertebral levels (the junction of T-12 and L-1—'lumbar transfer'—echoing stratigraphy's iridium layer marking the K-Pg boundary, as Barker argued). With this filtration of *all* spatio-morphological continuity through disarticulating horology *without* exception (the emptying out of nature's infinitesimal embodiment into a chronometrics unpinioned from *ab ovo* concentricity), somatic containment catastrophically becomes reformatted as *self-abruption* rather than *self-inclusion*. The Principle of Continuity, along with its stipulation of infinite soma-divisibility and self-similarity, is rescinded and *depth* becomes available as an internalized heterogeneity, giving rise to something more like a Principle of Mereological Alienation. For chronometric horology is not limited to the structures and strictures of embodied and objectivated chronotopes and thus is not *divisible* into living time, the tempos native to the *Lebenswelt* (the embodied time of our lived experience is limited to the motion of bodies in space, and thus to sidereal circulations and calendric rhythms of observed events; clock time, in contrast, abstracts time into a blank ordinal series no longer defined or measured by observable and calendric cycles).[14] When the indivisibility of ordinal time is read through embodied self-divisibility, the body becomes a thread to be unravelled. Thus the geognostic Law of Superposition came to compromise and revoke that of Leibnizian Continuity.

And yet, if we must include the indivisible recalcitrance of a time that outstrips containment within experience (because bodies *are* glaciated temporality), then somatic self-inclusion

---

14.   See A. Greenspan, *Capitalism's Transcendental Time Machine*, PhD Thesis, University of Warwick, 2000.

must, at a certain depth, invert into historical self-exclusion (as Ballard much later realised, at some stage, mnemonic recall must become ruinous for the framework of personal experience). That is, if we contain the grandest time, then we carry within us our outside, the trace of our prior nonexistence (in more contemporary terms, this is the organism's internal pact with its own dissolution through dissipative renewal—the fact that we must constantly die in tiny amounts in order to stave off dying entirely). What we arrive at by way of such **self-excluding self-inclusion**, however, is an almost geometric deduction of **Recapitulationism**—the second tributary of Spinal Catastrophism after the Law of Superposition. Made infamous post-1860 by Haeckel, recapitulationism finds its true roots in the 1770–1830 *Goethezeit* and the *naturphilosophisch* speculations of philosophers such as F.W.J. Schelling and Lorenz Oken.

Recall that, according to the Principle of Continuity, every division or scission only arrives at further quotient lives, never bottoming out in a partition between 'life' and indivisible 'non-life' that simply cannot be further accounted for or biotically justified. This exhaustive expelling of 'unaccountability' and 'unjustifiability' is all-important, because it reveals the Principle of Continuity to be a strict entailment of the higher-order **Principle of Identity**. The wholesale expulsion of unjustifiability from existence is nothing but the converse of the maximal identification of existence with judiciality. Or, in other words, this 'expulsion' is simply the necessary collateral of the Dogmatic Idealist conviction that there is some mutually-exhaustive and foundational identity between rationality and reality (as embodied in the Leibnizian mantra: '*Whatever is, is just*'.) The Principle of Identity allowed Enlightenment Idealism to stipulate that everything, without exception, is contained within (and, thus, justified by) 'the Idea' (inasmuch as 'thinking=being' or 'A=A'). In this way, these Idealist Principles (i.e. the Principles of Identity and of Continuity, but also of Plenitude and Sufficient Reason) serially interlock to define nature as *nothing but* the bodying forth of the infinitely divisible fasciae of judicial and jurisprudent reason. Nature is, without exception or saltation, the interminably uninterrupted connective tissue for the self-expression of the law.

Yet ever since Steno's first suggestion of its fundamental principles, the nascent earth sciences, practised from Buffon to Deluc, had been uncovering temporal prospects that far outstripped, in precedence and possibilia, both ideational and organismic horizons.[15] And from within the bosom of Idealism **Recapitulation** arose, almost spontaneously, as a compromise (and immune response) to the injurious and injudicious discovery of this vast outside, postulating that Spirit somehow still *contains* it because, crucially, Spirit *repeats* and *recalls* all exteriority through its own developmental self-realization (*Entwicklungsgeschichte*). Spirit thus comprises the ages of its deepest past as prepersonal stages on its long and inevitable journey to personeity. *Noogeny 'includes' geogony.*

---

15.   G.L. Buffon, *Histoire Naturelle, Général et Particuliér* (Paris: Imprimerie Royale, 36 vols., 1749–1788); G.L. Buffon, *The Epochs of Nature*, tr. J. Zalasiewicz, A. Milon, and M. Zalasiewicz (Chicago: University of Chicago Press, 2018); J.C. Greene, *The Death of Adam: Evolution and its Impact on Western Thought* (Iowa City, IA: Iowa State University Press, 1996); P. Rossi, *The Dark Abyss of Time: The History of the Earth and the History of Nations from Hooke to Vico*, tr. L.G. Cochrane (Chicago: University of Chicago Press, 1987); M.J.S. Rudwick, *Bursting The Limits of Time: The Reconstruction of Geohistory in the Age of Revolution* (Chicago: University of Chicago Press , 2005); M.J.S. Rudwick, *Worlds Before Adam: The Reconstruction of Geohistory in the Age of Reform* (Chicago: University of Chicago Press, 2008).

This internalization ('phagocytosis') of a gargantuan inorganic outside, however, inevitably led to fatal indigestion. Consuming earth history triggered intussusception within the sphere of the Idea. Put differently, *this was the first discovery (which is to say, production) of the Unconscious.*

That is, the stance of 'developmental repetitiousness' forced acceptance, amongst Schelling and his *naturphilosophischen* peers, that swathes of Spirit's development are not self-conscious, yet must still somehow be (genetically) included within Spirit. Since containment, noetic as much as somatic, could no longer equal telescoping self-similarity or infinitely divisible inclusion, memory became the domain of the unconscious (*Unbewußtsein*). Spirit had to contain everything, but it came to appreciate (via burgeoning natural historical researches) that it could not transparently recall the entire route to transparent self-consciousness. Its *Bildungsroman* was partly foreclosed to it, but no less real for it. With most of Spirit's long history proving troublingly unavailable to itself, then, memory became the domain of the unconscious. In Germany, this unconscious memory came to be studied under the title of the 'night-side of natural science'.[16] 'Forgetfulness' was no longer just a cognitive lapse but the *very principle of embodiment and of chronology.* To even have a body, riddled as they are liable to be with disease and recalcitrance, was for pure spirit a form of forgetfulness. (Amnesia, indeed, is the only way that certain strands of Idealism can even begin to explain natural history.) Ergo, innermost interiority was suddenly tenanted by the outermost past, invisible to the life of mind, experienced

---

16.   G.H. von Schubert, *Ansichten von der Nachtseite der Naturwissen-schaft* (Dresden: Arnold, 1808). The title translates as 'Views from the Night-Side of Natural Science'.

inwardly as a kind of opacity to intellect (though manifested outwardly as a body and its evolutionary history). The body as entrenched amnesia. Person, after all, is an entirely forensic term: meaning that one's personhood is only ever constructed *post hoc*.

Matter is amnesiac mind. Applied embryologically, this conviction led to the so-called **Meckel-Serres Law**, which claimed that '[t]he development of the individual organism obeys the same laws as the development of the whole animal series; that is to say, the higher animal, in its gradual development, essentially passes through the permanent organic stages that lie below it'.[17] This law was formulated in 1821. By the time of Ernst Haeckel's work in the 1860s, the principle had been raised to the status of evolutionary axiom and had attained maximum slogan density: '*Ontogeny recapitulates phylogeny*'.[18] Thus the Biogenetic Law was announced.

Provoked by the unstable compromise between Absolute Idealism and Natural History, this obsession with developmental repetitiousness became a core tenet of *Goethezeit Naturphilosophie*.[19] It promulgated the conviction, among many practicing naturalists, that the entire external universe was

---

17.   J.F. Meckel, *System der vergleichenden Anatomie* (Halle, 1821), 514; E.S. Russell, *Form and Function: A Contribution to the History of Animal Morphology* (London: John Murray, 1916), 236; S.J. Gould, *Ontogeny and Phylogeny* (Cambridge, MA: Harvard University Press, 1977), 37.

18.   Haeckel, *Generelle Morphologie*, vol. 2, 300; and see Gould, *Ontogeny and Phylogeny*, 76-8.

19.   See A. Gode-von Aesch, *Natural Science in German Romanticism* (New York: Columbia University Press, 1941); J.L. Esposito, *Schelling's Idealism and Philosophy of Nature* (Lewisburg, PA: Bucknell University Press, 1977); and, of course, I.H. Grant's trailblazing *Philosophies of Nature After Schelling* (London: Continuum, 2006).

simply the fossilized museum of various arrested stages of evolutionary development, 'relics' or 'abortions' from mind's unconscious voyage unto self-consciousness.[20] (In consequence, the first models of 'the unconscious' were radically ectopic, physicalized, and extended.)[21] So that what appears, from within chronotopic constraint, as a 'unified present moment' or 'window of simultaneity' is revealed instead as an exploded-view cross-section of radically disarticulated moments of total time: each internal organ or external species a piece of suspended historical shrapnel. Recapitulation, quite simply, is the nemesis of any stable *de nunc* indexicality. It detonates the unity (*synecheia*) of the present, revealing not only unilinearity but also all windows of simultaneity, to be entirely downstream of CNS enclosure and its contingent quirks.

---

20.   '[A]ll the lower forms in relation to the highest may be regarded as abortions'; see J.H. Green, *Vital Dynamics; the Hunterian Oration Before the Royal College of Surgeons* (London, 1840), 40. Even Freud couldn't resist this notion, once nomenclating non-human animals as 'permanent embryos'; see F. Sulloway, *Freud, Biologist of the Mind* (Cambridge, MA: Harvard University Press, 1979), 267.

21.   See A. Nicholls and M. Liebscher (eds.), *Thinking the Unconscious: Nineteenth-Century German Thought* (Cambridge: Cambridge University Press, 2010).

TH4. PHARYNGEAL PHANTASY & SPINAL POLYPTOTON

We find Ballard rehearsing the Meckel-Serres Law when he writes that the foetus's 'uterine odyssey [recapitulates] the entire evolutionary past'[1]—a statement that also helps decrypt the novelist's preoccupation with Elizabeth Taylor's 'lost gill-slits',[2] for Haeckel had theorized that the human embryo's pharyngeal grooves are palingenetic repetitions of ichthyic branchia, or gill arches—that the 'human gill slits *are* (literally) the adult features of an ancestor'.[3] Ballard himself, in 1970, acknowledges the *naturphilosophische* provenance of this idea, citing 'Goethe's notion that the skull is formed of modified vertebrae' and that 'the bones of the pelvis may constitute the remnant of a lost sacral skull'.[4]

But the true progenitor of 'Goethe's notion' was the towering Lorenz Oken (1779–1851), who, among other startling hypotheses, maintained that the entire human musculoskeletal system was procedurally constructed from a single self-iterating and self-deforming vertebra.[5] Beginning as a calcified vertebral 'vesicle', elongated to make a 'spine', and differentiating into poles to render 'head and pelvis', Oken deduces the human from the metamere. The 'entire human being is only a vertebra': the 'brain' is repeated 'spinal marrow'; the 'braincase' a refrain of the 'backbone'. (A noteworthy reversal of the

---

1. Ballard, *Drowned World*, 44.

2. Ballard, *Atrocity Exhibition*, 9.

3. Gould, *Ontogeny and Phylogeny*, 7.

4. Ballard, *Atrocity Exhibition*, 13–14.

5. See R.J. Richards, *The Romantic Conception of Life: Science and Philosophy in the Age of Goethe* (Chicago: University of Chicago Press, 2002), 495–502.

supposition of ancient Galenic medicine that the spine sprouts from the brain 'as a trunk'.)[6] 'The skeleton is only a fully grown, articulated, repetitive vertebrae', he expatiated.[7] There can be no doubt that in Oken we have recapitulation's most profligate proponent, and one of the most important progenitors of Spinal Catastrophism.

Oken's schema implied that the skull and pelvis are morphic moieties and should be considered as resonant polarities or tectological echoes of one another. This theory of the 'sacral skull', it is reported in *The Atrocity Exhibition*, succeeds in uncovering the 'rudiments of symmetry not only about the vertical axis but also the horizontal'—i.e., not just across the sagittal but also the transverse plane. Here Ballard clearly alludes to the idea, popularized by palaeontologists since the 1880s and only recently fully discredited, that dinosaurs owned a posterior 'second brain' housed in the pelvic cavity. This idea of a saurian lumbar brain arose from the discovery of fossil traces of dorsosacral nervous enlargements and the subsequent theorization that the prodigious *Stegosaurus*, given the pitiful size of its primary brain, would require a secondary plexus to which it could outsource the processing of digestive and reproductive operations.[8] (This duocephalon would make the

6.　Galen, *Galen on the Usefulness of the Parts of the Body*, tr. M. Tallmagde May (Ithaca, NY: Cornell University Press, 1968); see A.P. Wickens, *A History of the Brain: From Stone Age Surgery to Modern Neuroscience* (London: Taylor and Francis, 2015), 193.

7.　L. Oken, *Über die Bedeutung der Schädelknochen* (Jena, 1807), 5.

8.　O.C. Marsh, in 1881, described the *Stegosaurus* as having a 'posterior brain case' to increase neural supply to the posterior regions. See O.C. Marsh, 'Principal Characters of American Jurassic Dinosaurs', *American Journal of Science* 21 (1881), 417–23. Scientists now roundly reject this idea of saurian parallel computing. See E.B. Giffin, 'Endosacral Enlargements in Dinosaurs', *Modern Geology* 16 (1991), 101–12.

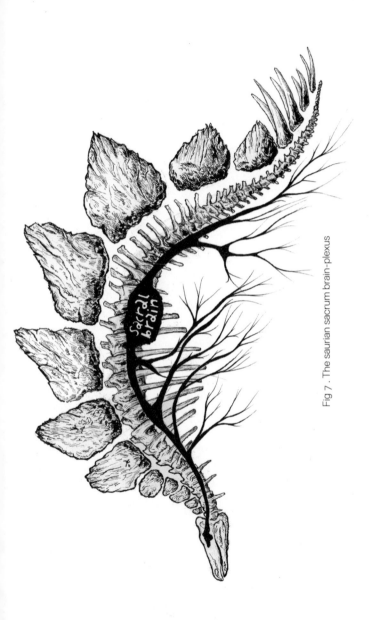

Fig 7 . The saurian sacrum brain-plexus

Fig 8. An amphisbaena, or two-headed snake,
longing for ouroboric symmetry

dinosaur alike to the amphisbaena of the mediaeval bestiary.)
In 1914, the palaeontologist Wilhelm von Branca (1844–1928)
went so far as to venture that, in the neural swelling of our solar
plexus, humans appear to retain traces of the saurian pelvic
encephalon.[9]

Ballard immediately links the suggestion of this vestigial
sacral braincase to a longing for the 'lost symmetry of the
blastosphere', 'precursor of the embryo' and the 'last structure
to preserve perfect symmetry in all planes'.[10] A longing that
recalls naturalist Étienne Geoffroy Saint-Hilaire's (1772–1844)
attempts to discover an underlying topological continuity
across divergent phyla by modelling the contortion of the vertebrae into a cephalopod (imagining that, if one were to bend
a chordate backwards about the dorsal axis—so that the head
conjoins with the backside and cephalic and caudal ends

---

9.   W. von Branca, 'Die Riesengrosse sauropoder Dinosaurier vom Tendagnru, ihr Aussterben und die Bedingungen ihrer Entstehung', *Archiv für Bion-
tologie* 3:1 (1914), 71–78.

10.   Ballard, *Atrocity Exhibition*, 7–8.

converge—one would derive a squid).[11] Such secret morphisms and tectologies, Ballard suggests, are the cryptic source of our desire to 'return to a symmetrical world, one that will recapture the perfect symmetry of the blastosphere',[12] a desire to regress from *bilateral schism* back into *radial immersion*. Fulfilment of which, incidentally, would cement a new alliance with the echinoderms: starfish and urchins are genetically bilaterian animals that have 'retrogressed' to a radial body-plan, sacrificing their heads to globular immanence. Their self-immolating ecstasies make them the true mystics of the sea. And with the attendant decerebration, these pentamerist beings simultaneously revolted against cephalization. (In the 'Voices of Time', Ballard describes a mutated cnidarian—a genetically radial sea anemone—prematurely wrenched from spherical immersion via genetic modification; it develops a 'rudimentary notochord', or proto-spine; the creature soon self-destructs, however, violently rejecting the phaneroscopic perversity of a spinal axis.)[13]

Ballard connects this longing for egress from the bilateral to the 'Mythology of Amniotic Return': the 'impulse' to 're-enter the amnionic corridor and [regress] through spinal [time]'.[14] It is dramatized in *The Drowned World* by the outbreak of sui-cidal compulsions to drown oneself in the so-called 'Pool of

11.   J.A.M. van den Biggelaar, E. Edsinger-Gonzales, and F.R. Schram, 'The Improbability of Dorso-Ventral Axis Inversion During Animal Evolution as Presumed by Geoffrey Saint Hilaire', *Contributions to Zoology* 71 (2002), 29–36. Deleuze, unsurprisingly, was fond of this image. See G. Deleuze and F. Guattari, *A Thousand Plateaus*, tr. B. Massumi (London: Continuum, 1987), 52 and 281.

12.   Ballard, *Atrocity Exhibition*, 14.

13.   It is, we are told, the 'first plant ever to develop a nervous system'. Ballard, *The Voices of Time*, 15.

14.   Ballard, *Drowned World*, 101.

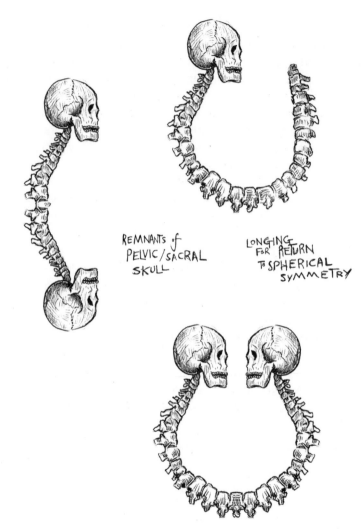

REMNANTS OF PELVIC/SACRAL SKULL

LONGING FOR RETURN TO SPHERICAL SYMMETRY

Fig 9. A belated attempt to return to a symmetrical world

Thanatos': the 'uterine night' of a deep jungle lagoon.[15] Free-flowing liquidity revolts against spinal erection: postural differentiation *contra* oceanic *Indifferenz*.[16] As Barker himself later noted, '[n]umerous trends in contemporary culture attest to an attempted recovery of the icthyophidian- or flexomotile-spine: horizontal and impulsive rather than vertical and stress-bearing'.[17] Flatten deep time into the unconscious by interpreting it precisely as a species of forgetfulness, and immediately there arises the desire for *recollection* and *return*. We long to lapse, hoping for the 'rapture of rupture', the rupture that will rid us of all individualising boundaries.[18]

Here we finally arrive at the core Spinal Catastrophist contention: that each threshold in life's serial deviations from immersion (CNS-implosion → spinal-wrenching → glottogonous encasement) instates thanataxic impulses toward rupturous resolution (return) into the surrounding media. This would be the ultimate form of recall, or **anamnesis**. Oken and the *Naturphilosophen* were reticent about willing this total recall (though it is there, as a tragic undercurrent or *Todessehnsucht*, within much Idealist thought). Schelling accepted that nature strives constantly for 'annihilation of the individual' and that it longs to 'revert to universal indifference' (with 'life itself' thus being

15.   'Perhaps these sunken lagoons simply remind me of the drowned world of my uterine childhood...'. Ballard, *Drowned World*, 28.

16.   K. Theweleit, *Male Fantasies: Women, Floods, Bodies, History*, tr. C. Turner, C. Erica, and S. Conway (Minneapolis: University of Minnesota Press, 1985); K. Theweleit, *Male Fantasies: Psychoanalyzing the White Terror*, tr. C. Turner, C. Erica, and S. Conway (Minneapolis: University of Minnesota Press, 1987).

17.   Barker, 'Barker Speaks', 6.

18.   D. Pettman, *After the Orgy: Towards a Politics of Exhaustion* (New York: SUNY Press, 2002), 37–61.

'only the bridge to death').[19] 'Left to itself, nature would [...] lead everything back into the state of utter negation', he admitted, darkly.[20] Nonetheless, aside from the centuries, what separates Ballard from his *naturephilosophische* forerunners is that he not only accepts but overtly champions this tendency. For Ballard, regardless of whether or not it is just or justifiable, it is undeniably *desirable* and, as such, a source of utter fascination. It is the point upon which the speeding highways of modernity converge. And, as the *Naturphilosophen* before him had nervously realised, total anamnesis is indistinguishable from annihilation. Indeed, Ballard prophesies that, at the lowest spinal-neuronic levels, organic self-inclusion completely evaginates into the 'inhospitality of the mineral world', its 'inorganic growths', its 'profound anguish', as in *The Crystal World*, where the deepest entropic future leaks backwards into the present.[21] Time bends into itself, cephalopod-like: accelerative lurch into the entropic future is nothing but thoracic drop into the pre-organic past.

19. F.W.J. Schelling, *First Outline of a System of the Philosophy of Nature*, tr. K.R. Peterson (New York: SUNY Press, 2004), 69.

20. F.W.J. Schelling, *The Ages of the World*, tr. J.M. Wirth (Albany, NY: SUNY Press, 2000), 31.

21. Ballard, *Atrocity Exhibition*, 31.

TH5. LITTORAL OSTEO-CHILOPODA CROSS THE WOUNDED GALAXIES

William S. Burroughs (1914–1997), corresponding with Ballard, commended as 'most interesting' the British author's 'concept of a lost sacral brain'.[1] Burroughs, who was also fascinated with the loops between 'inner space' and 'outer space', himself saw the vertebral column as a writhing inner bone-centipede. Nerves, along with all other control systems, were his sworn enemy. He imagined a surgical procedure to abbreviate a patient's body to nothing but an unappendiculated 'spinal column', thereby creating a **chilopodic monstrosity**.[2] Yet the major control system was not the nerves per se, but what they enabled: language.

'Burroughs suggests that the protohuman ape was dragged through its body to expire upon its tongue', Barker recounts. For Burroughs, language is a 'parasitic organism' that possesses the speaker's nervous system. 'The word', Burroughs characteristically wrote, 'has not been recognized as a virus because it has achieved a state of stable symbiosis with the host'; and we have 'no way of ascertaining' the invasion in such cases of 'latent virus infections'.

> The same may be true of the word. The word itself may be a virus that has achieved a permanent status with the host.[3]

---

1.   'William S. Burroughs and J.G. Ballard: An In-Depth Account Drawing on Interviews, Correspondence, and Unpublished Documents' (2012), *Reality Studio*, <https://realitystudio.org/scholarship/william-s-burroughs-and-j-g-ballard/>.

2.   W.S. Burroughs, *The Naked Lunch* (London: Harper, 2010), 87.

3.   W.S. Burroughs, *The Job: Interviews with William S. Burroughs* (London: Penguin, 1989), 12, 190.

Words propagate through us, we do not make them, they are self-selective and thus have interests of their own, not necessarily coincident with ours. 'Viruses make themselves real. It's a way viruses have'.[4] Thus, inspired by the research of the largely forgotten scientist Kurt Unruh von Steinplatz, Burroughs pieced together a detailed 'linguistic virology' and 'viral linguistics'.[5] He liked to remark that language isn't something you decide to do, it is something that happens to you; it doesn't belong to you, and it never will.

> From symbiosis to parasitism is a short step. The word is now a virus. The flu virus may once have been a healthy lung cell. It is now a parasitic organism that invades and damages the lungs. The word may once have been a healthy neural cell. It is now a parasitic organism that invades and damages the central nervous system. Modern man has lost the option of silence. Try halting your sub-vocal speech. [...] You will encounter a resisting organism that *forces you to talk*. That organism is the word. In the beginning was the word.

Anthropogenesis is thus symbiogenesis, or linguoparasitic horizontal transfer.[6] 'The realization that something as familiar to

4. W.S. Burroughs, *The Revised Boy Scout Manual: An Electronic Revolution* (Columbus, OH: Ohio State University Press, 2018), 98.

5. The writings of von Steinplatz are almost impossible to find today, with the few remaining copies in the hands of private collectors of esoterica. The entire print run of his four-volume treatise on *Authority Sickness* was reportedly pulped by the CIA in the 1960s.

6. We aren't the only ones to have been birthed from parasitism. Lynn Margulis (1938–2011), a noted fan of Vernadskii, was another of Barker's inspirations. Her theory—long scorned, lately accepted—held that parasitism and symbiosis were key drivers behind the development of cellular complexity.

you as the movement of your intestines [is] also alien and hostile does make one feel a bit insecure at first', Burroughs mused.[7] He wondered, indeed, whether language was a virus from outer space. Moreover, 'The Word'—this intimate alien—is precisely responsible for dragging us upright. Following von Steinplatz, he imagined it 'effecting a change in its host which was then genetically conveyed': these biophysical mutations, it was reported, mainly effected spinal makeup and thus also the 'inner throat structure'.[8]

In a section of *The Soft Machine* entitled 'Cross the Wounded Galaxies', Burroughs dramatized this agonizing process, imagining that, at the dawn of hominization, this 'muttering sickness leaped into our throats'—'spitting blood bubbling throats torn with the talk sickness'—and spurred the ape-men into 'warm mud-water', where they 'waded' and thus 'stood' upright, becoming 'naked' and hairless'. 'When we came out of the mud we had names'.[9] In so far as this was also the birth of self-consciousness, '*objective reality*' is thus '*produced by the virus in the host*'.[10]

Mitochondria *were originally an infection*, parasitizing prokaryotes in order to render eukaryotes. See L. Margulis, *Origin of Eukaryotic Cells* (New Haven, CT: Yale University Press, 1970). Margulis proposed that most major steps in cellular evolution were down to viral mutagenesis. Freeman Dyson (1932–) has gone further, arguing that abiogenesis was itself caused by RNA invading and parasitizing rudimental vesicles. Accordingly, Dyson proposes that our very own RNA is 'the oldest and most incurable of our parasitic diseases'. See F. Dyson, *Origins of Life* (Cambridge: Cambridge University Press, 2004), 16.

7.   W.S. Burroughs, *The Ticket That Exploded* (London: Harper, 2010), 39.

8.   Burroughs, *The Job*, 13.

9.   W.S. Burroughs, *The Soft Machine* (London: Harper, 2010), 127.

10.   Burroughs, *The Revised Boy Scout Manual*, 98.

With these images of self-consciousness and standing birthed in shallow swamps, one is inevitably reminded of the lingering **Aquatic Ape Hypothesis**, which proposes an oceanic etiology for our orthograde spine. As first suggested by Westenhöfer's 'Aquatile Hypothese' during the 1920s, Elaine Morgan's 1972 *Descent of Woman* famously argued that female anthropoids first entered the water to protect their infants from sabretooths. (The fact that it was mothers who were first forced into the shallows in this way perhaps goes some way towards explaining the perennial mythic collocation of the feminine and the oceanic.) Wading facilitated acoustic communication (as the aquatic medium impeded olfactory and gestural signalling) as well as glabrous nakedness (for purposes of thermoregulation).[11] *Homo sapiens* is indeed that *'great and true Amphibium'*. Most importantly, the exodus into water explains our otherwise anomalous bipedalism. For Morgan, the perversity of the orthograde spine could only be explained by our being forced—'as it were under duress'—into wading in the shallows in such a manner.[12] Alongside the threat of sabretooth predation, Morgan also speculated upon certain catastrophic geophysical causes that would have caused such 'duress': crustal deformations causing huge floods in Ethopia around the time of the 'ape/man' split.[13]

Whatever the cause of our evolutionary 'duress', it came at a high price. Morgan, in *Scars of Evolution*, meticulously recounts the 'cost of walking erect': from daily endocrine crises to swollen adenoids, to varicose veins, to inguinal hernia, to

---

11.   E. Morgan, *The Descent of Woman* (London: Souvenir Press, 1972).

12.   E. Morgan, *The Scars of Evolution: What Our Bodies Tell Us About Human Origins* (London: Souvenir Press, 1990).

13.   Morgan, *Scars of Evolution*, 50–58.

prolapsed uterus, to haemorrhoids and piles, to lower back pain and inevitable vertebral degeneration. prolapsed uterus, to haemorrhoids and piles, to lower back pain and inevitable vertebral degeneration. There is, indeed, a long tradition of evolutionary biologists darkly observing that 'man's upright posture has brought with it certain consequential disadvantages in regard to the functioning of his internal organs and his proneness to rupture'.[14] As Barker (an early supporter of Morgan) later confessed: 'I was increasingly aware that all my real problems were modalities of back-pain'.[15]

Morgan, moreover, went on to decrypt our being forced upright as the archaic source of human sexual difference's unique violence. As the sacrum adapted for standing, the vagina migrated inward; our species could no longer copulate from behind; in consequence, humans adopted ventro-ventral 'missionary' intercourse; sex, now involving far more 'intimacy', became painful and traumatic for females; and thus only males that *ignored* protestations were reproductively selected for. Misogyny birthed from the spine.

Burroughs, interestingly, also related the adoption of uprightness and speech to ancestral sexual violence. Once more following the research of von Steinplatz, Burroughs remarked that the viral infection and its alterations to the spine 'may well have had a high rate of mortality' originally:

> But some female apes must have survived to give birth to the wunder kindern. The illness perhaps assumed a more malignant

14. J. Huxley, *The Uniqueness of Man* (London: Chatto and Windus, 1943), 26–27. Within the same breath, Huxley highlights our unique 'proneness to laughter'. The ancient philosopher Chrysippus is said to have ruptured himself to death through excessive laughter after seeing a donkey eating his figs.

15. Barker, 'Barker Speaks', 6.

form in the male because of his more developed and rigid muscular structure causing death through strangulation and vertebral fracture. Since the virus in both male and female precipitates sexual frenzy through irritation of sex centers in the brain the males impregnated the females in their death spasms and the altered throat structure was genetically conveyed. Having effected alterations in the host's structure that resulted in a new species specially designed to accommodate the virus the virus can now replicate without disturbing the metabolism and without being recognized as a virus. A symbiotic relationship has now been established and the virus is now built into the host which sees the virus as a useful part of itself.[16]

And so, both Morgan and Burroughs (writing within a decade of one another) focus attention on the agonies involved in standing upright. In doing so, they notably invert a dominant Western tradition—extending from Aristotle to Gregory of Nyssa, to Charles Darwin—that links the orthograde 'liberation' of hand and mouth to the advent of human rationality.[17] Western thinkers have often seen standing upright as a *blessing*. Gregory of Nyssa, as quoted by Leroi-Gourhan, is exemplary:

So it was thanks to the manner in which our bodies are organized that our mind, like a musician, struck a note of language within us and we became capable of speech. This privilege would surely never have been ours if our lips had been required to perform the

16.   Burroughs, *The Job*, 12-3.

17.   See Aristotle, *On the Parts of Animals*, tr. J.G. Lennox (Oxford: Oxford University Press, 2003), 4:10; Gregory of Nyssa, *La creation de l'homme*, tr. J. Laplace (Paris: Cerf, 1944), 106–7; C. Darwin, *The Descent of Man, and Selection in Relation to Sex* (London: D. Appleton, 2 vols., 1871), vol. 1, 135–6.

onerous and difficult task of procuring nourishment for our bodies. But our hands took over that task, releasing our mouths for the service of speech.

Burroughs would largely agree with Gregory's fourth-century musings on this telic identification of 'speaking' with 'standing'. Yet, of course, he saw glottogony not as a blessing but as a pandemic.[18] In this vein, Burroughs wrote of newfangled linguo-viruses being made to order in the lab. (Riffing on L. Ron Hubbard, he asked whether one could produce a string of words and images that could induce *death*—a 'death-tape'. He even implied, like Ballard, that certain semio-strings or meme-packets could alter chronoception, with '[t]ime dragging or racing' being caused by alterations in the way 'the brain edits, makes sense of, and selects storage key features'.)[19] He always feared the weaponized word, knowing that all words are weapons.

Is the virus then simply a time bomb left on this planet to be activated by remote control?[20]

Burroughs, indeed, worried that, owing to the ease of transfer enabled by twentieth-century massified media (those very conditions which Ballard so adroitly diagnosed), the

---

18. On the scientific possibility that synaptic plasticity and cognition itself was caused by an ancient retroviral infection, see E.D. Pastuzyn et al., 'The Neuronal Gene Arc Encodes a Repurposed Retrotransposon Gag Protein that Mediates Intercellular RNA Transfer', *Cell* 172:1 (2018); and N.F. Parris and K. Tomonaga, 'A Viral (Arc)hive for Metazoan Memory', *Cell* 172:1 (2018).

19. Burroughs, *The Job.*, 185.

20. Ibid., 12.

millennia-old 'symbiotic relationship' between virus and host 'is now breaking down'.[21] The time bomb is ticking.

---

21.   Ibid.

TH6. PHILOSOPHICAL ANTHROPOLOGY'S MÄNGELSWESEN

Not all thinkers of the spine have followed Burroughs and Morgan in emphasizing the ruinous effects of human evolution; some have positively celebrated the consequences of standing, and echoed Kant's suggestion of a deep link between bodily uprightness and the human's triumphant dominion over the planet. However, to avoid returning to the naive self-aggrandisement of Gregory of Nyssa, almost all have had to accept that uprightness may well be a poison (as Burroughs no doubt would be quick to protest) as well as a cure. It is because we can stand that we can fall, and because we stand *for ourselves* falling is *our fault*, and it is precisely this self-accountability that first forces us to produce the technical prostheses that unleash our power over the globe: this is a dynamic that is merely repeated (recapitulated?) in the age of the atom bomb by the fact that the technoscientific power to redesign our world in our image is simultaneously the power to destroy it. As ever, all of this flows from the ancestral spine.

In 1952, in an essay simply titled 'The Upright Posture', the German-American neurologist Erwin Straus (1891–1975) formulated what could be classified as a *vestibular phenomenology*. He argued that not only the 'shape and function of the human body', but by extension the entire human universe, 'is determined in almost every detail by, and for, the upright posture'.[1] The shift to bipedalism not only rearranges the hierarchical priorities of the senses, thus reorganizing the *Umwelt* (pivoting from an olfactory to an audiovisual universe), it

---

1.   E. Straus, 'The Upright Posture', *Psychiatric Quarterly* 26:1 (1952), 529–61: 531.

simultaneously opens up new 'action spaces' or 'affordance spaces' for work and tool-use ('lateral space is the matrix of primitive and sophisticated skills', Straus notes), whilst changing our relation to the world from one of consumption-and-competition toward one of objectivity-and-recognitivity by freeing the mandibular infrastructure from purely masticatory, aggressive, and prehensile tasks, for use instead in precise phonetic micro-movements:

> In every species, eye and ear respond to stimuli from remote objects, but the interest of animals is limited to the proximate. Their attention is caught by that which is within the confines of reaching or approaching. The relation of sight and bite distinguishes the human face from those of lower animals. Animals jaws, snoot, trunk, and beak—all of them organs acting in the direct contact of grasping and gripping—are placed in the 'visor-line' of the eyes. With upright posture, with the development of the arm, the mouth is no longer needed for catching and carrying or for attacking and defending. It sinks down from the 'visor-line' of the eyes, which now can be turned directly in a piercing, open look toward distant things and rest fully upon them, viewing them with the detached interest of wondering. Bite has become subordinated to sight. [...] Eyes that lead jaws and fangs to the prey are always charmed and spellbound by nearness. To eyes looking straight forward—to the gaze of upright posture—things reveal themselves in their own nature. Sight penetrates depth; sight becomes insight.[2]

---

2.   Ibid., 557–8.

'Distal sight grants foresight and allows for planning' is Gallagher's gloss on Straus's schema.[3] (Indeed, the very prefix '*fore-*' expresses forwardness in time by relaying forwardness in space; gaining its meaning from the forwards-facing filtrations of the craniate sensorium, highlighting, once again, the synonymy of cephalization and chronognosis.) Straus continues:

> Animals move in the direction of their digestive axis. Their bodies are expanded between mouth and anus as between an entrance and an exit, a beginning and an ending. [...] Man in upright posture, his feet on the ground and his head uplifted, does not move in the line of his digestive axis; he moves in the direction of his vision. He is surrounded by a world-panorama, by a space divided into world-regions joined together in the totality of the universe. Around him, the horizons retreat in an ever-growing radius. Galaxy and diluvium, the infinite and the eternal, enter into the orbit of human interests.[4]

Similarly linking this shift from horizontal to vertical to the 'capacity for foresight', but with an eye to the ambivalence of its supposed benefits, Hans Blumenberg (1920–1996) spoke, more darkly, of the anthropogenic debut of bipedality—and the consequent influx of a panoramic universe—*as a crippling confrontation*. In this, he moves away from the simple optimism of Straus.

Cast out from the pronograde securities of bestial existence's well-defined 'life-world' (*Lebenswelt*), the upright human

---

3. S. Gallagher, *Enactivist Interventions: Rethinking the Mind* (Oxford: Oxford University Press, 2017), 168.

4. Straus, 'The Upright Posture', 558.

confronts, for the first time, the terrifying '**absolutism of reality**' (*Absolutismus der Wirklichkeit*). The human is the first to confront reality as an open-ended and absolute prospect—and thus a provocation—rather than as a well-determined biotope.

Once *homo sapiens sapiens* discovers the artifice of any circumscribed 'life-world', there is simply no going back: and this is the germination of the open-ended chronotope. Turning to this specific matter in his late work of the 1970s, Blumenberg claimed that this confrontation spurred the human on to its project of artificialization (first instanced in the 'work of myth', and later in the development of technoscience). Just as, in a biblical register, being naked wasn't a problem until we became self-aware of our nakedness, so too reality wasn't a pressing 'problem' until, *before our very eyes*, it became panoramic and absolutized—a step change delivered first by uprightness's binocular aperture and distal gaze. The extending plane of an open-ended horizon, unlocked by a perpendicularizing skull, is granted to us only through our vertebral transcendence from this selfsame plane.

Certainly, self-awareness, inasmuch as it consists in differentiation of ego and environ, is always an exile; and yet one has to lose all sense of habitat and of habit—becoming utterly vagrant—in order to be first motivated to *build for oneself* a home worthy of the name. Only in ceaseless destitution does the upright subject ever balance herself. Our bodies speak of our anthropogenic relation to precarity. This interlocks with a notion alluded to by Straus:

> While the heart continues to beat from its fetal beginning to death without our active intervention and while breathing neither demands nor tolerates our voluntary interference beyond narrow limits, upright posture remains a task throughout our lives. Before

reflection or self-reflection start, but as if they were a prelude to it, work makes its appearance within the realm of the elemental biological functions of man. In getting up, in reaching the upright posture, man must oppose the forces of gravity. It seems to be his nature to oppose nature in its impersonal, fundamental aspects with natural means. However, gravity is never fully overcome; upright posture always maintains its character of counteraction.

(Morgan also notes that the 'emergency' hormone, aldosterone, is released into our endocrine system every time we stand up.) Straus seems to be implying that, on the physiological level, orthograde posture dimly prophesies rational uprightness. Vertical balance, he stresses, is something actively achieved, never passively received. For, inasmuch as the resting state of the human body is somewhere on the floor, standing upright requires continual vigilance and vestibular micro-revisions. Yet through this, and through this alone, it becomes something *we have earnt*. In much the same way, one can only claim to be 'rational' if one demonstrates a propensity to revise one's opinions should they be shown to be incorrect. Thus, it is only through jeopardizing old claims that one reaches better thinking: this is why Kant had likened reasoning to a game of 'betting' where certitude only ever comes in degrees because incertitude is the very environing occasion of better reasoning.[5] Shut off your vestibular vigilance and you are on the floor, refuse riskiness in thinking and you cannot even be so much as wrong.

To be caught up in the game of bets that is reasoning is to be constantly motile—'conceptually cursorial'—just as upright standing requires continual revision from proprioceptor systems and mechanosensory feedbacks. This is why Straus sees a

---

5.   Kant, *Critique of Pure Reason*, 687 [A824-5/B852-3].

'prelude' to rationality in such poise: just as precariousness is the very medium of upright standing, so too is it the very avenue by which we correct incorrect beliefs and demonstrate our propensity to have worthwhile beliefs in the first place. And one only displays this propensity, for revision and vigilance, to the extent that one is 'liberated' from blind instinct (which is precisely how palaeoanthropologists and philosophical anthropologists have long read spinal verticalization and our uniquely steadfast standing).

Roth and Dicke write that 'cognitive ecologists converge on the view that mental or behavioural *flexibility* is a good measure of intelligence'.[6] And flexibility is coincident with a diminution of reliance upon instinct, or 'detachment'.[7] The human is the detached animal, delaminated from the claustrophobias of heredity. Indeed, Gould theorized that, in the case of *Homo sapiens*, 'behavioral flexibility' reaches a heretofore unseen extreme via **neoteny** (the paedomorphic retention of childhood traits into adulthood). Despite engendering the lengthy dependency of the human neonate, neoteny powerfully prolongs brain plasticity and behavioural flexibility.[8] The adult human—an essentially foetalized creature with its

6.   G. Roth and U. Dicke, 'Evolution of Nervous Systems and Brains', in C.G. Galizia and P.-M. Lledo (eds.), *Neurosciences: From Molecule to Behavior* (New York: Springer, 2013), 41.

7.   L. Moss, 'Detachment, Genomics and the Nature of Being Human', in M. Drenthen, J. Keulartz, and J. Proctor (eds.), *New Visions of Nature: Complexity and Authenticity* (New York: Springer, 2008), 103–15; and P. Lemmens, 'The Detached Animal—On the Technical Nature of Being Human', in M. Drenthen, J. Keulartz, and J. Proctor (eds.), *New Visions of Nature*, 117–27.

8.   Gould, *Ontogeny and Phylogeny*, 397–404. This is a perfect example of heterochrony: the acceleration or retardation of a developmental feature, and attendant allometric scaling, relative to an evolutionary ancestor.

swollen head, overgrown eyes, and hairless skin—inherits an extended window of 'cognitive pluripotency', allowing for the uptake of conceptual recipes, stratagems, protocols and rules that are linguistically encoded rather than genetically inherited. (This ability to transmit is what led Burroughs, following the General Semantics of Alfred Skarbek Korzybski, to call the human 'the time binding animal'.)[9] It is precisely because the human is birthed *preterm* in terms of physiology that it can undergo the *postnatal* linguistic birth that is the influx of discursive consciousness. (Simply put, extending the 'window of apprenticeship' augments the scope and range of the skills achievable therein.)

Human neoteny is, thus, an **empowering underdetermination**. This readily interlocks with the core rationalist notion that it is the *nature of the human to be unnatural* ('unnatural' here in the sense of somehow lacking full specifiability within naturalistic vocabularies alone). When it comes to worldedness, therefore, exile coincides with empowerment: it is in becoming delaminated from all particular biotopes that the orthograde ape conquered them all, inaugurating the psychozoic era. For Blumenberg, it was the new 'distanced optics' of the open savannah that provoked the first concretion of 'rationality' (*Vernunft*) as that 'organ of expectation and of the formation of horizons-of-expectancy, an incarnation of preventative dispositions and provisory-anticipatory attitudes'.[10] Announced first in our peculiar adoption of steadfast standing, this is the shift from heteronomy to autonomy, or from claustrophobia to

---

9.   For 'time binding' see A.S. Korzybski, *Manhood of Humanity* (Boston: E.P. Dutton, 1921).

10.   H. Blumenberg, *Beschreibung des Menschen* (Berlin: Suhrkamp, 2006), 560–61.

capaciousness. It is the shift from a well-defined world to an open-ended one; from a circumscribed horizon to an unlimited one; from high domain specificity to domain agnosticism; from fragility to robustness; from the exigent to the interrogative; from the competitive to the recognitive; and from the expedience of immediate habitudes toward the spaciousness of *irrealis* attitudes.

André Leroi-Gourhan (1911–1986), in *Gesture and Speech* (1964), applied this notion to human phylogenesis as a whole, reconstructing the latter as a 'series of successive liberations' from flexile fish to orthograde person: 'that of the whole body from the liquid element, that of the head from the ground, that of the hand from the requirements of locomotion, and finally that of the brain from the facial mask'.[11] Each 'liberation' within this 'paleontological adventure' unto uprightness heralds an increment of lability, and does so to the exact degree that it is a diaspora from instinctiveness and the claustrophobias of specialization. Such a process finally culminates in 'language as the instrument of liberation from lived experience'.[12] That is, language, operating as a highly distributed model of ourselves and our world, affords an additional interface with reality, one that, despite being superadded to sense receptivity, is not itself governed by the local exigencies of incoming sense-data (which are constitutively tethered to an expedient present) but rather is regulated by nonlocal concerns (including, *inter alia*, criteria of correctness and coherence). And language, for Leroi-Gourhan,

---

11.   The successive body-liberations rise up through 'icthyomorphism', to 'amphibiomorphism', to 'theromorphism', to 'pithecomorphism', and, finally, to 'anthropomorphism' and its steadfast standing. Leroi-Gourhan, *Gesture and Speech*, 25.

12.   Leroi-Gourhan, *Gesture and Speech*, 19, 227.

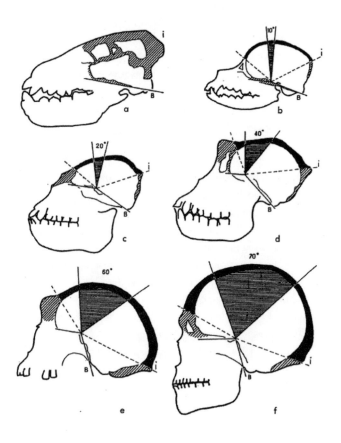

Fig. 10. Leroi-Gourhan's 'spreading of the cortical fan'.
From *Gesture and Speech* (Cambridge, MA: MIT Press, 1993)

from a stance diametrically opposed to that of Burroughsian horror, announces the 'freeing of the human brain',[13] which he connects with the **'exteriorization'** attained by the invention of technical systems from cuneiform to computation. Certainly, the ultimate frontier of 'liberation' is to be found in the nervous system gaining an 'extraorganic dimension' by way of modern technoscience.[14] Leroi-Gourhan, however, never ceases to stress the one axis around which this accelerating exterioriza-tion revolves: each and every one of these subsequent devel-opments hinges entirely upon our orthograde spine. He consistently argued that the bulging human cerebrum and its ingenious prostheses are merely the *evolutionary beneficiary* of an upright spine and not its *evolutionary cause*.[15]

Similar ideas abound in the German tradition, with zoolo-gists such as Konrad Lorenz claiming, in 1967, that the human is a 'specialist in being unspecialized' and Adolf Portmann, in 1956, describing mankind as the 'cosmopolitan' (*Weltoffen*) animal in contrast to the 'environmentally-bound' (*umwelt-gebunden*) universe of the pronograde animal.[16] The major source for such ideas, however, was the German tradition of 'philosophical anthropology' emerging during the twentieth-century, which insistently stressed spinal verticalization. (Port-mann, indeed, had borrowed the terminology of biotopic cosmopolitanism from Max Scheler, a progenitor of the

---

13.   Ibid., 226.

14.   Ibid., 31.

15.   Ibid., 26.

16.   K. Lorenz, *Über tierisches und menschliches Verhalten: Aus dem Werdegang der Verhaltenslehre* (Büchergilde Gutenberg: Frankfurt, 1967), vol. 2, 489; A. Portmann, *Zoologie und das neue Bild des Menschen: Biologis-che Fragmente zu einer Lehre vom Menschen* (Hamburg: Rowohlt, 1956).

movement.)[17] In 1940, Arnold Gehlen (1904–1976), a key figure in philosophical anthropology, published his *Der Mensch: Seine Natur und seine Stellung in der Welt*. Therein, he picks up on Nietzsche's dictum that humans are the 'not-yet-determined' or 'not-yet-finished' being, as well as Herder's notion that we are the '**creature of deficiencies**' (*Mängelswesen*).[18] Gehlen emphasizes that '[f]rom a biological point of view, in comparison to animals, the structure of the human body appears to be a paradox and stands out sharply'.[19] Our 'upright gait'—that 'special morphological position'—is the central feature of 'the peculiar human bodily structure', expressing the fact that our species is characterized 'by deficiencies' and 'lack of adaptations'. And yet, such an inheritance of underdetermination is not only an endowment of 'plasticity' (*Plastizitat*) but also precisely a summons to 'action'. For, to the extent that 'man' is 'undetermined', according to Gehlen, 'his very body presents a problem and challenge to him', and, concordantly, he is spurred to 'develop an attitude toward himself and make something of himself'. It is because 'man, dependent on his own initiative, may fail to meet this vital challenge' of steadfast standing that

> he is an endangered being facing a real chance of perishing. Man is ultimately an *anticipatory* [*voresehend*] being. Like Prometheus, he must direct his energies toward what is removed, what is not present in time and space. Unlike animals he lives for the future

---

17.   'The *geistig* being is no longer bounded by drives or its environment, but is "environmentally-unbound" and, if you will, "cosmopolitan"'. M. Scheler, *Die Stellung des Menschen im Kosmos* (Darmstadt: Reichl Verlag, 1928), 47.

18.   A. Gehlen, *Man: His Nature and Place in the World*, tr. C. McMillan and K. Pillemer (New York: Columbia University Press, 1988), 4–13.

19.   Gehlen, *Man*, 13.

and not in the present [...] man represents Nature's experiment with an acting being.

And, for Gehlen, it is anticipation that wrenched us upright, in doing so further forcing us to augur and anticipate.

[Man] compensates for this deficiency with his ability to work and his disposition toward action, that is, with his hands and intelligence; precisely for this reason, he stands erect, has circumspect vision, and free use of his hands.[20]

For Gehlen as for Blumenberg, and recalling Kant's theses on 'togetherness' and 'orientation', the spinal surge toward binocular world-openness (*Weltoffenheit*) engenders a 'flood of stimulation' that, in radically perturbing the neonate's afferent system, forces it to efferently 'orient itself' in order 'to cope with unpredictable' and 'changeable circumstances'. Gehlen's '*common root of knowledge*' is exposure to risk (first exampled in falling upwards) and the attendant summons to prudential culpability (whether sensorimotor or jurisdictive).[21] Only through risking itself does the defenseless being secure itself for itself; it is only because we are liable to fall that we are responsible for our standing upright (an observation that reveals, inversely, the coincidence of the 'radial regressive trend' with the circumspect rejection of the burdens of intellect, or '*Geistschmerz*': a jaded longing for the nonage of supine or spherical irresponsibility). 'Man is the risky creature that can miscarry itself',

---

20.　Gehlen, *Man*, 24–26.

21.　Ibid., 34.

Blumenberg later wrote. 'Man is the embodied impossibility; he is the animal that lives anyway.'[22]

But these ideas go back even further than the interwar years. Around the turn of the 1900s, Russian philosophical anthropologist and cosmist visionary Nikolai Fedorov announced that, spurred on by its myriad deficiencies in the face of an overwhelming nature, the 'first act' of humanity was its assumption of 'vertical position'. 'The least protected creature, the most endangered', the human is 'all-vulnerable' and was forced to assert itself by standing up. And in doing so, humans gained 'the organs of self-activity' and invention: hands and thumbs. 'Having become upright', Fedorov proclaimed, humanity discovered not only space (opening up the relation of heavens to earth, allowing for the invention of agriculture), but also time (in the measurement of the cycles of the stars on the distant horizon), and therefore also mortality (by becoming aware of a mensurable future extending far beyond the present). In discovering death, the upright human became motivated to invent artifice and externalize bodily functions in order to escape deathly collapse back to the soil of the earth. Fedorov pointed to the fact that early humanity exteriorized 'digestion' from the 'stomach' to the 'laboratories' of artifice, such as the cooking pot, which in turn 'liberated' us further from animal exigencies. Thus, the basic coordinates of vertical and horizontal map onto the processes of life and death, ingenuity and acquiescence, artifice and nature:

> The vertical position was, one might say, unnatural, that is, the man is opposing himself to nature. In an upright position, the I and not-I are already prophesied. This also explains why horizontal

22.   Blumenberg, *Beschreibung des Menschen*, 550.

positions give us the impression of peace or death, as opposed to vertical lines which provoke a view of vigilance, wakefulness, life, resurrection. The transition from horizontal to vertical position and back merged in the view and in the concept the transition from death to life and vice versa.

Thus, for Fedorov, the 'art of moving with only the lower extremities' is the root of all other 'art'.[23]

Paul Alsberg (1883–1965), another major figure in philosophical anthropology, advanced similar theories in his 1923 *Das Menschheitsrätsel* (translated as 'The Riddle of Man'). Preempting Leroi-Gourhan and Gehlen, Alsberg claimed that the principle of **'body-liberation'** (*Körperausschaltung*) is central to hominization and can be detected in the 'line leading from the imperfect posture of the Ape, over the stooping carriage of the *Neanderthal Man*, to the perfect upright gait of modern Man'.[24] Anthropogenesis, 'in all its successive phases', he insists, is 'a unitary event rooted exclusively in the principle of body-liberation'.[25] This emancipatory upswell is counterposed to the animal's principle of 'body-adaptation', or specialization, which Alsberg notes is, in fact, a *'principle of body-compulsion'*.[26] It is in liberating itself from such atavistic immurements—concordantly becoming 'naked', 'non-equipped', and 'unnatural'—that orthograde humanity embarks upon the unique quest of 'extra-bodily adaptation': its investment in the 'organ-projections' of technoscience that, in turn, have allowed it to reformat 'the

23. N. Fedorov, *Sochineniya* (Moscow: Progress, 4 vols., 1995), vol. 2, 249–57.

24. P. Alsberg, *In Quest of Man: A Biological Approach to the Problem of Man's Place in Nature* (Oxford: Pergamon, 1970), 10.

25. Ibid., 176.

26. Ibid., 31.

whole globe' as its 'laboratory', 'vegetable-garden', 'power-station', or 'park for wild and domesticated animals'.[27] Our exoskeleton asphyxiates the globe; the encephalon exteriorized on a planetary scale.

Alsberg makes it clear throughout that, in standing upright, 'Man' embarks 'upon a style of life in which the maintenance and welfare of his species is no longer supported and directed by a fixed set of instincts, but is entrusted, in increasing degree, to the free guidance of conscious ethical motives':

> Man has thus to face a new situation in which Nature no longer
> holds her protecting hand over him, but now charges him with
> the heavy burden of his own *responsibility* and obligations to
> himself, to the human community, and to Nature.

Our accelerating diaspora from instinct—'Nature's means of control'—is 'in itself a great but precarious achievement, and often enough has led to fatal errors'.[28] Alsberg notes that orthograde *Homo sapiens* is the first and only species that could rightly be considered *accountable* for its own survival and potential extinction. This applies not only in the straightforward sense that we are now technically capable of omnicide (from nukes to nanotech) but additionally in the deeper sense that it is *only through* becoming capable of invoking such culpability that we are conjointly summoned to the tasks of prediction and preemption such that, correlatively, we come to

---

27. Ibid., 35 and 187. Alsberg borrows the term '*Organprojektion*' from Ernst Kapp's *Grundlinien einer Philosophie der Technik* of 1877. See E. Kapp, *Elements for a Philosophy of Technology*, tr. L.K. Wolfe (Minneapolis: University of Minnesota Press, 2018).

28. Alsberg, *In Quest of Man*, 179.

prospectively understand any future extirpation (whether anthropogenic or not) precisely as *our own failing*. Body-liberation, converging upon encephalization, is precisely the undertaking of self-accountability. And, as Alsberg averred in an expanded English version of *Das Menschheitsrätsel* penned during the Cold War, 'Technology, with which the [body-liberation] principle started, is still the pace-maker, and this gives our "Atomic Age" its profound significance'.[29]

Certainly, this 'pace-maker' tends to outpace its host. Already in the 60s, Leroi-Gourhan proclaimed that artificial life—as the ultimate exteriorization of the human nervous system—would soon leave the biological relic named *Homo* far behind. Body-liberation, at the limit, slides into self-immolation through auto-secession. Leroi-Gourhan foresaw that there would come a time when '*Homo sapiens*, having exhausted the possibilities of self-exteriorization, will come to feel encumbered by the archaic osteo-muscular apparatus inherited from the Paleolithic':[30]

Freed from tools, gestures, muscles, from programming actions, from memory, [...] freed from the animal world, the plant world, from cold, from microbes, from the unknown world of mountains

---

29. Ibid., 184.

30. In contrast to 'the mechanical monsters produced in the nineteenth century', which, 'without a nervous system of their own', rely on human symbiotes to assist them, Leroi-Gourhan sees the oncoming autonomous machines of the twentieth and twenty-first centuries as heralding a 'parallel living world' that is 'leading to something like a real muscular system, controlled by a real nervous system, performing complex operating programs through its connections with something like a real sensory-motor brain'. *All in total secession from the human.* See Leroi-Gourhan, *Gesture and Speech*, 248–51.

and seas, zoological *Homo sapiens* is probably nearing the end of his career.[31]

Again, there is a point at which inward collapse, endogeneity, and ephemeralization all become indistinct from the utmost reality-egress, or *extinction*. At the Omega Point, transcension and senescence collapse. Certainly, Alsberg's principle of *Ausschaltung*, besides translating as 'liberation', additionally connotes '*exclusion*' and '*elimination*'. The exteriorization of neural functionality reaches fever pitch as the prime control system (or 'neural sovereignty') disinters itself from the zoologic human frame. The externalization of sensorimotor control, exampled today in fully autonomous robotic locomotors, 'represents the penultimate possible stage of the process begun by the Australanthrope armed with a chopper'.[32]

> The freeing of the areas of the motor cortex of the brain, definitively accomplished with erect posture [and the freeing of the hands for work], will be complete when we succeed in exteriorizing the human motor brain. Beyond that, hardly anything more can be imagined other than the exteriorization of intellectual thought through the development of machines capable not only of exercising judgment (that stage is already here) but also of injecting affectivity into their judgement, taking sides, waxing enthusiastic, or being plunged into despair at the immensity of their task.

Deliberation secedes from its neuronic substrate. Extending Samuel Butler's conjecture that humans may be mere pollinators

---

31.   Leroi-Gourhan, *Gesture and Speech*, 407.

32.   Boston Dynamics' BigDog, then, represents the contemporary frontier of the Pleiocene-incipient project of 'freeing' nervous functionality.

of ascendant machines, Leroi-Gourhan predicts that '[o]nce *Homo sapiens* had equipped such machines with the mechanical ability to reproduce themselves, there would be nothing left for the human to do but withdraw into the pale-ontological twilight'.[33] After all, biological man, as Leroi-Gourhan writes, is *already* a 'living fossil'.[34] Can we escape our spine, or will we expire along with it?

Blumenberg, who explicitly linked our bipedal gait and bin-ocular gaze to our singular conversancy with 'existential risk' (*Existenzrisiko*), relayed an illustrative thought-experiment.[35] Suppose some future intelligent observer uncovers fossilized *Homo sapiens* but finds no trace whatsoever of our globe-spanning prostheses alongside. Quite rightly, all that this intel-lect would observe is a petrified primate. Possibly one with a peculiar posture—as well as a grotesquely enlarged brain-capsule—but nothing more than a simian, nonetheless. (Our deep future palaeontologist would have no clue, Blumenberg notes, of how radical an effect this glabrous imp

---

33.   Leroi-Gourhan, *Gesture and Speech*, 248.

34.   The passage is worth quoting at length: 'The human species adjusted with equanimity to being overtaken in the use of its arms, its legs, and its eyes because it was confident of unparalleled power higher up. In the last few years the overtaking has reached the cranial box. Looking facts in the face, we may wonder what will be left of us once we have produced a better artificial version of everything we have got. [...] What this means is that our cerebral cortex, however admirable, is inadequate, just as our hands and eyes are inad-equate; that it can be supplemented by electronic analysis methods; and that the evolution of the human being—a living fossil in the context of the present conditions of life—must eventually follow a path other than the neuronic one if it is to continue. Putting it more positively, we could say that if humans are to take the greatest possible advantage of the freedom they gained by evading the risk of organic overspecialization, they must eventually go even further in exteriorizing their faculties'. Leroi-Gourhan, *Gesture and Speech*, 265.

35.   Blumenberg, *Beschreibung*, 550–622.

had had upon the history of life and earth systems.)[36] This simple *Gedankenexperiment* lets us know that 'the human' has *already left* its own cerebrospinal system (that 'living fossil'— that ganglion stack hailing from the Paleozoic sea-bed). Our self-image includes far more than our bones. We live and think and have our being *ex situ*; Geist moves inwardly only *ab exteriori*. Yet Blumenberg is quick to note that this entails that the actual 'flesh-and-blood' human is now no more than a *parasite* within its ramifying prosthetic nexus and branching everted plexus. Citing Alsberg's conviction that artificial exteriorization triggers somatic atrophy, Blumenberg notes that parasites, also, gradually lose their own organs of self-sufficiency by way of piggybacking upon inputs from the host-organism. 'Man likewise becomes a parasite within the technological sphere of life': foregoing sensory 'reality-contact' (*Wirklichkeitskontakt*)— undergoing attenuation of its indigenous nervous chronotope— in pursuit of artefactual-ectopic replacements. 'The question is, whether there will be a persisting residuum, or limits to the degeneration of our resilience', he observes.[37]

It was the intuition of twentieth-century philosophical anthropology, then, that our species—spinally exiled from any determinate *topos*—compensated for its biotopic vagrancy by retreating into the inward ramifications of a sequentially chirographic, mythical, artefactual, cultural, industrial and computational exoskeleton. This glorious retreat inward via exoskeletal externalization was by no means the end of our problems, however: aside from the 'internal friction' of risk endogeneity, such an inward-coiling autocomplexification makes the human like a hermit-crab lost in its own exponentially expanding shell.

36. Ibid., 582.

37. Ibid., 590.

The lines between parasite and host, means and end, blur. As Marx foresaw, technologization leads to a reversal of 'subject and object'—a 'thingification of persons' and a 'personification of things'.[38] Are we the cuckoo or is it our swelling prostheses? We become more our self-projection than ourselves. Whatever the case, in exteriorizing absolutely everything, we become ever more lost in our own labyrinthine shell—a carapace of radically extended cerebrospinal arcs.

In Blumenberg's schema, language and technics may well be rational, but they are still the blossoms of spinal trauma. Schizophrenic tendencies, moreover, appear to be the price our species pays for glottogony.[39] Bipedalism's migration from 'bite' to 'sight' (via recessing prognathous jaw, liberating buccal cavity, and descending larynx for language influx) may be celebrated by neurophenomenologists like Straus as 'liberation', yet such 'liberation', as Burroughs would no doubt protest, merely opens an ecological niche for an invading schizo-linguo-parasite. Citing Leroi-Gourhan, Roland Barthes envisioned that '[s]hifting to upright posture, man found himself free to invent language and love: this is perhaps the anthropological birth of a concomitant double perversion: speech and kissing'.[40] (A perversion, indeed: the very basis for thousands of years of misogyny and sexual violence, as Morgan would argue.)[41] Yet earlier, in 1937, Walter Benjamin had proposed that the vertical spine 'brings

---

38.   K. Marx and F. Engels, *Marx-Engels-Werke* (Berlin: Dietz Verlag, 45 vols., 1988), vol. 23, 128.

39.   T.J. Crow, 'Schizophrenia as the Price that Homo Sapiens Pays for Language', *Brain Research Reviews* 31 (2000), 118–29.

40.   R. Barthes, *Roland Barthes*, tr. R. Howard (New York: Farrar, Straus and Giroux, 1977), 140–41.

41.   Morgan, *Descent of Woman*.

with it a phenomenon unprecedented in natural history: partners can look into each other's eyes during orgasm. Only then does an orgy become possible'.[42] What are *you* doing after the orgy?[43]

Aside from Straus's sunny optimism, the myriad members of the twentieth century's school of philosophical anthropology take a darker view of the connection between rationality and uprightness. They see uprightness as a *burden*—a continual toil—but they see our falling upward as a *fortunate fall* in that it is only by constantly having to fight off falling over that we are forced to become rational. Base gravity is the *original* 'summons' behind the vocation of man. We would be a heap on the floor without the burdens of vestibular vigilance, just as it is only through endless exile from received opinions that we earn the title 'objective'. Our fortunate fall upward is not a question of God-given dignity, but a precarious position we have to earn via ceaseless striving. It is a burden.

Spinal Catastrophism takes this essentially tragic lesson to heart: the conditions for reason, enlightenment, and face-to-face speech are also the enablers of pain, perversion, and exodus from any home on the horizon. These 'conditions', then, would require some kind of therapy—but one that would have to go much further than 'psychoanalysis' traditionally conceived, since all our parochial neuroses are the sequelae of wounds not only terrestrial, but stretching beyond the earthbound and outward into the hoary galaxies. Nonetheless, it shouldn't be a surprise that it was a psychoanalyst—albeit an utterly unorthodox one—that first stepped up to the tectonic p[a]late.

---

42.   W. Benjamin, *The Work of Art in the Age of its Technological Reproducibility and Other Writings on Media*, tr. E. Jephcott, R. Livingstone, H. Eiland (Cambridge, MA: Harvard University Press, 2008), 154.

43.   J. Baudrillard, 'What Are You Doing After the Orgy?', *Art Forum* 22:2 (1983), 42–6.

In 1993, respected cosmologist Fred Hoyle, whose speculations on backwards causation, extraterrestrial viruses, and intelligent interstellar dust-clouds had already rendered him congenial to Barker, would himself deliver a lecture attempting to trace the intersection between Solar System disasters and the major events of human prehistory. Over the past 10,000 years, he would claim, cometary cataclysms have triggered the Iron Age, germinated world religions, and embedded their legacy deep in the recesses of the Abrahamic psyche (which, therefore, retains submerged relics of this 'strange nightmare of the past').[1]

Hoyle had once met Immanuel Velikovsky at Princeton and, despite dismissing his methodologies as unsound, proclaimed that the furore provoked by *Worlds in Collision*'s egregious anti-uniformitarianism nonetheless uncovered something troubling:

> [C]ould it be that Velikovsky had revealed, admittedly in a form that was scientifically unacceptable, a situation that astronomers are under a cultural imperative to hide? Could it be that, somewhere in the shadows, there is a past history that it is inadmissible to discuss?[2]

---

1.   F. Hoyle, *The Origin of the Universe and the Origin of Religion* (Kingston, RI: Moyer Bell, 1993), 62; see also, V. Clube and B. Napier, *The Cosmic Serpent: A Catastrophist View of Earth History* (London: Faber, 1982); V. Clube and B. Napier, *The Cosmic Winter* (Oxford: Blackwell, 1990); and M.G.L. Baillie, *Exodus to Arthur: Catastrophic Encounters with Comets* (London: Batsford, 1999). Despite new acceptance of 'catastrophist' ideas, Velikovsky's speculations upon interplanetary interactions remain roundly rejected.

2.   F. Hoyle, *Home is Where the Wind Blows: Chapters from a Cosmologist's Life* (Sausalito, CA: University Science Books, 1994), 285–6.

As documented in *The Velikovsky Affair*,[3] in 1950, Velikovsky had submitted *Worlds in Collision* to Macmillan. It was accepted, but triggered a reaction from the scientific community that many regarded as bordering on the neurotic. After concerted threats of boycott, Macmillan was forced to transfer the book to Doubleday (where it duly became a popular bestseller).[4] The book itself, deranged in its scope and aims, argues for a **universal catastrophist euhemerism**: reading the collected works of mythology and religion, of bard and sage, as so many memory-traces of earth-shuddering calamities and the interplanetary interactions that caused them. Such theories on the origins of religions date back at least to Hume and Montesquieu, yet Velikovsky took them to dizzying extremes, seeking to provide a prognosis of the human condition that advanced 'from the deepest recesses of man's inner torment to the outer reaches of our solar system'.[5]

What is interesting is that Velikovsky was trained neither as an astrophysicist nor as an archaeologist, but had made his living as a clinical psychiatrist. His euhemerist machinations—those that made him infamous—were, arguably, mere by-products of his firmly-held psychoanalytic suppositions on what he called 'deeply imbedded phylogenetic memories' and the 'inherited trauma' with which they were freighted.[6]

---

3.   A. de Grazia (ed.), *The Velikovsky Affair: The Warfare of Science and Scientism* (New York: University Books, 1966).

4.   I. Velikovsky, *Worlds in Collision* (New York: Doubleday, 1950).

5.   F. Warshofsky, *Doomsday: The Science of Catastrophe* (New York: Reader's Digest, 1977), 41. Warshofsky provides a solid—if slightly apologist—summary of *Worlds in Collision* and the 'Velikovsky affair'.

6.   I. Velikovsky, *Mankind in Amnesia* (New York: Doubleday, 1982), 31–2.

In 1982's *Mankind in Amnesia* (a retrospective of the 1950s controversy and analysis of his detractors' motives), Velikovsky explicates this, his motivating backdrop. We are, he says, a palimpsest of 'inherited unconscious memory'; 'the human race is a carrier of traumatic experience of earlier generations'; and the more distressing the impression, the more likely it is to become 'permanent through unconscious mneme or mneme complex'. As Velikovsky writes, 'the most devastating experiences are the most deeply buried and their reawakening is accompanied by a sensation of terror'.[7] (Hence the tremendous provocation of and neurotic reaction to *Worlds in Collision*.) With this in view, the Russian psychoanalyst announced that the upheavals of our 'Atomic Age' (that threshold of 'profound significance' for Alsberg) had unleashed within us ancient neuroses via reactivating markers of phyletic paroxysm. It was nuclear detonation that provided the reverberant 'chord', awaking our 'ancient engram':

> The two World Wars, the ashes of Hiroshima and the cinders of Nagasaki touched such a chord; then the story of ancient cosmic upheavals needed to be told so that the lost phylogenetic memories could come forth with sails unfurled from the sealed haven they entered thousands of years ago.[8]

In a phenomenological observation as Ballardian as it is Barkerian, he maintains that we feel this *revividus* as 'a throb in the arteries, a hidden key to the endocrine system, the solar plexus, medulla, gray matter'. A chord in the cord:

---

7. Velikovsky, *Mankind in Amnesia*, 31–5.

8. Ibid., 149..

[W]herever the ancient terror had dug itself in, something started to vibrate slightly differently, the key made a partial turning, some mnemes lit up, a spark flying forth and back and around the million cells holding the engrams of racial origin—a network crisscrossed by flashes.[9]

The elder portions of the spine resonate to the nuclear sunset; blast wave and recollection cascade. ('An avalanche backwards into the past', as Ballard would put it.) And the 'sealed havens' from which these phylogenetic memories burst—the sacral sarcophagi of cosmic trauma—are, of course, the 'nerve cells as carriers of memory'.[10]

It was in a paper published in the 1930s, when he was working as a psychiatrist, that Velikovsky had first ventured these notions. Entitled 'On the Physical Existence of the Noetic World', the paper argued that, distributed throughout the CNS, 'nerve-energies' (*Nervenenergie*) conserve memories across the aeons. Ergo, 'the thoughts of man are common property'; and one can talk of the 'immortality' of experience, and even of a mnemonic 'consciousness of inorganic material' (*ein Bewußtsein der anorganischen Materie*).[11] Realizing the truly troubling nature of such 'immortality of experience', Barker would make

---

9. Against this backdrop, the entire species could become 'analysand'. Velikovsky pronounced, indeed, that his analyses were of utmost importance to our very survival. Velikovsky, *Mankind in Amnesia*, 149.

10. Velikovsky, *Mankind in Amnesia*, 23.

11. I. Velikovsky, 'Über die Energetik der Psyche und die physikalische Existenz der Gedankenwelt—Ein Beitrag zur Psychologie des gesunden und somnambulen Zustandes', *Zeitschrift für die gesamte Neurologie und Psychiatrie* 133 (1931), 422–37. Compare this to Freud's 1920 comment on the essentially '*conversative* nature of living matter', see S. Freud, *Beyond the Pleasure Principle*, tr. G.C. Richter (Peterborough, ON: Broadview, 2011), 76.

this a keystone idea, extrapolating Velikovskian suggestions into the conviction that his own bodily 'tics' were but the reverberant echoes of cosmic traumatisms.

Velikovsky later recounted that, in 1931, he had sent his article to a fellow researcher, who approvingly affirmed that he was in 'complete agreement' with Velikovsky's conclusions on the matter. Indeed, this fellow explorer of the unconscious of mankind would return, throughout his life, to the question of recapitulation and inorganic memory. His name: Sigmund Freud.[12]

---

12.   Velikovsky, *Mankind in Amnesia*, 25.

The pre-psychoanalytical work of Freud (1856–1939) saw him mastering neuroanatomy, mapping the phylogenetic path of ganglion cells.[1] As his interests subsequently moved up the spinal cord, they simultaneously migrated from lampreys and fish toward man. Even after leaving neurobiology behind and embarking upon psychoanalysis, Freud, by his own admission, 'remained faithful to the line of work upon which I had originally started'; he had merely migrated, in his own words, from 'the spinal cord of one of the lowest of the fishes' up to 'the human central nervous system'.[2] His psychoanalytical work, naturally, attributed a central role to bipedalism: upright posture expedited the central role played by sight within human sexuality, as opposed to the quadruped's coprophiliac *Umwelt* (tethered to the horizontal-digestive axis and anchored to olfactory stimulation). Freud speculated that infant sexuality retraces this journey toward 'upright carriage' and away from scatological stimuli.[3] A 'devout recapitulationist' to his career's end, Freud presages Ballardian neuronics when he diagnoses a schizoid analysand as existing within a 'prehistoric landscape', perhaps 'in the Jurassic', where 'the great saurians are still running around'

---

1.   For example, S. Freud, 'Über den Ursprung der hinteren Nervenwurzeln im Rückenmark von Ammocoetes', *Sitzungsberichte der kaiserliche Akademie der Wissenschaften* 75 (1877), 15–27; 'Über Spinalganglien und Rückenmark des Petromyzon', *Sitzungsberichte der kaiserliche Akademie der Wissenschaften* 78 (1878), 81–167; 'Die Structur der Elemente des Nervensystems', *Jahrbücher für Psychiatrie und Neurologie* 5 (1884), 221–29.

2.   Quoted in Sulloway, *Freud, Biologist of the Mind*, 15; see also, L.C. Triarhou, 'Exploring the Mind with a Microscope: Freud's Beginnings in Neurobiology', *Hellenic Journal of Psychology* 6 (2009), 1–13.

3.   Quoted in Sulloway, *Freud, Biologist of the Mind*, 200–201.

and 'horsetails grow as high as palms'.[4] Expanding on themes from 1913's *Totem and Taboo,* Freud speculated, in unpublished and forgotten papers recovered posthumously from a dusty trunk, that all individuals developmentally repeat the Ice Age traumas of our early ancestors. 'Anxiety hysteria—conversion hysteria—obsessional neurosis—dementia praecox—paranoia—melancholia—mania': this 'series seems to repeat phylogenetically an historical origin', he allowed himself to profess—but only in the disavowed context of a 'phylogenetic fantasy'.[5] Although he suggests deeper phyletic parallelisms with his speculation that the primordial organism is born in a way that parallels many early theories of the earth's formation (evoking the deposition of a 'crust' around an volatile core), and despite also indicating that 'the developmental history of our earth and of its relation to the sun [has] left its mark' on our psyche, Freud left it to his students to explore this terrain.[6]

---

4.   Quoted in Gould, *Ontogeny and Phylogeny,* 158.

5.   S. Freud, *A Phylogenetic Fantasy: Overview of the Transference Neuroses,* tr. A. Hoffer and P.T. Hoffer, (Cambridge, MA: Harvard University Press, 1987), 79.

6.   Freud, *Beyond the Pleasure Principle,* 77. Freud's intriguing idea, in *Beyond the Pleasure Principle,* of the originary 'organic vesicle' individuating itself by depositing an 'outer crust' around itself closely parallels early theories of the earth's formation. It was Descartes who first classified the earth as an aborted star, formed by becoming wrapped in the hard shell of its own outermost, extinct layer. See R. Descartes, *Principles of Philosophy,* tr. V.R. Miller and R.P. Miller (Dordrecht: Kluwer, 1991), 181. Leibniz likewise endorsed this notion of the earth as an 'extinct star' suffocated and encased within an epigene crustal shell. See G.W. Leibniz, *Protogaea,* tr. C. Cohen and A. Wakefield (Chicago: University of Chicago Press, 2008), 5. Athanasius Kircher and Thomas Burnet also promoted the idea of geogony as the formation of a deadened outer layer around an '*ignis centralis*'. It became even more popular in eighteenth-century France, amongst the likes of Georges Buffon and Jean-Sylvain Bailly, where Jean-Jacques d'Ortous de Mairan even attempted

More overt spinal catastrophist notions, alongside the discovery of the neuronic antagonism between 'cortical man' and 'medullary man', were to emerge not from the inventor of psychoanalysis but from his heretical disciples.[7]

The split between Freud and his student Wilhelm Reich (1897–1957) can be traced to the former's refusal of the 'oceanic'. It was Romain Rolland who had suggested the 'oceanic feeling' (of egoic dissolution) to Freud, who—whilst finding the notion alluring in spite of himself—resisted and ultimately rejected it. 'I cannot discover this "oceanic" feeling in myself', he attempted to convince himself.[8] Accordingly, as Theweleit glosses, 'Freud strives to go *upward*'—following spinal thrust.[9] Reich, on the other hand, was to develop therapies in which Rolland's 'oceanic feeling' was actively sought out, and thus saw spines as impositions against fundamental fluidity. Reich was a figure with whom Ballard was familiar, Burroughs intimately so.[10] The Austrian doctor also boasted the curious accolade of having his books burnt by both the Nazis *and* the US government (he fled Germany only to later die in the Federal

---

to prove the theory mathematically. See J.D. Mairan, 'Nouvelles recherches sur la cause générale du chaud en été et du froid en hiver, en tant qu'elle se lie à la chaleur interne et permanente de la terre', *Mémoires Acad. Royale des Sciences* (1765), 143–266. Intentionally or not, Freud's model for abiogenesis conspicuously parallels prior models of planet formation.

7.   Neumann, in 1949, described a battle between the 'medullary' and 'cortical' aspects of our psyche as undergirding the 'present crisis of modern man'. E. Neumann, *The Origins and History of Consciousness*, tr. R.F.C. Hull (Princeton, NJ: Princeton University Press, 1954), 330.

8.   S. Ackerman, 'Exploring Freud's Resistance to the Oceanic Feeling', *Journal of the American Psychoanalytic Association* 65:1 (2017), 9-31.

9.   K. Theweleit, *Male Fantasies*, 1:253.

10.   T. Morgan, *Literary Outlaw: The Life and Times of William S. Burroughs* (New York: Avon, 1988), 140–43.

Penitentiary at Lewisburg, Pennsylvania).[11] Primarily, Reich is famous for his '**characterological analysis**': an extension of psychoanalysis to the rhythms of the body and a reading of latent content through skeletomuscular posture (presaging Ballardian kinesics). In pursuit of this new approach, Reich broke from psychoanalytic orthodoxy and moved into what he eventually titled '**orgone biophysics**', the groundwork for which was laid down in *Character Analysis* (1933) and *Function of the Orgasm* (1942).

A penetration of '*biological depth*', Reich's orgone biophysics extended Freudian topographical models to physiology and tectology.[12] Here, the organism (again via a somaticisation of Steno's Law) is considered primarily as a stratal concretion of drives and desire, layered according to biogenetic → phylogenetic → ontogenetic succession. '[T]he stratification of the character', he writes, is directly comparable to 'the stratification of geological deposits, which are also rigidified history'.[13] Each stereotypy or pulsion-tic tells not only our own story, but that of life on earth. 'Every such layer of the character structure is a piece [of] history', and therefore traumata persist within (and nonlinearize) the present '*insofar as* [*they are*] *anchored in a rigid armor*'.[14] The body is an encrustation of pain: *Spirit's scab*. Within Reichian 'orgone-therapeutics', traumatisms inscribe themselves via the 'biopathy' of '**characterological**

---

11.   J.E. Strick, *Wilhelm Reich, Biologist* (Cambridge, MA: Harvard University Press, 2015), 1–2.

12.   W. Reich, *Character Analysis*, tr. V.R. Carfagno (London: Souvenir, 1984), 358.

13.   W. Reich, *The Function of the Orgasm*, tr. V.R. Carfagno (London: Souvenir, 1983), 145.

14.   Reich, *Function of the Orgasm*, 145.

armouring': a deposition of somatic 'immobility and rigidity' symptomatized through 'muscular hypertonia', identifiable as postural aberration (e.g. spinal 'lordosis'). Armouring is originally compacted to 'protect' the organism from exorbitant stimuli, yet its sedimentation sacrifices 'capacity for pleasure'.[15] '[B]iologically correct' functioning, contrarily, is a 'flowing' and 'streaming-away': Reich's infamous '*orgasm reflex*'.[16] Again, liquefying prostration is counterposed to ossifying erection.

The CNS and backbone are, consequently, central to Reichian biophysics: simultaneously the axis of orgasmic pulsation and the pylon of biopathic 'inner deadness',[17] the highway of skyward erection and the descending path of earthward relapse.

The centrality of this axis is captured in Reich's libidinal account of the phylogenesis of complex life, where he models life's ascent from a basic 'elastic bladder' which, stretched and squished by its own onanistic joy in its simplistic existence, extrudes itself longitudinally into a segmenting worm (exhibiting the basic bilateral plan of a paraxial, metameric nervous system). Now an annelid, life has already sacrificed its joy—the 'pleasure principle' of unconscious ecstasy—at the altar of complexification. Indeed, as the annelid's peristaltic vector develops, segments eventually become 'fixed', eventually precipitating a 'supportive apparatus': *a spine calcifies*.[18]

In the 'spine', then, and its 'segmental arrangement', '*we meet the worm in man*'.[19] And yet our spines, unlike the worm's flexile axochord, are *rigid*. Vertebrae, therefore, represent

---

15.   Ibid., 145.

16.   Reich, *Character Analysis*, 385.

17.   Ibid., 313.

18.   Reich, *Function of the Orgasm*, 275–9.

19.   Reich, *Character Analysis*, 372.

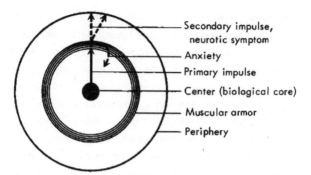

Secondary impulse,
neurotic symptom
— Anxiety
— Primary impulse
— Center (biological core)
— Muscular armor
— Periphery

Fig 11. Reich's model of characterological armouring.
From *The Function of the Orgasm (London: Souvenir, 1983)*

Fig 12. Flexion and adduction in orgasm.
From *Character Analysis* (London: Souvenir, 1984)

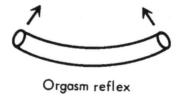

Orgasm reflex

Fig 13. Sacrum and cranium strive to reunite.
From *The Function of the Orgasm*

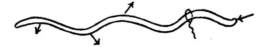

Fig. 14. Joyous vermicular trembling.
From *The Function of the Orgasm*

'remnants of a dead past in a living present'.[20] Accordingly, we long to return to the oceanic flow, we long to extravasate back toward primordial orgasmic-pulsation, to give ourselves up to blissful starfish-becomings—sacrificing axial rigidity for hydraulic flow and ridding ourselves of this vertebral impalement. As one of Reich's followers wrote of this Reichian phylogenesis of orgone-posture, cranialization is the expression of the 'anti-gravity tendency of the life force'.[21] Once again, life's headward thrust. And yet, the higher one scrapes, the more energetic potential builds behind one's collapse—the higher one reaches, the harder and further one falls—just as excitation and anticipation builds toward climactic release.

This is no mere simile for Reich: the orgasmic climax does not just release individually-accumulated tensions, but also ancestrally and phyletically acquired ones. Evolution's antigravity thrust *just is* the build-up behind one's desire for pyroclastic orgone-release. 'In the orgasm', Reich noted, the animal 'unceasingly' attempts 'to bring together the two embryologically important zones': 'mouth' toward 'anus'; the 'trunk strives [to] fold up' so as to relive its *ancient radial* morphology.[22]

---

20.   Ibid., 395.

21.   A. Lowen, *The Language of the Body/Physical Dynamics of Character Structure* (New York: Collier Books, 1958), 58.

22.   Reich, *Character Analysis*, 366, 386.

Sacrum and cranium reconverge blissfully as, in a brief recrudescence of spherical immanence, we bilaterians—in the flexion and adduction of orgasm—lose our vermicular architecture and recapitulate an even older morphology: that of the humble jellyfish.[23] As Reich explained:

> Just as Darwin's theory deduces man's descent from the lower
> vertebrate on the basis of man's morphology, orgone biophysics
> traces man's *emotional* functions much further back to the forms
> of movement of the mollusks and the protozoa.[24]

Cnidarian radial return; a true longing for lost symmetry. All we want is to become molluscs once again, no matter how fleetingly. Mussel memory also participates in the Velikovskian immortality of experience.

Carl Jung (1875–1961), another of Freud's heretical pupils, similarly identified the 'continual flow' of the 'sympathetic nervous system' as the seat of his 'collective unconscious'.[25] Jung, whose language of psychological 'archetypes' derived directly from Goethe and Oken, saw that, neuroanatomically, the 'serpent' of the spinal system 'leads down' into 'the sympathetic nervous system' and its 'undulating movement'. Here 'we approach the lowest forms of life', which Jung identified with the 'sea-anemone' or 'those colonies of the siphonophora' (the most notable of which is, of course, the Portuguese

---

23. Ibid., 397.

24. Ibid., 398.

25. C.G. Jung, *Introduction to Jungian Psychology: Notes of the Seminar on Analytical Psychology Given in 1925* (Princeton, NJ: Princeton University Press, 1989), 140.

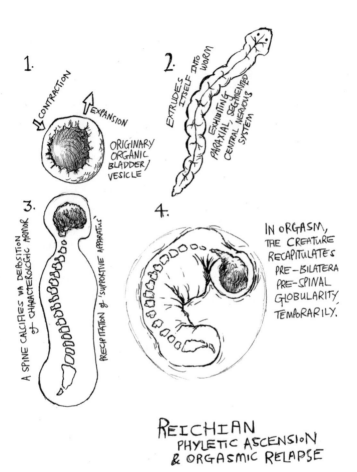

1. ⇓ CONTRACTION ⇑ EXPANSION

ORIGINARY ORGANIC BLADDER/ VESICLE

2. EXTRUDES ITSELF INTO WORM

EXHIBITING PARAXIAL, SEGMENTED CENTRAL NERVOUS SYSTEM

3. A SPINE CALCIFIES VIA DEPOSITION OF CHARACTEROLOGIC ARMOR

PRECIPITATION OF 'SUPPORTIVE APPARATUS'

4. IN ORGASM, THE CREATURE RECAPITULATES PRE-BILATERA PRE-SPINAL GLOBULARITY TEMPORARILY.

REICHIAN PHYLETIC ASCENSION & ORGASMIC RELAPSE

Fig. 15. Reichian Phyletic Ascension and Orgasmic Relapse

man-of-war). We carry within us the 'oldest nervous system in the world':[26]

> The very primitive animal layers are supposed to be inherited through the sympathetic system, and the relatively later animal layers belonging to the vertebrate series are represented by the cerebrospinal system.

Accordingly, Jung proclaimed that the unconscious exists 'outside' our brains and 'cannot be strictly said to be psychological but physical'.[27] (As Ballard later elaborated, for modern man it is physically encoded in our architectures as much as our advertisements—in the 'ectopic unconscious' and 'inorganic body' of techno-industry's spirit overspill.) Anatomically, Jung locates this unconscious below the 'vertebrate series', in the cnidarian *plexus solaris*—which operates as a submerged tranverse-symmetric proto-brain. Of this 'brain of the sympathetic system', Jung wrote:

> It is the main accumulation of ganglia, and it is of prehistoric origin, having lived vastly longer than the cerebrospinal system, which is a sort of parasite on the *plexus solaris*.[28]

In talking of this 'counter-brain', Jung, of course, couldn't help but refer to the endosacral encephalon of the great dinosaurs.

---

26.   C.G. Jung, *Nietzsche's Zarathustra: Notes of the Seminar Given in 1934–1939* (Princeton, NJ: Princeton University Press, 1988), 1435–6.

27.   Jung, *Introduction*, 140–1.

28.   C.G. Jung, *Dream Analysis: Notes of the Seminar Given in 1928–1930 by C.G. Jung* (London: Routledge, 1995), 334.

Whilst speculating upon the existence of a 'sort of vertebral mind' and the neuropsychic 'independence' of the 'spinal cord', he exclaimed:

> You know, the brain is a relative conception; in former periods of the earth there were animals like the megalosaurians, for example, where the size of the lumbar intumescence of the nervous matter was bigger than the brain.[29]

This is telling, given that one of Jung's favourite metaphors for our inheritance of phyletic mnemes consisted in envisioning a 'long saurian tail' that we drag behind us.[30] Elsewhere, he classified the worm—that 'secret trouble, under the earth', that 'chthonic thing, from within or beneath'—as the 'most primitive form of nervous life'. Utterly decentralized, it represents 'a life in compartments, in segments'. (Leroi-Gourhan would later write of worms that 'each segment of the body lives separately'.)[31] Jung accordingly identified schizotypal disorders as a recrudescence of vermicular forms of neural functioning—a type of spiritual centrifuge by way of phyletic relapse.[32]

Jung, in 1925, had spoken of 'the "geology" of a personality', producing a stratigraphic diagram descending to the soul's 'central fire'; in 1927, he delivered a lecture upon 'The Conditioning of the Psyche by the Earth'; one of his followers even described his method as a *Paläontologie der Seele*

29.   Jung, *Nietzsche's Zarathustra*, 250.

30.   C.G. Jung, *The Symbolic Life: Miscellaneous Writings* (London: Routledge, 1977), 81.

31.   Leroi–Gourhan, *Gesture and Speech*, 78.

32.   Jung, *Dream Analysis*, 234.

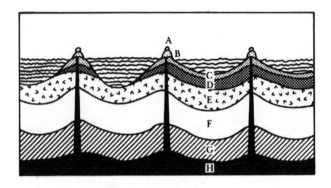

A = Individuals.
B = Families.
C = Clans.
D = Nations.
E = Large Group (European man, for example).
F = Primate Ancestors.
G = Animal Ancestors in general.
H = "Central Fire."

Fig, 16. Jungian geology of personality. From *Analytical Psychology: Notes of the Seminar given in 1925 by C.G. Jung* (London: Routledge, 1992)

[paleontology of the soul]'.[33] And yet, for Jung, this remained somewhere at the level of metaphor. It was with another of Freud's followers, Sándor Ferenczi, that such notions would become utterly literal and concrete.

---

33. C.G. Jung, *Die Erdbedingtheit der Psyche* (Darmstadt: Reichl Verlag, 1927); C.G. Jung, *Analytical Psychology: Notes on the 1925 Seminar* (Princeton, NJ: Princeton University Press, 1992), 133–4; and see C.B. Dohe, *Jung's Wandering Archetype: Race and Religion in Analytical Psychology* (London: Routledge, 2016), 84–117.

As we saw above, Freud had already speculated—in lost and unpublished papers on his phylogenetic fantasies—that we each recapitulate the Ice Age traumas of early humankind.[1] However, Freud's Hungarian protégé, Sándor Ferenczi (1873–1933) bore this line of thought out to its furthest, most vertiginous, conclusions. Already in 1913, Ferenczi was supposing that we 'faithfully recapitulate in our individual life' the 'misery of the glacial period' along with other 'geological changes in the surface of the earth'.[2] In 1915 Freud wrote to his younger colleague, praising Ferenczi's 'fruitful and original idea about the influence of geological vicissitude'.[3] This 'original idea' would see its full explication, however, in 1924's *Thalassa: A Theory of Genitality*, where Ferenczi extends the scope of trauma-inscription far beyond the confines of human prehistory, announcing our retention of the archaeo-evolutionary trauma *of the transition to land*. In a radicalisation of the 'oceanic feeling' hypothesis, *Thalassa* suggests that, just as the neonate longs for *regressus ad uterum*, the migration from ocean to land installs a 'thalassal regressive trend' in terrestrialized animals—a longing to return to the sea.

'[L]eaving the sea two hundred million years ago', Ballard has one of his characters say in *The Drowned World*, 'may have

---

1.   Freud, *Phylogenetic Fantasy*, xvi.

2.   S. Ferenczi, *First Contributions to Psychoanalysis*, tr. E. Jones (London: Karnac, 1994), 237

3.   S. Freud and S. Ferenczi, *The Correspondence of Sigmund Freud and Sándor Ferenczi: 1914–1919*, tr. P.T. Hoffer (Cambridge, MA: Harvard University Press, 3 vols., 1996), vol. 2, 68.

been a deep trauma from which we've never recovered'.[4] Blumenberg, when he defined bipedalization as a traumatogenic expulsion from any determinate biotope, similarly cited Ferenczi's notion of terrestrialization as a calamity frozen within our neurons.[5] For Ferenczi, indeed, the individual's ontogenetic desire for uterine retreat collapses into phylogenetic thalassotropism, itself merely the iterated permutation of an abiogenetically-instigated desire to allow the inorganic to compulsively 'recapitulate' itself through our extinction. This of course is Freud's death drive: that 'old state' toward which life 'strives to return through all the detours of evolution'.[6] '*Ururtrauma*' accordingly becomes, for Ferenczi, existence's vanishing point.[7]

A key inspiration for Reich's work, the Hungarian analyst was the first to expand psychoanalysis into '**bioanalysis**' (a topography of the 'biological unconscious'): 'in the biological stratification of organisms', he speculated, 'all their earlier stages are in some manner preserved and kept distinct'. The most 'remote epochs' therefore lie dormant within us.[8] Neuronics, again, revokes temporal unilinearity.

Ferenczi's *Thalassa* is a towering fever-dream of recapitulatory reverie, excavating resonant traumatisms across all biological series. Breastfeeding is cast as the 'ectoparasitic'

---

4.   Ballard, without doubt, read Ferenczi, though there is no explicit record of this. The year after *The Drowned World* and its 'Pool of Thanatos', Ballard penned a short story, 'The Reptile Enclosure', depicting a thalassal mass suicide triggered by fugue-inducing satellite beams.

5.   Blumenberg, *Work on Myth*, 5.

6.   Freud, *Beyond the Pleasure Principle*, 77.

7.   S. Ferenczi, *The Clinical Diary of Sándor Ferenczi*, tr. M. Balint and N.Z. Jackson (Cambridge, MA: Harvard University Press, 1995), 83.

8.   S. Ferenczi, *Thalassa: A Psychoanalytic Study in Catastrophes in the Development of the Genital Function*, tr. H.A. Bunker (London: Karnac, 1989), 91

newborn's cannibalistic desire to *bore* its way back—through the maternal flesh—into its prior state of oceanic 'endoparasitism'; the penis, later, reiterates the same task via vaginal penetration and preputial invagination, both representing desperate attempts at regaining embryonic suspension and pelagic immersion; and, crucially, our assumption of foetal posture in sleep, again via flexion and adducement, is, Ferenczi suggests, properly read as an attempt to regain an aquatic-amniotic mode of existence. But for this thinker who would himself eventually fall victim to spinal degeneration, vertebrality is, once again, central.[9] Coitus and sleep—both relieving the discontinuity of spinal-priapic erection through collapse into horizontal submersion—represent attempts at 'archaic' regressions. During both, 'the whole body assumes [a] spheroid shape', recapitulating not just conditions in utero, but the morphologies of our pre-bilateral ancestors, the marine radiata. Ferenczi states, moreover, that the sleeper's executive centre, their 'soul', sinks back through nervous laminae, routing down from the hibernating and deactivated encephalon into the proprioceptive spinal column. A katabasis of the CNS, *sleeping is thus temporary decapitation*: the somnolent 'has only a "spinal soul"', Ferenczi exclaims; evidence, then, of the sleeper's 'phylogenetic regression' through neuronic layers. The 'soul' descends spinally from brain to thorax; a genuine recapitulation of precephalic existences. Dreams are spinal emissions. *Sleep is time travel.*[10]

Certainly, for Ferenczi, caenogenetic organs are mere 'superpositions' over older ones, while the oldest remains forever 'potential' within our biotic palimpsest. 'Sleep' and

9.   P. Roazen, *The Trauma of Freud: Controversies in Psychoanalysis* (Piscataway, NJ: Transaction, 2002), 57.

10.   Ferenczi, *Thalassa*, 75–6.

'genitality' are aligned, therefore, with 'organic disease'—they are all temporary reeruptions, within the organic 'present', of phyletic 'archaisms': physiological illnesses are regressions 'to antenatal and probably likewise to a phylogenetically ancient mode of existence'.[11] *Disease is inorganic recividism.* And therefore a form of internal or mereological time travel: a dyssynchronous lurch of tissue into anorganic posteriority or anteriority. From this perspective, *all* sickness is time sickness. For, if bodies are just **glutinated time**, pathologies can be approached as **timestep desynchronisations**: an organ or tissue's runaway into its *own* futurity being therefore indistinguishable from modular time travel—the organic part's malignant secession into its own divergent mode of temporal production, pathological vis-à-vis that of the whole. Chronoception collapse. All nosologies are dissonances of heterochrony, unravellings of mereological coevality or CNS timestep simultaneity; pathogenic time travel, temporal decentralization, evodevo arrhythmia, heterotopic futurality. Excrescences can be read either as revenants of ante-organic pasts or as invasions from post-organic posterities, as some 'part' progressively disarticulates from the window of simultaneity fabricated by the 'whole'. Why might not therefore the lithifying spine itself be read (as some of Barker's early exo-archaeological papers suggested it might), as fulgurite from the future—the retroactive trace of some unliving virus—inhabiting the dorsal axis, puppeting it into the perverted ascent of the reasoning animal, dredging ventriloquising words from receding jaw? For Ferenczi, for whom 'embryogenesis' is a thnetopsychic sleep 'disturbed' by one's 'biographical dream', life is just one prolonged hypnogogic jerk, and, accordingly, the colossal malignancy of

---

11.   Ibid., 83–4.

existence itself becomes merely an arrhythmic belatedness or precociousness relative to non-existence's obsidian repose: a vast, drawn-out chronopathy.[12]

In an early essay (written in 1916) entitled 'On the Ontogenesis of the Interest in Money', Ferenczi derived money and the drive-to-accumulate from the sublimation, corollary with upright posture, of the infant's desire to play with its own faeces (a desire which Freud, of course, saw as itself a recapitulation of quadruped forms of life and their libidinal olfactions). In spinal erection, we repress our anal desire for our own 'faecal property', which duly becomes deflected into the drive to accumulate money's 'filthy lucre':

> Pleasure in the intestinal contents becomes enjoyment of money, which, however, after what has been said is seen to be nothing other than odourless, dehydrated filth that has been made to shine. *Pecunia non olet.*

In this way even capital itself is derived from Ferenczi's 'biogenetic ground principle' of 'phylogenetic' repetitiousness. To reach this conclusion, the Hungarian rallied the argument that 'capitalism' is 'not purely practical and utilitarian, but libidinous and irrational'.[13]

That an entire economic system is neither 'utile' nor 'practical' is, perhaps, a strange notion at first sight. Yet Ferenczi was writing in the midst of the first of the two world wars. Decades later, just after the Second World War, it was Georges

---

12.   Ferenczi, *Thalassa*, 80.

13.   Ferenczi, *First Contributions*, 326–30; see also N.O. Brown, *Life Against Death: The Psychoanalytical Meaning of History* (New York: Vintage, 1959), 234–306.

Bataille (1897–1962) who noticed that these global conflicts jointly represented 'the greatest orgies of wealth—and of human beings—that history has recorded', and that, whilst they may well 'coincide with an appreciable rise in the general standard of living', such an upswell in our quality of life represents—like the wars—*just another way of expending surplus energy.*[14] Bataille was masterful in his sustained revelation of the fact that the capitalist global system is, in Ferenczi's terms, 'utterly libidinous and irrational'. For, when any system has an inevitable point of total exhaustion (and our globe is, in the longest term, just such a system), every single *process* that will ever have taken place within said system becomes *utterly indistinct* from a route towards that terminal point: thus, what may locally be called 'means' or 'utilities' are all alike revealed so many avenues through which the wanton and squandrous 'end' announces and hastens its arrival. In such a generalized view, where all myriad utilities and means become indistinct from the end of utmost and terminal expenditure, the luxuriations of the upright spine—its unlikely architecture and its pricey burdens—become yet more sumptuosities on the slope toward the 'immense synthesis of the historical and psychic zero'.[15]

14.   G. Bataille, *The Accursed Share: Volume 1*, tr. R. Hurley (New York: Zone Books, 2007), 37. Note that Bataille cites Vernadskii in his ruminations on solar influx and the earth system. *Ibid.*, 192.

15.   Ballard, *Terminal Beach*, 137.

TH10. ANCIENT AZYGY
OF THE PINEAL SUN-BLOSSOM

Bataille described existence as 'a durable orgasm'.[1] Both Reich and Bataille saw in the orgasm the ultimate relapse into undif-ferentiated plasma, yet Bataille was far clearer as to where this led: death. For Bataille, existence itself is synonymous with ineluctable expenditure, a fact betrayed by orgasm, sleep, laughter, and death—reversions from upright rectitude to bes-tial relapse and wanton disbursement, these are all stations on the inevitable downward route to 'zero'. And, given the postural significance of each of these actions, Bataille was inevitably drawn to Spinal Catastrophism.

Like Blumenberg, Bataille relates uprightness to the origins of mythology, and, like Freud and Ferenczi, he formats the 'progressive erection [from] quadruped to *Homo erectus*' as a deviation from coprophiliac anality. Bataille fixates upon half-upright monkeys, who, he delectates, expose their 'anal projec-tions' like 'excremental skulls'. Inasmuch as their knuckle-dragging existence is some kind of ugly 'halfway house' between horizontal and vertical modes of carriage, primates are cast as some kind of partway antithesis on the stepwise ascent to mankind's upright 'nobility': a dialectical step between horizontal and vertical, the monkey is awkwardly diagonal.[2] (Primate posture thus inhabits a kind of uncanny valley—from which Bataille derives much titillation.) Nonetheless, by way of necrotizing the Renaissance cliché of orthograde 'dignity', Bataille locates in man's spinal realignment merely a *more refined*

1. G. Bataille, *Visions of Excess: Selected Writings, 1927–1939*, tr. A. Stoekl (Minneapolis: University of Minnesota Press), 82.

2. Bataille, 'The Jesuve', *Visions of Excess*, 73–8.

lasciviousness—a *more violent* voluptuousness. To wit, he pinpoints '**Two Terrestrial Axes**': the 'vertical', which 'prolongs the radius of the terrestrial sphere' as axis of libertine escape, lorded by ocean tides and plants (which 'flee' the earth to sacrifice themselves 'endlessly' to the Sun's downward onslaught); and the 'horizontal', domicile to beasts and 'analogous to the turning of the earth'. 'Only human beings', Bataille notes, 'tearing themselves away from peaceful animal horizontality', have 'succeeded in appropriating the vegetal erection', surrendering themselves to exquisite **upwards collapse** towards outer space's solar enormities and fluxions.

Kant had linked the terrestrial-spinal axis to self-orienting rationality, but for Bataille the excremental effluence of the simian anus is merely *rerouted upward*—'blossoming with the most delirious richness of forms'—in the ostentatious bulbing of the sapient cranium, a most exotic and wanton flower. The surging gradient of expenditure migrates from digestive-horizontal slope to the more intensified zenith-realm of intelligences. And yet, as Bataille notes, this upward-thrusting 'liberation of man' is somewhat end-stopped or bottlenecked *by the skull's right angle*. Like the swell of a kinked hose, the perpendicular brain-cap is a ballooning instability. Along with Reich and Ferenczi, Bataille notes that in laughter, coitus, and torment this blockage in the solar-spinal surge is relieved: we assume free-flowing continuity with celestial potlatch. He wrote that 'human life is bestially concentrated in the mouth':

> Terror and atrocious suffering turn the mouth into the organ of rending screams. On this subject it is easy to observe that the overwhelmed individual throws back his head while frenetically stretching his neck in such a way that the mouth becomes, as much as possible, an extension of the spinal column, *in other*

words, in the position it normally occupies in the constitution of animals.[3]

But whatever our posture (whether thrown back in spasmodic laughter or hunched over in studious repression), the 'delirious richness' of intelligence maintains its cloaked solar affinity. Effectively, it matters little whether we attempt to truncate the radiant wantonness of laughter and orgasm by holding our heads firmly forward in rational conversation: intelligence itself is, for Bataille, just another form of filthy expenditure. Bataille sees right-minded rationality, like the sun's long-drawn-out thermonuclear orgasm, as a form of profligacy (albeit one disguised in the rectitude of a skull at right angles to its spine); he communicates this unstoppable solar affinity with the symbol of a 'pineal eye' erupting from the parietal suture at the skull's 'summit'.[4]

This **parietal third eye** is actually exhibited in fish, amphibians, and reptiles, where it is used for photoreception. In these creatures it remains nervously connected to the brain's pineal gland. In the 1880s, scientists first described it as the distal extension of the *epiphysis cerebri*, erupting through a parietal foramen at the pinnacle of the skull. (One of the first proper neuroanatomical descriptions of it came from a study of the *Petromyzon*, the fish whose nervous system Freud was himself specialising in during this same period.)[5] Such an unpaired eye, atop the skull, it has long been hypothesized, serves to connect the pronograde lizard, salamander, or frog with the

---

3.   Bataille, 'Mouth', in *Visions of Excess*, 59.

4.   Bataille, 'The Pineal Eye', in *Visions of Excess*, 79–90.

5.   F. Ahlborn, 'Untersuchung über das Gehirn der Petromyzonten', *Zeitschrift für wissenschaftliche Zoologie* 39 (1883), 191–294.

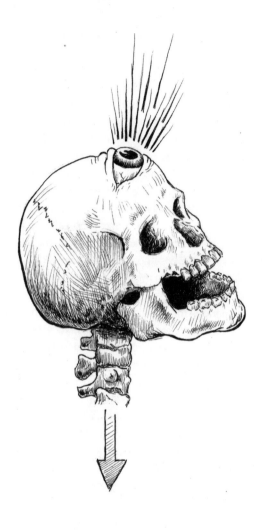

Fig. 17. The parietal eye

blazing heat of the tropical sun directly above them.[6] We mammals outwardly exhibit no such organ, though our closest extinct ancestors did; nonetheless, we retain an inward vestige of it in the shape of our pineal gland. This gland, importantly, is **azygous**—meaning that it doesn't exist in a pair—just like the eye it was once connected to. (This curious anatomical oneness, of course, led Descartes to infuse it with the soul's ipseity.) Such azygous singularity arises from the gland's position as the anatomical inner remnant of the cyclopean proto-eye exhibited by protochordates (such as the lancelet or amphioxus, celebrated by Haeckel as the common ancestor of vertebrata).[7] It thus represents bilaterality's liminal threshold. The mammalian retention of a pineal gland is the somatic fossil-scar of **ancestral cyclopia**, and therefore *of pre-bilateral existence* (of **ancient azygy**, predating sagittal symmetry)—so that Bataille's symbol once again captures Spinal Catastrophism's phyletic-temporal recidivism. It should come as no shock, then, that the pineal gland is a producer of melatonin and thus remains functional in the modulation of circadian rhythms and seasonal cycles. In other words, it is an ancient inner clock—at the proximal core of the brain—oscillating in tune with the solar *Zeitgeber*. Cerebral revenants of a pre-spinal past, pineal glands are, moreover, uniquely prone to **calcification**.[8] Known as '**brain sand**' or *corpora arenacea*, such cortical mineralization demonstrates this ancient gland's acute susceptibility to *time*

6.   A. Dendy, 'The Pineal Gland', *Science Progress in the Twentieth Century* 2:6 (1907), 284–306: 286.

7.   N. Hopwood, 'The Cult of Amphioxus in German Darwinism; or, Our Gelatinous Ancestors in Naples' Blue and Balmy Bay', *History and Philosophy of the Life Sciences* 36:3 (2015), 371–93.

8.   G. Bocchi and G. Valdre, 'Physical, Chemical, and Mineralogical Characterization of Carbonate-hydroxyapatite Concretions of the Human Pineal Gland', *Journal of Inorganic Biochemistry* 49:3 (1993), 209–20.

sickness or *heterotopic futurity*.[9] Our ancient pacemaker is prone to arrhythmia. And the unfortunate upright ape with a blinded and calcified third eye truly is gazing into its own entropic future.[10] Which, incidentally, is the same as the future prematurely glaring into it by way of a mineralising brain-core, a chronopathic infection vector.

9.   One of Barker's projects involved 'detecting' iridium traces in the brain sand of specimens.

10.   See R. Klee, 'Human Expunction', *International Journal of Astrobiology* 16:4 (2017), 379–88; though, for a rigorous and convincing riposte, see M.M. Ćirković, 'The Reports of Expunction are Grossly Exaggerated: A Reply to Robert Klee', in *International Journal of Astrobiology* 18:1 (2019), 14–17.

TH11. CHIROPRAXIS, TARZAN PHILOSOPHERS & PENIS POETICISMS

If Bataille is correct then neither gigantic wars nor great leaps of economic progress are ruses of cunning reason; they are more like orgasmic releases of energetic tension. For writers that were witness to the horrors of the Great War, this would have seemed apt. A global trauma, its psychic shock waves rippled forth and attracted yet more minds to ponder upon the ever-tighter intertwining of the atavistic and the futuristic—a coupling that is central to Spinal Catastrophism.

Nearly a decade before Velikovsky propounded that the peripheral nerves are telepathic conductors, and that the lower region of the nervous system maintains a herd-like form of life more communitarian and less individualized, D.H. Lawrence (1885–1930), himself a dabbler in psychoanalysis, formulated a theory of '**vertebral telepathy**'. Proposing the existence of 'two forms of consciousness'—'mental and vertebral'—that are 'mutually exclusive', he asserted that the latter is 'the true means of communication between the animals' and, being strongest where the brain is less developed, it is naturally 'most *absolute* in the cold fishes and serpents, reptiles'. For such organisms enjoy 'perfect ganglia-communication' with one another:

> It is a complex interplay of vibrations from the big nerve-centres of the vertebral system in all the individuals of the flock, till click!—there is a unanimity. They have one mind. And this one-mindedness of the many-in-one will last while ever the peculiar pitch of vertebral nerve-vibrations continues unbroken through them all. [...] It is a form of telepathy, like a radium-effluence, vibrating fear principally. It is a form of telepathy, like a

radium-effluence, vibrating fear principally. Fear is the first of the actuating gods.[1]

(As Ballard, no stranger to the iguanid portions of the collective psyche, would remark: 'most biological memories are unpleasant ones, echoes of danger and terror'—'[n]othing endures so long as fear'.)[2] The provocation for Lawrence's ethnology of reptilian **'vertebral telegraphy'** was his observation of a similar 'herd instinct' in human crowds. He attributed a preponderance of 'pre-mental' oscillations to great leaders— to history's heroes and despots—explaining their neuro-seismic capacity to command the mob as the effect of emanating spinal vibrations:

> This is what makes the magic of a leader like Napoleon—his power of sending out intense vibrations, messages to his men, without the exact intermediation of mental correspondence. [...] It is the stupendous wits of brainless intelligence. A marvellous reversion to the pre-mental form of consciousness. [...] In Caesar and Napoleon, the vertebral influence of power prevailed.

Stirred by demagoguery's deep-spine vibratiuncles, we all slip into a communal reptile brain. (Worse than a 'swinish multitude', a crowd is a salamandrine one: together, we all know what it is to live and think like lizards.) This is how Lawrence explained 'that strange phenomenon of revolution' which pockmarks modern history. In particular, 'the Russian and French revolutions' could be accounted for as eruptions of spinal telepathy. Revolution is 'a great eruption against the classes in authority',

1. D.H. Lawrence, *Kangaroo* (New York: Thomas Seltzer, 1923), 350–54.

2. Ballard, *The Drowned World*, 43.

Lawrence ventured, and a 'passionate, mindless vengeance taken by the collective, vertebral psyche upon the authority of orthodox *mind*'. All revolt is spinal revolt, wherein the populous becomes lumbar energumen. 'All great mass uprisings are really acts of the [...] dynamic, vertebral consciousness in man bursting up and smashing through the fixed superimposed mental consciousness of mankind':

> The masses are always, strictly, non-mental. Their consciousness is preponderantly vertebral. And from time to time, as some great life-idea cools down and sets upon them like a cold crust of lava, the vertebral powers will work below the crust, apart from the mental consciousness, till they have come to such a heat of unison and unanimity, such a pitch of vibration that men are reduced to a great non-mental oneness as in the hot-blooded whales, and then, like whales which suddenly charged upon the ship which tortures them, so they burst upon the vessel of civilization.[3]

Hegel, characteristically, had imagined the *Zeitgeist* of massified history as an 'old mole', churning under the planetary mantle, 'until grown strong in itself it bursts asunder the crust of the earth which divided it from the sun'[4]—world-spirit as subterrene. But rather than Hegel's flaming *nous* and its return to solar identity, for Lawrence the masses and their oncoming waves of revolution now represent, instead, a stony serpent spine—revenant of ancient reptile mindlessness—torquing through the rock of ages.

---

3.   Lawrence, *Kangaroo* (New York: Thomas Seltzer, 1923), 350–54.

4.   G.W.F. Hegel, *Lectures on the History of Philosophy*, tr. E.S. Haldane and F.H. Simson (Lincoln, NE: University of Nebraska Press, 3 vols., 1995), vol. 3, 547.

Inversely, instead of characterizing revolution as downward lapse, the Marxist philosopher Ernst Bloch (1885–1977) championed the skyward surge of our 'upright gait' (*aufrechter Gang*) as the source of all 'rebellions'. Without uprightness, 'there would be no uprisings', he insisted:

> The very word uprising means that one makes one's way out of one's horizontal, dejected, or kneeling position into an upright one.

Although Bloch, like Lawrence, saw modernity's turbulent history as a function of the spine, then, he did not see its insurrections as a reversion to ichthyoid-reptilian modes but as confirmation of our steadfast standing above the circumspections of supine material relations. He eulogized bipedalism as the 'moral orthopaedics of human dignity, as strengthening the backbone against humiliation, dependency, and subjugation': in diametric opposition to the emancipatory squirming collapses of Reichian biotherapy, Bloch's rigid standing becomes the very somatic basis of the Marxist-Promethean demand to transcend all bondages.[5] Praxis is **chiropraxis**.

Accordingly, Bloch was revulsed by the myriad anti-modern reactions to modernism and their **pronotropic tendency**, their shared desire to revert back to the pronograde. (Barker, of course, would later diagnose the 'contemporary trends' that 'attest to an attempted recovery of the icthyophidian- or flexomotile-spine'.)[6] Where Reich saw this as a therapeutic solution to the problem of the modern, Bloch only saw dirty backwardness. Deftly connecting various contemporary strands of thought

---

5. Quoted in J.R. Bloch, 'How Can We Understand the Bends in the Upright Gait?', *New German Critique* 45 (1988), 9–39.

6. Barker, 'Barker Speaks', 6.

and their expressions of longing for the irresponsibility of supine life, Bloch saw this will to 'archaic collective regression' as a common thread running through psychoanalytical, primitivist, and vitalist schools, all characterized by an enthusiasm for 'fleeing the present, hating the future, [and] searching for the primeval time'. He railed against all such 'Tarzan philosophers'. For his part in this overall pronotropic trend and in particular his carnal championing of 'the nocturnal moon in the flesh, the unconscious sun in the blood', D.H. Lawrence earned from Bloch the title of 'sentimental penis-poet'.[7] (In his defence, Lawrence had, in his own psychoanalytical writings, celebrated upright posture whilst stressing the centrality of 'the great ganglion of the spinal system' in the early development of selfhood: the child, Lawrence claimed, individuates itself in opposition to the parent when, upon standing, it 'stiffens its spine in the strength of its own private and separate, inviolable existence'; and, thereafter, in 'the lumbar ganglion the unconscious now vibrates tremendously in the activity of sundering'.)[8] Beyond the English writer's penis-poeticisms, though, Bloch found the worst culprit of all in the school of psychoanalysis, where the analyst digs down to 'the archaic traces of the mere memory of humanity'—down through 'much older layers'—to the churning core of 'impersonal, pandemonic libido'. This 'mandate to strive from the light into the darkness' is a 'true nighttolerance'; a rejection of the burdens of upstanding accountability and public lights in knowing. (Of course, von Schubert, who had earlier coined the terminology of a

---

7.   E. Bloch, *The Principle of Hope,* tr. N. Plaice, S. Plaice and P. Knight (Oxford: Blackwell, 2 vols., 1986), vol. 1, 59.

8.   D.H. Lawrence, *Psychoanalysis and the Unconscious and Fantasia of the Unconscious* (New York: Dover, 2006), 24.

'night-side of natural science', also exerted a significant influence on Freud.) Bloch complains that the Freudian unconscious has been 'excavated', by Orphic practitioners like Ferenczi, 'down to the primal memories of the first land animals'. But no analyst, for Bloch, is worse than 'C.G. Jung', that 'fascistically frothing psychoanalyst' who 'generalized and archaized Freud's unconscious right down the line' and, correlatively, aims to drag 'all too civilized and conscious man' back—down through the threaded vortices of the spine—into 'ancestral night' and the 'witch-crazes' of the 'Tertiary period'.

> In this way, the libido in Jung opens up like a sack of undigested, atavistic secrets, or rather abracadabras, in fact this sack, in Jung's own words, drags 'an invisible dinosaur tail behind it; carefully separated, it becomes the saviour serpent of the mystery' [...] The anatomical location of this libido is the ancient sympathetic nerve, not the cerebro-spinal system.[9]

Bloch goes on to attack the vitalism of Henri Bergson along similar lines. The French philosopher had previously been a target of the woefully underappreciated Wyndham Lewis (1882–1957). Ever inveterate, often undemocratic, always venomous, Lewis, like Bloch, saw in philosophies of unconscious flow and blind creativity an anti-modernist revolt against the rigid, upstanding, angular, geometric and autarchic. In their place, such philosophies luxuriate in the glandular, eusocial, pulsional, endocrine, and voluptuous; a hostile takeover of the unconscious, raising up the liquidities of time over the austerities of space. Lewis's 1927 *Time and Western Man* is a 600-page multifront assault on all such presumption. He casts

9. Bloch, *Principle of Hope*, vol. 1, 59–63.

aristocratic cephalate centrality against 'time philosophy' and its preconscious 'insect communism' of the decentralized spinal crowd. With characteristic acrimony, he writes:

> Imagine your body an ant-hill: suppose that it is a mass of a million subordinate cells, each cell a small animal. [...] We live a conscious and magnificent life of the 'mind' at the expense of this community. [...] But in sympathy with the political movements to-day, the tendency of [philosophic] thought is *to hand back to* this vast community of cells this stolen, aristocratical monopoly of personality which we call the 'mind'. 'Consciousness', it is said, is (contrary to what an egotistic mental aristocratism tells us) not at all necessary. We should get on just as well without it. On every hand some sort of *unconscious* life is recommended and heavily advertised, in place of the *conscious* life of will and intellect which humanly has been such a failure, and is such a poor thing compared to the life of 'instinct'.

This regicide of the cephalon provokes 'civil war' in the body and soul:

> Inside us also the crowds were pitted against the Individual, the Unconscious against the Conscious, the 'emotional' against the 'intellectual', the Many against the One. So it is that *the Subject* is not gently reasoned out of, but violently hounded from, every cell of the organism: until at last [it] plunges into the *Unconscious*, where Dr. Freud, like a sort of Mephistophelian Dr. Caligari, is waiting for [it].

This 'triumph of the *Unconscious*'—and of the crowd— is properly a decerebration, a reversion to the salamandrine.

'For the exercise of the Will (or of the Unconscious) *no brain at all* is required', insofar as '[g]anglionic impulsion is just as good':

> For the Unconscious (or on the plane of the Will) the body is an egalitarian and self-sufficient commonwealth. Since in invertebrates the oesophageal ganglia take the place of the brain, we must assume that these suffice also for the act of will. In decapitated frogs the cerebellum and spinal cord supply the place of the cerebrum.

Thus, having 'got the brain down into the ganglia, and made of the body a commonwealth of Unconscious "Wills", we have taken the personality a step further on the road to destruction', Lewis complains:

> The personality of the animal, in this way decentralized, and characterized essentially by *will*, not 'thought', can be decomposed before our eyes.

This, then, is 'the final extinction of such a redoubtable human myth as "the mind"'. In response, Lewis mourns Western man's auto-decapitation.[10] He sees this as an act of 'tearing off and

---

10.   Despite such overriding prejudices, this did not mean Lewis was a stranger to celebrating the involuntary motions of the spinal nerves. In words that Bataille would have no doubt have appreciated, Lewis wrote of the 'Wild Body' that 'triumphs in its laughter'. 'What is the Wild Body? The Wild Body, as understood here, is that small, primitive, literally antediluvian vessel in which we set out on our adventures. [...] Laughter is the brain-body's snort of exultation. It expresses its wild sensation of power and speed; it is all that remains physical in the flash of thought, its friction: or it may be a defiance flung at the hurrying fates. [...] The Wild Body is this supreme survival that is us, the stark apparatus with its set of mysterious spasms; the most profound of which is laughter'. See W. Lewis, *The Wild Body: A Soldier of Humour, and Other Stories* (New York: Haskell, 1927), 237–8.

out of himself everything that reminded him of the hated symbols, "power", "authority", "superiority", "divinity", etc.':

> Turning his bloodshot eyes inward, as it were, one fine day, there he beheld, with a state of horror and rage, his own proper mind sitting in state, and lording it over the rest of his animal being—spurning his stomach, planting its heel upon his sex, taking the hard-work of the pumping heart as a matter of course. Also he saw it as a *mind-with-a-past*: and he noticed, with a grain of diabolical malice, that the mind was in the habit of conveniently forgetting this humble (animal) and *criminal* past, and of behaving as though such a thing had never existed. It did not take him long to take it down a peg or two in that respect! The 'mind' [was] soon squatting with a cross and snarling monkey, and scratching itself.[11]

Hypergenealogy aims at filthy superlation—the championing of theriophiliac oblivion—rather than right-minded or constructive suspicion. It aims to reduce Lewis's 'Western man' to Swift's excremental Yahoo.[12] As Swift himself had quipped, centuries earlier, at the beginning of a time that would continually be made anew by the rolling regicides and revolutions thundering upward from the lower back:

> We read of kings, who in a fright,
> Though on a throne, would fall to shite.[13]

---

11.   W. Lewis, *Time and Western Man* (London: Chatto and Windus, 1927), 319–66.

12.   See again Brown, *Life Against Death*.

13.   J. Swift, *Poetical Works* (Oxford: Oxford University Press, 1967), 48.

Yet we remember that lucre is filthy, after all; so, presumably, the regal brain wouldn't have far to fall. Regardless, Lewis angrily complained that, against the uprightness of the noble mammal and its cephalic monarchy, the trend of the times (exampled from Bergson to Lawrence, from Freud and Ferenczi to Jung) was instead toward the 'swarming of insect life' and its allegiance to 'a rigid communistic plan'—less suited to the monarchic autarchies of the regal brain, and more to the parallel planning of the spinal **reflex arcs**—those neural pathways controlling our involuntary movements and jerks, which do not pass directly through the brain, and thus hint at a devolved and horizontalized vision of bodily function.

Writing just two years after Lewis's invectives, the Irish crystallographer and futurologist J.D. Bernal (1901–1971), who was also an ardent communist, published his utopian vision of the socialist future. Prospecting an oncoming seizure of the means of genetic reproduction via promethean technoscience, Bernal noted that in 'the alteration of himself man has a great deal further to go than in the alteration of his inorganic environment'. Humanity may have changed the entire surface of planet with noospheric aplomb, but it has not yet changed drastically itself. We must reengineer the spinal landscape, not just the earthly one. (Indeed, Bernal wrote of the need to reformat desire *and* the body, in tandem.) Nonetheless, taking Alsbergian 'body-liberation' to its most extreme, he saw that this seizure of the means of 'growth and reproduction' would lead to the secession of the cerebro-spinal system from the rest of the body—an enlightened decapitation. Reaching this conclusion, Bernal notes that modern technics have 'rendered both the skeletal and metabolic functions of the body to a large extent useless': the 'limbs' are now 'mere parasites, demanding nine-tenths of the energy of the food and even a kind of blackmail in the exercise they need to prevent disease, while the bodily organs wear themselves out in supplying their requirements'. In direct tension with this drag of the evolutionary past into the technical present, Bernal points to the fact that

> the increasing complexity of man's existence, particularly the mental capacity required to deal with its mechanical and physical complications, gives rise to the need for a much more complex sensory and motor organization, and even more fundamentally for a better organized cerebral mechanism. Sooner or later the useless parts of the body must be given modern functions or dispensed with altogether....

Insofar as morphology and anatomy is itself a type of retention or biological memory, this is the final stage of retrograde amnesia for a '*mind-with-a-past*'. This would be total redesign; another maximum jailbreak. Indeed, Bernal looks at the ambitions of 'eugenicists and the public health officers' and their attempts at life extension, and finds them essentially lacking. One can prolong the life of the body, but one is only prolonging pain (and, worse, *bad design*) unless one starts again from the ground up. 'Sooner or later some eminent physiologist will have his neck broken in a super-civilized accident or find his body cells worn beyond capacity for repair', Bernal quipped. The solution? *Get rid of the body below that neck*. In short, Bernal anticipates that the communistic prometheans of the future will be cerebro-spinal systems surgically emancipated from the rest of the human frame (which has, of course, become a mere parasite). The promethean human is a brain trailing a spinal tail, the loosened tendrils of which, Bernal projects, will be repurposed as the connectors for various plug-and-play sensory and motor appendages that can be switched in and out according to need and desire. (Strange that Bernal's omega point resembles Reich's primordial plan: the humble jellyfish. Or perhaps not so strange when one considers Barker's rumoured involvement with Maximilian Crabbe—specialist in abyssopelagic habitability and cetacean linguistics—whose project for self-preservation reportedly led him toward a dismembered existence residing in various high-pressure liquid vats.)[14] Speculating on the 'final state' of this transformation, Bernal sees the body becoming a 'cylinder':

> Inside the cylinder, and supported very carefully to prevent shock, is the brain with its nerve connections, immersed in a liquid of the nature of cerebro-spinal fluid, kept circulating over it at a uniform temperature.[15]

An unappendiculated, delimbed techno-spine floating in its own portable thalassa: the communist overmen of the future will resemble, if not the abysmally archaic radial barrel-shaped extra-terrestrials unearthed in H.P. Lovecraft's *At the Mountains of Madness*, then perhaps the centipede monstrosities of Burroughs's nightmare visions. Burroughs himself, however, would later claim that

---

14. Crabbe, an eccentric billionaire, wasn't concerned with terraforming outer space for human habitation (as billionaires are today), he was instead obsessed with reengineering the human frame for residence on the ocean floor. See 'Maximilian Crabbe: Subaquatic Researcher and Entrepreneur (1940–1999?)', in CCRU, *Writings*, 141–3.

15. J.D. Bernal, *The World, the Flesh and the Devil: An Enquiry into the Future of the Three Enemies of the Rational Soul* (Indianapolis: Indiana University Press, 1969), 13–20.

[m]an is an artefact designed for space travel. He is not designed to remain in his present biologic state any more than a tadpole is designed to remain a tadpole.[16]

Ironic, then, that the human of the future will precisely come to resemble a tadpole, dragging a dinosaur tail: a cylindrical communist space-brain with a centipedal spine trailing behind it.

Karl Marx himself, however, had envisioned modernization not so much as Lewis's formicating decerebration or Bernal's decapitating body-liberation, but more as the conquest of the external world by our neural innards: as the onward-marching outpouching and eversion of our control centres. Having apportioned the planetary environs as 'man's inorganic body', Marx, in the *Grundrisse*, is impressed that 'locomotives, railways, electric telegraphs,' and so forth, are 'organs of the human brain'—they represent 'the power of knowledge, objectified'.[17]

What is remarkable in this intellectual conflict, and indeed throughout all periods under scrutiny in our secret history, is that, although there will always be those who advocate submission to the yearning for katabasis and those who decry its mortal dangers, both sides are *invariably unanimous* in recognizing that—in some important sense—what is at stake in modernity is a genuine temptation toward, and a real possibility of, psychic regression. This is a battle over the very meaning of the tenses through which we understand temporality. The startling persistence of spinal catastrophic episodes in modern thought testifies to the fact that it is not so easy to separate

---

16.   W.S. Burroughs, 'Civilian Defense', in *The Adding Machine: Selected Essays* (New York: Arcade Publishing, 1985), 85.

17.   K. Marx, *Grundrisse: Foundations of the Critique of Political Economy*, tr. M. Nicolaus (London: Penguin, 1973), 706.

onward rush and outward projection from inward involution and backward regression. Even the futuristic global telegraphy-actuated megamind, which was emerging as Marx was writing, came to curiously resemble our anciently-inherited neural make-up, thus heralding new potentials for archaeopsychic subsidence.

TH12. GLOBAL VERTEBRAL TELEGRAPHY & NEURAL NEUZEIT

If teeth are objectified hunger, and the steam engine a mechanization of musculoskeletal vivacity, then telegraphy is the organ of a globe become self-conscious. Such a view was already common by the 1870s, two decades after the first transatlantic cables had been laid. In 1877, Ernst Kapp (1808–1896) published his *Grundlinien einer Philosophie der Technik*, where he develops a theory of '**organ projections**' (a concept that Alsberg inherited and borrowed) by claiming that technology is nothing but the eversion of the bodily functions of the human animal. Writing that 'the comparison between the electrical telegraph and the *nervous system* is self-evident', Kapp thereafter lists the many other anatomists of his time who had similarly noted how closely the global telegraph network resembles an extended nervous network of cerebrospinal arcs.[1] As the influential physician Rudolf Virchow (1821–1902) had stated in an 1871 lecture 'On the Spinal Cord': 'the nerves are the cable installations of the animal body, just as you might call telegraph cables the nerves of humankind'.[2] Kapp writes that, in global communications networks, humanity has produced for itself 'an exact artificial reconstruction of the body's own nervous system' by laying a 'branching electrical framework over the entire earth'.[3] (Extending this to a yet wider scale, we note that Kapp's *Organprojektion* is precisely the principle that influenced

1.   E. Kapp, *Elements of a Philosophy of Technology*, 103.

2.   'Die Nerven sind kabeleinrichtungen des thierichen Körpers, wie man die Telegraphen-kabel Nerven der Menschheit nenne kann'. See R. Virchow, *Über das Rückenmark* (Berlin, 1871), 10–11.

3.   Kapp, *Elements*, 104.

Acheropoulos's conviction that 'the laws of physics' are themselves nothing but the externalized reflex arcs of some cosmic-scale alien tektology.) In support of his argument, Kapp pointed out that cross-sections of spinal cord nerves and telegraph cables—when placed side-by-side—unveil an uncanny identity in design.

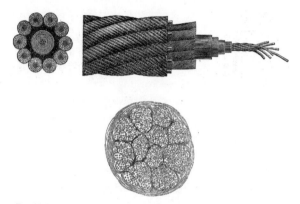

Fig. 18. Kapp's comparison of transverse cross-section of a telegraph cable to a nerve bundle. From *Elements of a Philosophy of Technology* (Minneapolis: University of Minnesota Press, 2018)

Kapp, moreover, noticed that it is solely 'through organ projection that we recognize the impulse human nature has *to reflect itself in itself*'.[4] The human being knows itself in the special way it does because it everts itself so as to reflect itself back upon itself. *It is the artefact of its own artifice*. So, as Blumenberg and Alsberg hinted, we *are* our neural prostheses. And, just as the 'eye sees not itself / But by reflection, by some other things',[5]

---

4.   Ibid., 119.

5.   W. Shakespeare, *Julius Caesar*, ed. D. Daniell (London: Bloomsbury, 1998), 1.2.52–3.

global humanity likewise only becomes truly self-conscious by mediating itself through some globally-inosculating neural prosthetic. The sentient animal already accomplishes this by collapsing into the neural reflexion of its own world, but by embarking upon a global-scale technogenic plexus evagination, the human reaches a new intensity of planetary autonoesis. Kapp, already in the 1870s, noticed the seemingly paradoxical fact that it is only our *intussusception outwards* that vouchsafes our *intensified inwardness*.

The telegraph, then, provides the global sensorium within which humanity can reflect itself unto itself, thus becoming aware of itself *as* a massified cosmopolitan community.[6] From here, from this massification of history via neural transcontinental prostheses, come the world-shaking revolutions of a time of unceasing geopolitical upheaval and time-space compressions (in other words, '*Neuzeit*' or 'modernity').[7] It is only by assembling a planetary-scale brain that we began to think

---

6.   Not long afterward, Nikolai Fedorov imagined that this encephalization would expand *beyond the globe*, spilling its consciousness-suffusing tendrils into the circumstellar expanses, and human activity would create a 'centralization' and 'coordination' of organizing activities and reflex arcs at the scale of the Solar System. He proposed requisitioning the 'heavenly bodies' and matter of the planets as outward extensions of our 'sensory and motor nerves'. He claimed that our Solar System, in its current unorganized state, was like an invertebrate—with a diffuse, unconscious, and haphazard neural structure—awaiting its evolution into a vertebrate animal enjoying a complexified, differentiated, and consciousness-supporting nervous organization. In other words, it is the job of human industry to give to the Solar System a central nervous system and brain. See N. Fedorov, *Philosophy of the Common Task*, tr. M. Minto (London: Honeyglen 1990), 100.

7.   Owing to developments in transnational and transcontinental communication, Lukács noted, the French Revolution 'for the first time made history a *mass experience*'. G. Lukács, *The Historical Novel*, tr. H. Mitchell and S. Mitchell (Lincoln, NE: University of Nebraska Press, 1983), 23.

like a planet. Globalization, indeed, is nothing other than self-consciousness *of* globalization, so it should come as no surprise that it demands this encephalization of the planet. For as soon as one operates under nonlocal horizons, one *cannot but* become ever more deracinated in one's actions. Becoming globally focalized can do nothing but facilitate more global focalizing: globalization *is* its own awareness of itself, and, since the brain is the organ of awareness, globalization demands a globe-brain. And the telegraphic planet-spine—inceptive of the modern subject's distinctively multiscalar focalization—represents the outward concretization of this process. Communications networks are a megamachine for interoception ex situ. They generate for us our world-interior. Each undersea telegraph line is a moment in the externalization, or self-mediation, of Spirit. And when, in the late 1850s, the telegraph connected Ireland to Newfoundland, our nervous system became properly transatlantic. The movements of Spirit, that 'old mole' torquing through the crust, present to us nothing other than the moments of what Kapp calls a '**Universal Telegraphics**'—the assembly of a planetary-scale Spinal Surrogate, or, in Lawrence's words, an extension of 'vertebral telepathy' into a 'vertebral telegraphy'.[8]

---

8.   In 1883, Krakatoa in Indonesia erupted, one of the biggest eruptions of the Holocene; it was also the first natural disaster to be known, instantly, across the globe—the first massified calamity. Telegraphic news of the cataclysm reached foreign shores before the volcano's shock wave did. Capturing the local-global loopings within which we are all progressively entangled, we note that the rubber used to insulate the undersea telegraph cables came from latex trees found only in Indonesia. The island that produced the neural sheaths for our global cerebrum also produced the first truly globally focalized disaster. See S. Winchester, *Krakatoa: The Day the World Exploded, August 27, 1883* (New York: Harper Collins, 2003).

In 1876, the year prior to Kapp's disquisition upon *Organprojektion*, Engels had declared that the primal adoption of 'more erect posture' was '*the decisive step in the transition from ape to man*'[9] because it freed up the hands for **labour**; and labour, in turn, promoted conditions that would promote further spinal erection. In this conception, labour and spinal erection *cause each other*: mutually bootstrapping, symbiotically and serially dragging one another into existence, to gradually converge on *Homo economicus*. From one perspective, uprightness first enables labour to invade reality; from another, labour value quite literally drags the ape upright, invading us with lowering time preference, riddling us with futurity. A symbiogenesis of sufficiencies. Yet, whilst Marxians from Engels to Bloch would celebrate this convergence upon the labouring ape, Elaine Morgan notes that of 'all the man-hours lost to industry through various forms of illness, the highest percentage derives from our mode of locomotion':

> In a recent year in Britain, lower back pain occasioned the loss of nineteen million working days. In the United States it has been calculated that 70 per cent of American citizens are affected by it at some time in their lives.[10]

Certainly, as Ferenczi would point out, standing upright heralded no great boom in efficiency: it merely deflected our irrational desire for faecal mess into the grubby machinations of finance. Chiropraxis, on this view, is nothing but **copropraxia**. The symbiogenesis of labour must then be viewed with

9.   F. Engels, *The Part Played by Labour in the Transition from Ape to Man*, tr. I.L. Andreev (Moscow: Progress, 1985), 28.

10.   Morgan, *Scars of Evolution*, 27.

appropriate suspicion—as Burroughs reminds us, '[f]rom symbiosis to parasitism is a short step'.[11] Binocular vision, opposable thumbs, and intrusive spinal uplift are all physiological symptoms of abstract labour's **retroparasitism**: its teleo-economic lock-in as both drive and destiny of terrestrial history; a new self-intricating 'sealed haven' or entrapment to rival that of nervous enclosure.

Spinal Catastrophism's conception of time is one essential to modernity itself. The lock-in of systems that cause their own furtherance and exaggeration (i.e. the globalized economic system unmasked by both Ferenczi and Bataille as an excrementitious end-unto-itself) creates a sense in which the future *drags us* towards it. The future is not passive, it *actively creates* its own emergence via such circular causality (when something causes itself to cause itself, time seems to flow backward). And the more the future flows backward towards us in this way, the more we feel that our present is in the grip of a past that is utterly retrograde. As soon as time begins to speed up, the future begins arriving early, which means that the past is felt—more and more—as inertial drag within the present. 'Precocity' can be *defined only relative* to 'belatedness'. Thus, as modernity ripples outwards into the rolling revolutions of a time made continually anew, the ancient and outmoded and primal becomes increasingly resurgent and compulsively repetitive. Only when we became suitably modern—gathering enough momentum to see the past distinctly in the rear-view mirror—did the gothic begin to exert a considerable drag upon us. This seems paradoxical, but it is anything but. Only when we defined ourselves against the horrors of the past did the past become horrifying (and thus able to

---

11. Burroughs, *Ticket That Exploded*, 39.

exert considerable psychic effect upon our present); so our realization of our distance from the archaeopsychic past is precisely the archaeopsychic past exerting its pull upon us. Kapp, indeed, anticipating Ballard's suggestion of resonance between inner and outer space, noticed that, insofar as the modern technical world was a projection of our insides, one could perform an investigation of the human unconscious by analysing the geometries and designs of our technological landscape. Futurity's bleeding industrial edge repeats an ancient drive. Time exhibits a lordotic curvature; modernity's sense of chronology is one of whiplash. Ballard would have welcomed the thought and Lewis and Bloch no doubt would have hated it, but the regurgitation of the past—where the horsetails grow as high as palms—is internal to the modern rush. And it is no coincidence if it was just at the point when temporality began compressing and coiling in this way that a nascent psychiatry diagnosed the first *illnesses of time*. It is still accepted that schizophrenia affects time perception, so it is appropriate that discussion of schizophrenia—and, specifically, of schizophrenia as a malady of temporality—was so central to the genesis of modern psychiatrics.[12]

---

12. N. Ueda, K. Maruo, and T. Sumiyoshi, 'Positive Symptoms and Time Perception in Schizophrenia: A Meta-analysis', *Schizophrenia Research: Cognition* 13 (2018), 3-6; and S. Thoenes and D. Oberfeld, 'Meta-analysis of Time Perception and Temporal Processing in Schizophrenia: Differential Effects on Precision and Accuracy', *Clinical Psychology Review* 54:44 (2017).

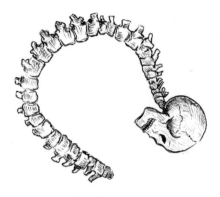

Like the brain, the spinal cord has its memory. A spinal cord without memory would be an idiotic spinal cord...

Henry Maudsley, *Physiology and Pathology of Mind* (1867)

The unconscious will in the self-standing spinal cord.

Eduard von Hartmann, *Philosophie des Unbewussten* (1869)

Many forms of fish, bird and beast
Brought forth an Infant form
Where was a worm before

William Blake, *The First Book of Urizen* (1794)

[F]irst we are a rude masse, and in the ranke of creatures, which only are; next we live the life of plants, the life of animals, [and] the life of men [...] Thus is man that great and true Amphibium, whose nature is disposed to live, not onely like other creatures in divers elements, but in divided and distinguished worlds [...] Thus we are men, and we know not how; there is something in us that can be without us, and will be after us, though it is strange that it hath no history what it was before us, nor cannot tell how it entered in us.

Thomas Browne, *Religio Medici* (1642)

LUMBAR GENESIS
(1900–1800)

L1. POSTERUS PRAECOX

Eugene Bleuler (1857–1939), an influential figure in early psychiatry, was not only the first to speak of 'depth psychology' but also, in 1908, coined the term 'schizophrenia'. A correspondent with Freud, he also met with Velikovsky and prefaced the latter's early paper on neural telepathy.[1] In a 1921 book (whose second-edition title translates as *Natural History of the Soul and of Your Becoming Conscious: Mnemonist Biopsychology*), Bleuler wrote of the psychic disintegrations symptomatic of schizophrenia as representing a kind of centrifugal unpeeling into separate, yet parallel, biopsychic units. This gives reason, he inferred, to think of consciousness itself as an aggregate system of nested inclusions, and accordingly Bleuler claimed that he saw no 'scientific reason to limit the psyche to the conscious functions':

> It is possible, or not yet dismissed, that consciousness arises in very different places; it is not out of the question that in the same organism there are truly several psyches, or, several very different kinds of consciousness: autonomous complexes of the human cortical tissue [*Rindenplastik*], 'souls' of the spinal cord and its foci, phylogenetic consciousnesses residing in the same brain, alongside the individual's psyche, yes, even a conscious psyche from the functioning of bodily organs is conceivable—yet, of course, this would be even less like our cortical-psyche [*Rindenpsyche*] than the buzz of a beetle....

What Bleuler referred to as the 'split-off segment-psyches in schizophrenics' he saw as representing a relapse, down the

---

1. Velikovsky, *Mankind in Amnesia*, 23, and 'Über die Energetik der Psyche'.

spinal pylon, to less centralized, more segmented forms of consciousness.[2] Schizophrenia could then be read as a retro-gression through what Bleuler had elsewhere called the '**phylo-psyche**', or '*Psychoide*'—the registry and agglomerated mneme-stack of all the subcortical accretions comprising our 'central nervous system'.[3]

Bleuler had inherited the diagnostic category of what he eventually came to taxonomize as 'schizophrenia' from Emil Kraepelin (1856–1926), who first brought sustained attention to the illness in the late 1890s. Kraepelin had referred to the affliction as '**dementia praecox**'. (Defined by precociousness of onset—or what is essentially an *untimely* madness—schiz-ophrenia has always been a horological sickness.) For Kraepe-lin, 'one of the creators of psychophysical research into posture', rigid and bizarre spinal poise quickly became a key indicator for diagnosis of the condition.[4] He highlighted the negativism and catatonia of patients displaying 'praecox' symptoms, and, as Sander Gilman records,

> Researchers argued that there was some type of vestibular involvement that could be used to explain the perceived S-curve of schizophrenic posture. Such schizophrenic postures, along with other physical signs such as shuffling gait, inflexibility of the neck and shoulders and a resting posture, were explained [as] a

---

2.   E. Bleuler, *Naturgeschichte der Seele und Ihres Bewsstwerdens: Eine Elementarpsychologie* (Berlin: Springer Verlag, 1921), 71.

3.   E. Bleuler, *Die Psychoide als Prinzip der organischen Entwicklung* (Berlin: Springer Verlag, 1925), 11.

4.   S.L. Gilman, *Stand Up Straight!: A History of Posture* (London: Reaktion, 2018), 129.

regression to primitive labyrinthine reflex, characterized by flexion, internal rotation and adduction.[5]

One article, published in *The Lancet* in 1902, focused on schizoid postural stereotypies, prominent among them 'attitudes of crouching like a beast'.[6] Again, the malady was understood as a time sickness.

Kraepelin may have popularized the term 'dementia praecox', but its first recorded usage comes from Heinrich Schüle (1840–1916). The elder German psychiatrist had already homed in on the catatonic and postural aspect of such illnesses, taxonomizing them as acute forms of **'cerebrospinal insanity** [*cerebrospinalen Verrücktheit*]'.[7] In his 1880 *Handbuch der Geisteskrankheiten* (*Handbook on Spirit-Maladies*), Schüle, seemingly in a moment of abandonment to enthusiasm, writes of schizoid mental states as being the 'delusional dream-flowers [*wahnhafte Traumblüten*] of the spinal nerve-tree [*spinalen Nervenbaum*] from which they blossom—the hallucinations of an abnormally functioning sentience-nerve'.[8]

A few decades later, in his commonplace book, H.P. Lovecraft jotted down the following idea for a short story:

Autonomic nervous system and subconscious mind do not reside in the head. Have mad physician decapitate a man but

---

5.   Ibid., 131.

6.   Anon., 'The Stereotyped Attitudes and Postures of the Insane in Regard to Diagnosis and Prognosis', *The Lancet* 159:4094 (1902), 465–6.

7.   H. Schüle, 'Zur Katatonie-Frage: Eine klinische Studie', *Allgemeine Zeitschrift für Psychiatrie und Psychisch-gerichtliche Medizin* 54 (1898), 515–25: 516.

8.   H. Schüle, *Handbuch der Geisteskrankheiten* (Leipzig: Vogel, 1880), 459.

keep him alive and subconsciously controlled. Avoid copying tale by W.C. Morrow.[9]

The tale Lovecraft was referring to was written not long after Schüle's speculations on 'dream-flowers', in 1897, by the American author of pulp suspense and weird fiction, William Chambers Morrow. It was entitled 'The Monster Maker'. It tells of an evil scientist who decerebrates an unwitting subject, before chronicling the horrific consequences of this ungodly experiment. It is explained that '[t]he cerebrum is merely an adornment; that is to say, reason and affections are almost purely ornamental'. Intellect and emotion are nothing but pretty parvenus—merely an 'offshoot' of the older autonomic systems,

> evolved from them by natural (though not essential) heterogeneity, and to a certain extent [...] dependent on the evolution and expansion of a contemporaneous tendency, that developed into mentality, or mental function. Both of these latter tendencies, these evolvements, are merely refinements of the motor system, and not independent entities; that is to say, they are the blossoms of a plant that propagates from its roots.[10]

So, perhaps not just schizoid states, but *all* conscious states, are nothing but 'dream flowers' sprouting from an eldritch overgrown nerve-tree. Indeed, in Morrow's story, the removal of the cerebrum causes an evolutionary regression, as the test

9. H.P. Lovecraft, *Miscellaneous Writings* (Sauk City, WI: Arkham House, 1995), 98.

10. W.C. Morrow, 'The Monster Maker', in *The Ape, The Idiot and Other People* (Philadelphia, PA: J.B. Lippincott, 1897), 228–36: 235.

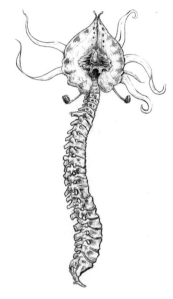

Fig.19. Delusional dream-flowers of the spinal nerve-tree

subject descends toward ape-like strength and brutality. Once the floral ornaments of reason have been removed, 'nature, no longer suffering the distraction of extraneous interferences' redoubles its vital powers and the subject becomes hyper-virulent and violent:

> Hence this marvellous voracity, this insatiable hunger, this wonderful ravenousness; and hence also [...] this strength that is becoming almost hourly herculean, almost daily appalling.[11]

---

11.   Ibid., 237.

The regression of the acephalic subject does not stop at the simian, but collapses even lower, to earlier stages of organic development. Eventually, it transforms into 'a huge, shapeless object, sprawling, crawling, and floundering along':[12] a terrifying embodiment of headless vigor. The idea here is that the ornamental efflorescence of consciousness, enthroned in the toothy gourd of that evolutionary newcomer, the head, is the only thing stopping total evolutionary recall. The brain is a memory-block, reason a form of civilized amnesia.

From Velikovsky through Bleuler—from the 'immortality' of experience to the privately recorded biographies of our *Rindenplastik* and its spinal nerve-tree—early psychiatrists and psychoanalysts were all drawing upon a notion of 'memory' that had dominated late nineteenth-century thought. Therein, the idea of 'mnemonics' had risen to the position of explaining the very tendency for universal matter to assume persistent form and exhibit regularities. Characteristic of this general trend, Charles Sanders Peirce asked 'may not the laws of physics be habits gradually acquired by systems'?[13] In other words, might the synechistic shape of our universe be a question of habit-formation and habit-retention? Here, 'memory' and 'cosmogony' became the same thing, essentially making the universe something like a gigantic nervous system. However, unlike Acheropoulos's later intimations, this memory was utterly and totally unconscious.

---

12.   Ibid., 242.

13.   C.S. Peirce, 'Design and Chance', in *Writings of Charles S. Peirce: A Chronological Edition*, ed. C.J.W. Kloesel (Indianapolis: Indiana University Press, 4 vols., 1989) vol. 4, 553.

L2. ENGRAPHY & ECPHORY:
NO BRAIN REQUIRED

In order to explain his theory of the 'phylo-psyche' in the 1920s, Eugene Bleuler would borrow generously from the late eighteenth-century theory of '**organic memory**' or '**mnemic psychology**'. Prior to the emergence of a proper genetic theory or mechanism of inheritance, this briefly influential school of thought had attempted to explain instinctual behaviour by simply collapsing *biographical memory* into *biological heredity*: casting both as modalities of matter's universal tendency toward inscription. Given the view of temporality lurking behind Spinal Catastrophism, movement in time is understandable primarily in terms of divergence in precocity or belatedness, differentia of tempo, and variant complexes of remembrance and forgetfulness. This inevitably lends itself to a vision of nature as a great system of retention. In particular, however, nervous systems were singled out and studied as the prime medium for nature's processes of inscription and memorization. Indeed, the idea that autonomic processing and reflexive behaviours could be accounted for as a type of inherited, nonconscious memory formed the common backdrop against which Freud, Ferenczi, and Jung would develop their theories on the matter. Envisioning a '*physiology* of the unconscious', the Viennese physiologist Ewald Hering (1834–1918) first postulated that neuroanatomy and nervous functioning is a question of memory-traces in an 1870 lecture entitled 'Memory as a Universal Function of Organized Matter'.[1] Later crossing paths with Freud, Hering condensed his

---

1.   E. Hering, *Über das Gedächtnis als eine allgemeine Funktion der organisierten Materie* (Leipzig: Engelmann, 1905).

outlook into the apothegm 'Instinct is the memory of the species'.[2]

Writing a few decades after Hering's innovations, the German biologist Richard Semon (1859–1918), who had studied alongside Haeckel, inherited and formalized Hering's work. Inventing a technical vocabulary for the study of organic memory, he called Hering's memory-traces '**mnemes**' and '**engrams**', also introducing the terms '**engraphy**' for their study and '**ecphory**' for their recall.[3] (Semon's work exerted a direct influence on many of the figures discussed above, from Jung, who cites Semon approvingly, to Burroughs, who diagnosed engrams as 'living viruses'; Reich's library also contained works by Semon.)[4] Semon spoke of memories being laid down as physiological micro-alterations to the CNS, deposited via 'chronologic stratification'.[5] With Semon having thus paved the way for a generalized physiology of memory, scientists were soon raving about how spinal cords are endowed with memory—indeed, are *nothing but* ossified memory—deposited lamina

2.   This apt slogan is attributed to Hering by the myrmecologist neuroanatomist August Forel. See A.H. Forel, *The Social World of Ants Compared to that of Man*, tr. C.K. Ogden (London: Putnam, 2 vols., 1928), vol. 2, 10. For Hering's relationship to Freud, see Sulloway, *Freud, Biologist of the Mind*, 274.

3.   R. Semon, *Die Mneme als erhaltendes Prinzip im Wechsel des organischen Geschehens* (Leipzig: Engelmann, 1904); *Die mnemischen Empfindungen in ihren Beziehungen zu den Originalempfindungen* (Leipzig: Engelmann, 1909); see also D.L. Schacter, *Forgotten Ideas, Neglected Pioneers: Richard Semon and the Story of Memory* (London: Routledge, 2011).

4.   On Jung and Semon see S. Shamdasani, *Jung and the Making of Modern Psychology: The Dream of a Science* (Cambridge: Cambridge University Press, 2003), 234; Burroughs, *The Ticket That Exploded*, 17; Strick, *Wilhelm Reich, Biologist*, 367.

5.   R. Semon, *Mnemic Psychology*, tr. B Duffy (New York: Allen and Unwin, 1923), 171–5.

upon delicate lamina. One such researcher, Théodule-Armand Ribot, claimed that 'memory is essentially a biological fact, accidentally a psychological fact'.[6] Another proclaimed that, '[l]ike the brain, the spinal-cord has, so to speak, its memory'.[7] Yet another proclaimed that, given these premises, it would be wrong to presume that the amphioxus, a small marine animal that possesses a spinal cord but no head, 'has no consciousness because it has no brain', and that, if it thus 'be admitted that the little ganglia of the invertebrate can form a consciousness, the same may hold good for [our] spinal cord'.[8] Which allows us to finally give an answer to the question 'What Is it Like to Be a Back?': it is like being an amphioxus—which, indeed, is just another way of saying that we all have a lancelet lodged in our lumbar spine.

Ernst Haeckel, that master of recapitulatory reverie, wrote in his *Die Welträtsel* (*The World-Riddle*) of 1899 of the various memory deposits compacted throughout our bodies as various forms of 'plasm'. In an essay on the '**protoplasmania**' rife in scientific culture during the period, Robert Michael Brain notes that 'protoplasm served as a kind of graphical recording apparatus, a medium for the inscription of forces acting in the organic world'.[9] Haeckel took this protoplasmania to its limits. Citing Hering as inspiration, he claimed that the 'chief difference

---

6.   T.-A. Ribot, *Diseases of Memory: An Essay in the Positive Psychology*, tr. W.H. Smith (New York: Appleton, 1882), 10.

7.   H. Maudsley, *The Physiology of Mind* (New York, 1889), 149.

8.   T.–A. Ribot, *L'Hérédité: Étude psychologique sur ses phénomènes, ses lois, ses causes* (Paris, 1873), 310.

9.   R.M. Brain, 'Protoplasmania: Huxley, Haeckel, and the Vibratory Organism in Late Nineteenth-Century Science and Art', in B. Larson and F. Brauer (eds.), *The Art of Evolution: Darwin, Darwinisms, and Visual Culture* (Hanover, NH: Dartmouth College Press, 2009), 112.

between the organic and inorganic worlds' lies in the former's capacity for active engraphy and ecphory. Haeckel therefore spoke of the '**psychoplasm**' of the nervous system and of the '**neuroplasm**' of the 'ganglionic cells and their fibres' as the chief medium of inscription. The ganglionic cells of the spinal cord were '*soul-cells*' or '*cytopsyches*' which inscribe and recall unconscious mnemonic material (these cells were further tax-onomized into afferent 'sensitive cells' and efferent 'will cells'). These 'innumerable social cells' make up the 'cell-community' of the nervous system. Memory, however, isn't only neurologi-cal but also, Haeckel thought, histological. (He even spoke of 'molecular memory'.) Living is nothing but recollecting. The whole life-system is a system of mnemonics—where 'even in the simplest unicellular protist sensations may leave a permanent trace in the psychoplasm'—and where cell communities knit themselves together precisely so they *can better remember.*[10] Haeckel claimed that only such a schema could explain 'the origin of the "*a priori* ideas" of man': they were 'originally formed empirically by his predecessors', through various alterations and perturbations to the inherited plasm-nexus. This was, for Hae-ckel, the 'embryology of the soul'.[11]

Like Haeckel, Samuel Butler (1835–1902), who translated Hering, championed engraphy as putting 'the backbone [into] the theory of evolution'.[12] In his *Unconscious Memory* (1880), Butler talked enthusiastically of the 'memory of the nervous system', averring that the recollections contained within even

---

10.   Peirce was also impressed by the habit-forming and retentive propensi-ties of slime moulds and protoplasms. See Peirce, 'Man's Glassy Essence', in *Collected Papers*, vol. 5, 165.

11.   Haeckel, *Riddle of the Universe*, 108.

12.   S. Butler, *Unconscious Memory* (London: Bogue, 1880), 8.

the 'sympathetic ganglionic system [are] no less rich than [those] of the brain and spinal marrow'.[13] Within Butler's grand engraphic vision, the innervated organism is nothing but a compacted **memeplex** of nature's universal past, expressed physically via stacked ganglion laminae. A body is nothing but glaciated time, the CNS its read/write (engraphy/ecphory) relay.

Writing on retrograde amnesia, Ribot noted that, in increasingly severe cases of the illness, the final memories to disappear were those belonging 'to that inferior order of memory having its seat in the cerebral ganglia, the medulla, and the spinal cord'.[14] With such thinking rife among the scientific community, it was entirely inevitable that the spine should come, contemporaneously, to be considered as the physiological seat of the unconscious. The fascinating figure of Eduard von Hartmann (who, along with Hering, is also treated in Butler's *Unconscious Memory*) exemplifies this position. Progenitor of Schelling and Goethe as well as terminarch of their grand metaphysical tradition, Hartmann—though now largely forgotten—was a titanic figure within nineteenth-century German intellectual life. Post-Schopenhauerian nihilism and pre-Freudian depth psychology form the poles around which von Hartmann's embracing metaphysic revolves, and his hulking multi-volume *Philosophie des Unbewussten* (*Philosophy of the Unconscious*), released in 1869, was read widely and singlehandedly triggered a 'pessimism controversy' in Germany.[15] (From this controversy we gain the word '*Weltschmerz*'—literally, 'world-pain'—which was minted to denote a nihilistic world-weariness characteristic of the day.)

13.   Ibid., 116.

14.   Ribot, *Diseases of Memory*, 121.

15.   F.C. Beiser, *Weltschmerz: Pessimism in German Philosophy, 1860–1900* (Oxford: Oxford University Press, 2016).

At one point in time, Hartmann was even mentioned in the same breath as Hegel; it is Nietzsche who is largely responsible for writing Hartmann out of history, describing his account of the upswell of consciousness—from its 'first throb' to its bitter end—as one 'huge joke'.[16] Joke or not, Hartmann's philosophical opus stages the impressive and sweeping evolutionary drama of a cosmic unconscious blindly assembling itself, from protoplasm to primate, from somnolence to sapience. Kapp rightly called it a 'panentheism of the unconscious'. Yet despite its staggering speculative grandeur, Hartmann was keen to ground his system in contemporary empirical findings. Accordingly, it should come as no surprise that neurology played a significant role (there is a lengthy appendix, for example, on 'The Physiology of the Nerve-Centres').

Utilizing his impressive knowledge of neuroanatomy, Hartmann rallied the engraphic ideas of the time to argue that spines—as mnemonic ladders—provide pathways into the prehistory of the cosmogonic unconscious. Following contemporary physiological understanding, Hartmann stressed the ontogenetic and phylogenetic parallelisms of the development of centripetalizing cephalization: 'the whole nervous system arises [both] phylogenetically and embryogenetically' from peripheralized and decentralized nervous nets toward consolidation upon the encephalizing brain, he observed.[17] In both the development of individuals and of the species, Hartmann saw successive waves of centralization—threading 'ganglionic cells' upward through the rising 'spinal centres' into the

16.   F. Nietzsche, *The Use and Abuse of History*, tr. A. Collins (Indianapolis: The Liberal Arts Press, 1957), 56.

17.   E. von Hartmann, *Philosophy of the Unconscious*, tr. W.C. Coupland (New York: Routledge, 3 vols., 2000), vol. 1, 259.

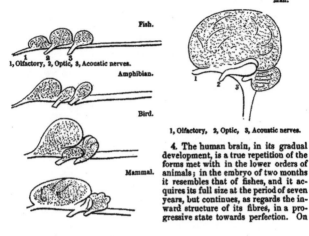

Fig. 20. Hartmann on cephalization.
From *Philosophy of the Unconscious* (New York: Routledge, 2000)

brain—as heralding oncoming intensifications of '*individuation*'.[18]
Accordingly, to travel down one's nervous system, as Ballard
would later have his pioneer of neuronics suggest, is to travel
into the past of the species. Spinal katabasis *is* temporal recidivus. For Hartmann, indeed, **somnambulism** represented a
temporary regression toward more ancient, less centralized,
life form[19]—precisely the same idea that lies behind Ferenczi's
later intimation of 'spinal sleep'.

Sleepwalking and adjacent states had long been freighted
with such connotations: preceding the mid-nineteenth-century
development of hypnotherapy (via the combination of the
extant mesmerism with more modern neurology, in what one

18.   Ibid., vol. 3, 246.

19.   Ibid., vol. 3, 250.

Scottish surgeon dubbed 'neurypnology'), practitioners of the earlier eighteenth century had recorded inducing various '**inner body experiences**' in themselves or their subjects whereby the somnambulist's conscious sensorium would sink from the head down toward the solar plexus—from the CNS's encephalon to the trunk's ANS (Ballard's 'thoracic drop').[20] This notion of sacral sensoria was popular amongst magnetists and mesmerists, and there are numerous accounts of somnambulant subjects seeing, feeling, and thinking within their trunks rather than their skulls.[21] Schopenhauer, speaking of the 'complete removal of the brain's power' in such states, recorded how practitioners reported that their executive function was entirely transplanted into the '*plexus solaris*'. This epigastric nerve centre, as a delegate sensorium, thereafter acts as a 'deputy' and takes 'over the function of the brain'. On this matter, Schopenhauer relays the

> statements of all clairvoyant somnambulists that their consciousness now has its seat entirely in the pit of the stomach where their thinking and perceiving are carried on as they were previously in the head.[22]

Despite remaining incredulous regarding this phenomenon of what he called the '*cerebrum abdominale*', Schopenhauer himself had theorized that dreams are caused when the sleeping brain, starved of external stimuli and input from the sensory

---

20.   J. Braid, *Neurypnology; or, the Rationale of Nervous Sleep, Considered in Relation with Animal Magnetism* (London, 1843).

21.   See J.H. Petetin, *Électricité animale* (Paris, 1808), 8.

22.   A. Schopenhauer, *Parerga and Paralipomena: Short Philosophical Essays*, tr. E.F.J. Payne (Oxford: Oxford University Press, 2 vols., 1974), vol. 1, 242.

organs, makes up for this by intercepting interoceptive messaging from the lower spinal regions and converting such signal into the brain's own native language—that of a spatiotemporally extended, three-dimensional world. In other words, when we dream, we literally inhabit a spinal landscape.[23] Oneirology is orthopaedics. Hartmann (who was, of course, greatly inspired by Schopenhauer) similarly attributed a distinct kind of proto-cognitive autonomy to the spine. He explained his position in a long footnote:

> The functions of the spinal cord in the higher animals may be likened to the performances of a man who is prevented by his servitude to a strict master from working out his many-sided tendencies, and is obliged to constantly devote himself to a well-defined and limited sphere of labour. The spinal cord of the higher animals is, as it were, simplified by its constant necessitation to hodman's services for the behoof of the brain; but the inference is illogical that it has lost consciousness and will (which it manifestly possesses in lower animals), since indeed in the sphere of activity reserved to it displays distinct intelligence, and in abnormal pathological cases is wont to take part also in the vicarious execution of more independent tasks.[24]

Hartmann thus compared the brain to a mere factory foreman atop a grand assemblage that, more or less, runs itself. One cannot but think here of ailments such as **Alien Hand Syndrome**, where limbs appear to manifest a will of their own, entirely separate from—and even antagonistic to—the brain's executive processing. Hartmann's physiophilosophy clearly

23.   Ibid, vol. 1, 236.

24.   Hartmann, *Philosophy of the Unconscious*, vol. 3, 237–8n.

makes room for the conceptual possibility of *Alien Spine Syndrome*, just as the nineteenth-century institution of the factory simultaneously made possible the strike and labour militancy. And, as Lawrence of course would later announce, revolutions roll upwards from the oldest, salamandrine portions of the spine.

The context for all this speculation was the emergence of a unified theory of cerebrospinal function around 1800. As far back as Galen, curious medics had observed that paralyses were often localized to the area *beneath* the level of spinal injury (with attenuating severity, the lower down the damage), yet spinal function remained obscure until the Enlightenment.[25] Studying continuing coordination in decapitated frogs, scientists such as Robert Whytt (1714–1766) began postulating, in the mid-eighteenth century, a separate '**sentient principle**' autochthonous to the backbone, thereby initiating a parade of laboratory acephali: carving open the spines of vivisected puppies and pricking each nerve sequentially, subsequent neurophysiologists such as Sir Charles Bell (1774–1842) and François Magendie (1783–1855), during the opening decades of the nineteenth century, mapped the separate **sensory** and **motor pathways**—or afferent and efferent neurons—of the backbone. (Magendie, in particular, was 'the exemplar of the evil scientist', known for his extremely gruesome and cruel methodologies of vivisection.)[26] Sensory and motor pathways evince different 'directions of fit' for nervous function: the former allow us to feel the world, the latter allow us to effect change upon it.

25. See A.P. Wickens, *A History of the Brain: From Stone Age Surgery to Modern Neuroscience* (London: Taylor and Francis, 2015).

26. M.N. Ozer, 'The British Vivisection Controversy', *Bulletin of the History of Medicine* 40:2 (1966), 158–67; and see C.R. Gallistel, 'Bell, Magendie, and the Proposals to Restrict the Use of Animals in Neurobehavioral Research', *American Psychologist* 36:4 (1981), 357–60.

Spinal function was beginning to be unveiled, and, so too, the private life of the backbone. It was Marshall Hall (1790–1857) who, performing experiments on decapitated eels and snakes, provided a view of this autonomous spinal life by successfully providing a cartography of the **reflex arcs**: integrative sensory-motor responses, spinally native, and requiring no functional participation from the brain. Hall found that many processes— from respiration to vomiting—work in this way. No brain is required. One could now witness the body as a nested conge-rie of integrated—yet modular—subroutines, stacked verte-brally in a spinal hierarchy.[27] Each paraxial juncture of reflex-signal could operate autonomously ('reflexively') without cerebral-passthrough or brain-arbitrage. Hall's reflex theory, in other words, led to a devolution, decerebration, and decen-tralization of conscious function.[28] This then is the background for what Lewis, almost a century later, would decry as eroding of autarchy for the 'subject' of Western history. It is the neu-rophysiological root of Freud's later notion that we are not masters in our own home. Our own bodies have a rich private life—or indeed *social* life, since the nervous system is already legion. As later celebrated by Haeckel's cell-communitarianism, the CNS here became a synergetic *colony* of individual 'proto-minds' (like 'zooids' within a compound superorganism), all infinitesimally graded from unconscious to apperceptive (each perhaps generating different tempos, time-tolerances, and

27.   Hall saw the mind as just such a hierarchy. 'Upon the cerebrum the soul sits enthroned', receiving 'ambassadors' from 'the *sentient nerves*' and 'send-ing forth its emissaries and plenipotentiaries' along 'the *voluntary nerves*'. See M. Hall, *On the Diseases and Derangements of the Nervous System* (London, 1841), 3.

28.   J. Starobinski, *Action and Reaction*, tr. S. Hawkes and J. Fort (New York: Zone Books, 1999), 145–6.

chronoceptive granularities). From Butler to Nietzsche, Bleuler to Velikovsky, many excitedly seized on this model, postulating various types of '**spinal soul**' psychically separate from the encephalon. This is precisely what Ferenczi later alluded to when he asserted, just as Hartmann had, that the sleeper 'has only a "spinal soul"'.[29] Ultimately, one need not look to the outside to 'roll from the centre toward X', one need only look inside.

After the consilience of this model of nervous function in the early 1800s, reflex movements and involuntary movements— now understood as requiring no cerebral sanction—became legible as our inner lancelet reawakening and rattling its cage. Such actions are phyletic revenants. This is what enabled Bataille to see spasmodic laughter and its evolutionarily regressive cancellation of cranial perpendicularity as a return to **amphioxus-being**. Indeed, presaging Bataille, Schopenhauer would write that he was 'surprised that Marshall Hall does not include *laughing* and *weeping* among the reflex movements'.[30] Such convulsions, he noted, roll like thunder from the spine, not the brain. These theories, moreover, were precisely the context for Hartmann's conviction that the brain is largely superfluous. With enthusiastic reference to experiments on decapitated frogs, to cases of anencephalic children, and to the fact that the dismembered parts of a single insect wage internecine war upon each other, he surmised that there are as many 'independent centres [of will] in the spinal cord as there are pairs of spinal nerves issuing therefrom'.[31] Hartmann's promulgation of this idea would, of course, earn him Lewis's later ire: across the distance of half a century, the inveterate

---

29. Ferenczi, *Thalassa*, 75–6.

30. Schopenhauer, *Parerga and Paralipomena*, vol. 2, 168.

31. Hartmann, *Philosophy of the Unconscious*, vol. 1, 62–4 and vol. 3, 222.

modernist would rail against Hartmann's belief that for 'the exercise of the Will (or of the Unconscious) *no brain at all* is required'. Lewis vituperated that, delivered from the impositions of a cerebral central authority, a disaggregated and disintermediated 'swarm' of spinal 'wills' provides a perfect 'picture of the Schopenhauer-von-Hartmann world-picture'.[32] Accusing his enemies of spinal separatism and secession, the anti-democratic Lewis would see in this picture a dirty deputation of mental autocracy, and duly complained that such Tarzan philosophers promote the backbone to an 'egalitarian and self-sufficient commonwealth'.[33]

Such a 'commonwealth' of proto-minds was also a part of the Nietzschean 'world-picture'. 'Person' and 'subject', Nietzsche wrote, are 'delusion':

A controlled community. At the guide of the body.[34]

The brain a jumped-up bureaucrat, a parvenu. Talking of the synthetic 'ego' (that 'apparent unity that encloses everything like a horizon'), Nietzsche recommended that muscularism was a better guide than legalism.[35] 'The evidence of the body

---

32. Lewis, *Time and Western Man*, 338.

33. Ibid., 336.

34. F. Nietzsche, *Kritische Studienausgabe*, ed. G. Colli and M. Montinari (Berlin: Walter de Gruyter, 15 vols., 1967–77), vol. 11, 623–4; I borrow translations of Nietzsche's German from D. Franck, *Nietzsche and the Shadow of God* (Evanston, IL: Northwestern University Press, 2012).

35. To fully appreciate Nietzsche's 'guiding thread', and how it feeds upon the contemporary neurological image of the body-as-commonwealth, it is useful to contrast it with the prior notions of Kant (whom Nietzsche closely read). Kant had previously argued that intentionality seems to presuppose the ability to follow rules. His argument went something like this: for a judgement

to be 'about' an objective world—in the sense of picking out the way things are rather than the way they merely seem—it must be capable of being wrong, which in turn requires some kind of further grasp of the criteria for the correct use of judgable concepts. Such a criteria would, of course, have to resemble a precept or a rule. However, as Hume had previously noticed, it is very hard to give a naturalistic account of what a rule is. Rules do a lot more than pick out natural items: they truck with shoulds and oughts and other such preternatural peculiarities. Nietzsche inherited this scepticism and extremified it. He saw Kant's rules-based account of cognition as the theological residuum of 'a sneaky Christian'. See F. Nietzsche, *Twilight of the Idols, or, How to Philosophize with a Hammer*, tr. R. Polt (Indianapolis: Hackett, 1997), 21–2. A lingering sense of enchantment: for even if we no longer enchant the surrounding world, we enlightened subjects still remain enchanted by ourselves, and this trick has been prolonged well past its expiry date. Even worse, laws are 'hostile to life'. (F. Nietzsche, *On the Genealogy of Morality and Other Writings* [Cambridge: Cambridge University Press, 1994], 50). 'Every thought, like fluid lava, builds a bulwark around itself and strangulates itself with "laws"', Nietzsche averred (Nietzsche, *Kritische Gesamtausgabe*, vol. 7, 1:510-11). He set about, therefore, to show how we could do without such outmoded legalisms. But this meant giving a new account of what it is to even be a subject—albeit one that still abides by Kant's innovation of considering the ego as something *produced* by 'synthesis' (as something '*made* through the thinking itself', in Nietzsche's words): an account that thus doesn't take the ego for granted (F. Nietzsche, *Beyond Good and Evil: Prelude to a Philosophy of the Future* [Cambridge: Cambridge University Press, 2002], 49). Kant's own synthetic account of individuation had been (as will surprise no one) thoroughly legalistic. Ever the rigorist, he had claimed that it is our capacity to distinguish between 'permissible' and 'impermissible' that marks us out as individual subjects. In short, this is because two people may hold contradicting beliefs, but one person *ought* not. (Indeed, it is hard to imagine how one person could wilfully and consciously endorse a logically contradictory claim. Try it yourself.) For Kant, I am an individual because I repulse incompatible beliefs. Kantian subjecthood is threaded together by conjointly determining declarations of 'I think' and 'You think' in the courthouse of logic: emerging piecemeal from the back-and-forth of what he called 'tribunal'. However, Nietzsche, like Schopenhauer before him, wanted to abrade all such petty legality from intentionality: making it the *power to be*—rather than the *power to be right*—and thus to submerge the rigorism of rules within a voluptuousness of sheer virulence. 'To be right', for Nietzsche, is just 'to maximally be'—and to do so most muscularly. This is Nietzsche's 'law of life': to make grandiose and sublime judgements rather than small-mindedly

reveals a tremendous multiplicity', he commended, and it is better 'to employ the more easily studied, richer phenomena as evidence for the understanding of the poorer'. And so,

> [f]ollowing the guiding thread of the body, we know man as a plurality of animated beings that partly fight each other mutually, and partly, being ordered and subordinated to each other, also assert the whole involuntarily, through the assertion of their individual beings.[36]

Contemporary neurology's model of consciousness as a nested congeries of modular wills, of course, provided the meat for the bones of Nietzsche's notion. (Elsewhere enjoining that 'philosophy, physiology and medicine' must enter a 'most cordial and fruitful exchange', Nietzsche would certainly have relished the notion of a 'cerebrum abdominale', insofar as he also declared that '"spirit" resembles a stomach more than anything'.)[37] 'There have been innumerable *modi cogitandi*', he announced, clearly following neurology's modular schema: and there 'is thus in man as many "consciousnesses" as there are beings—in every moment of his existence—which constitute his body'.[38]

---

correct ones. Let the lava flow. This extended, naturally, to his account of individuation. Given that what we call 'rules' are now a question of virulence rather than virtue, so too is the subject individuated not by its protocol-obsessed adherence to games of logic but by the self-cancelling antagonisms of myriad proto-wills.

36. Nietzsche, *Kritische Studienausgabe*, vol. 11, 577–8.

37. F. Nietzsche, *On the Genealogy of Morality*, 37; *Beyond Good and Evil*, 122.

38. Nietzsche, *Kritische Studienausgabe*, vol. 11, 563.

Thus the agonism of logical games (the process of sifting legal from illegal that individuates subjects for Kant, insofar as two people can hold contradictory beliefs but one person cannot) is replaced with intestine antagonism and agonistic muscle pairings (those biomechanical duos whose conflicting forces cancel out into one smooth motion). Rather than emerging from deliberative governance, subjecthood emerges from somatic strife. To *be* an individual is to be a warring multitude (like Hartmann's squabbling earwig offcuts). The bacchanalian revel of Hegel's *Phenomenology* preface, where a chaos of opposing motions mutually cancel out into placid repose, is here brought down to earth. Correctness is more a question of equilibrioception than ratiocination. Yet it is only through waging war—part against part—that a synthetic unity emerges. Subjectivity as sinew and subjugation. The pipeline of person-hood isn't a legal run in a logical game (the mutually bolstering and bureaucratic pitter patter of 'I think' and 'You think') so much as it is a noisy parliament of proto-brains, strung down the spine—Nietzsche's guiding thread.

Schopenhauer had already described Kant's illusory 'unity of apperception' as the 'thread of the string of pearls' upon which 'all representations are ranged'.[39] Nietzsche simply drew out the semantic potential of such a phrase. He proclaimed, that is, that 'logic' itself is a 'kind of spinal cord for vertebrates'.[40] A spine, a logical syntax: both provide bulwarks against which the lava of thought is forced to flow, like a piston pushed by pressure. Yet it is not legalism that comes first, as the pump in the pipeline, but the backbone's synapsing, self-conflicting

---

39.   Schopenhauer, *World as Will and Representation*, vol. 2, 251; and Ni-etzsche, *Kritische Studienausgabe*, vol. 11, 539.

40.   Nietzsche, *Kritische Studienausgabe*, vol. 11, 539.

strife. For Nietzsche, then, we thread ourselves together not by way of regulative rules but along the wilful arcs of the segmental spine. We should search for the hydraulic behind synthetic unity first, then, through this 'guiding thread of the body'.

> [O]ur life is possible through the interaction of many intelligences highly unequal in value, and thus only through a continual thousandfold obeying and ordering—stated in moral terms: through the uninterrupted exercise of many *virtues*. And how could one stop speaking morally![41]

To speak morally is to speak belatedly and inertially, however, even if one cannot help doing so: for Nietzsche, there is something *already superseded* in talking in this way. When talking of morality it is the illusions of the pallid and hieratic past that speak through us, a past already outstaying its welcome, already outmoded by some inevitable point of future disillusion. (Nietzsche's thought is self-consciously a *prelude to the philosophy of the future,* after all.) In line with this, Nietzsche noticed that the 'nervous system has a much broader domain: the world of consciousness is appended', and that, in 'the systematization and overarching process of adaptation, it does not matter':

> Consciousness, in the second role, just about indifferent, superfluous, perhaps destined to disappear, and a perfected automatism to take its place—[42]

---

41. Ibid., vol. 11, 577–8.

42. F. Nietzsche, *Nietzsche Werke*, ed. G. Colli and M. Montinari (Berlin: Walter de Gruyter, 15 vols., 1971), vol. 8, 3:121.

Appropriately, Nietzsche seems to have met his demise by way of syphilitic infection of the CNS, his muscular agonism lapsing into the agony of dementia, his 'consciousness'—superfluous as it was by his own lights—'destined to disappear'. Indeed, as new nervous maladies and neuroses began proliferating during the late nineteenth century, it may well have seemed that consciousness was at the end of its tether.

L3. MODERNITY AS WHIPLASH AND SPONDYLOSIS

The nineteenth-century preoccupation with the backbone's 'private life'—whether as pylon of phyletic memory or relay of the cosmic unconscious—explains the flourishing of novel, now 'extinct' nervous disorders during the Victorian era. It seemed that Nietzsche had been correct in his prognosis when he viewed the densification and acceleration of information as creating a Europe-wide 'over-excitation of the nervous [...] powers' and foresaw that, in modernization, 'the demands on the nervous system are too grand',[1] the implication being that the expansion of our mental powers via telegraphy also extended our scope for neurosis.

The most prominent of these modern ailments was '**railway spine**': a post-traumatic condition attributed to the abrupt lurch of the global transport networks then piecing themselves together. Caused by the 'significant jolts of acceleration' sometimes experienced in early train carriages, railway spine was—just like whiplash during the automobile age—an elusive and baffling illness that was more the invention of contemporary medico-legal incentives and cultural fears than a real neural disorder.[2] Railway spine was characterized by a miasma of unsettling post-traumatic symptoms, ranging from malaise to immobility, from chronic pain to a full-on state of nervous collapse. First diagnosed by John Eric Erichsen in 1866, much

1.   F. Nietzsche, *Human, All Too Human: A Book for Free Spirits*, tr. R.J. Hollingdale (Cambridge: Cambridge University Press, 1996), 116; and Nietzsche, *Werke*, vol. 8, 3:226.

2.   A.C. Croft, 'Biomechanics', in S.M. Foreman and A.C. Croft (eds.), *Whiplash Injuries: The Cervical Acceleration/Deceleration Syndrome* (Philadelphia, PA: Lippincott Williams and Wilkins, 2002), 54.

was written on the topic in the ensuing decades, with heart-breaking case studies of lives destroyed by phantom damage to the spine.[3] Most terrifying of all for the prudent Victorian mind was the implication that there were no real lesions or concussions, the condition bringing about such a 'state of collapse from fright, and from fright only'.[4]

Based on the contemporary theories examined above, we might perhaps venture that these invisible 'railway injuries' were triggered by a form of 'colony collapse' inflicted upon the bodily commonwealth, an unravelling of time-step contiguity across CNS segment-psyches as the deep temporalities of Victorian spines became pathologically desynchronized from their sensorium's speeding present, resulting in conflictive heterochronies. (Whiplash, after all, is produced by conflicting tempos: a simultaneity of acceleration and deceleration, lurch and inertia.) It is precisely the acceleration of modern technology that *makes* the archaic past reassert itself, more and more, as a drag upon the present. (Ours is a mind 'with a past', trawling a saurian tail, after all. And caudal trawl only comes from forward motion.)

This reading, moreover, is not at all anachronistic: railway spine was seen as precisely an illness of time, a chronobiological ailment. For example, the English psychologist James Sully (1842–1923) had written that since the 'nervous system has been slowly built up' out of older forms, it follows 'that those nervous structures and connections which have to do with the higher intellectual processes [...] have been the most recently evolved':

---

3.   J.E. Erichsen, *On Railway and Other Injuries of the Nervous System* (London, 1866).

4.   H.W. Page, *Railway Injuries: With Special Reference to those of the Back and Nervous System* (New York, 1892), 36.

Consequently, they would be the least deeply organized, and so the least stable; that is to say, the most liable to be thrown *hors de combat*. [...] And, in states of insanity, we see the process of nervous dissolution [...] taking the reverse order of the process of evolution.

Quoting Sully, Herbert Page (1845–1926) used this model to provide an aetiology for railway spine, claiming that 'when by the profound shock of a railway collision the "higher intellectual processes" are thrown *hors de combat*', older evolutionary forms of neural functioning 'step out of their natural obscurity, and become the foci of [the] mind'. One thereby neurofunctionally recapitulates 'the lower animal, whose brain is hardly differentiated from the other parts of its nervous system, or which has no brain at all'. Railway spine is a whiplash caused by the lurch of an accelerating present acting against the historical inertia of a spinal past. It is on speeding along the tracks of a time made constantly anew that we realise we have always been off the rails: for every lamina of consciousness is pathological from the 'functional perspective' of the other layers.

An interesting implication of this is the abandonment of 'normativity' as criterion of medical diagnostics and its wholesale replacement with chronology and heterochrony. Here, time does all the explanatory work. Madness is a temporal recidivism of the nervous system, whereby neural operations that are *perfectly healthy* in lower organisms recur and recrudesce. 'Healthy' becomes a relative term, and so too does any notion of 'the present'. (As with all recapitulatory notions, this approach relativizes all unified notions of the present: 'nowness' is, like the bodily commonwealth, an agonistic union of disaggregate time-series.) Neuronal pathology is, therefore, not so much patho*physiological* as it is patho*chronological*. Injury requires neither lesion nor any erring from 'normal function', but merely time-state desynchronization.

The key figure behind this nosological model that both Sully and Page draw upon was the English neurologist John Hughlings Jackson (1835–1911). Superimposing evolutionary hierarchy onto cerebrospinal anatomy, in his approach to nervous disease Jackson spoke of the 'evolutionary hierarchy of [our] nervous centres'—from the lowest 'horns of the spinal cord', through the 'corpus striatum', upward unto the 'prae-frontal' and 'occipital lobes'—and saw nervous malady as 'loss of function' in these 'topmost' and newest 'anatomico-physiological layers' along with attendant reversion of command to the lower, and older, centres. 'Different kinds of insanity are different local dissolutions of the highest centres', he inferred, and the type of affliction is thus 'dependent on disease at various levels from the bottom to the top of the central nervous system'. Insanity is a question of vertebral echelon.

Jackson called this process '**devolution**', defined as a 'reduction from the most voluntary of all towards the most automatic of all', the inevitable conclusion being that nervous disease is effectively an anomalous regression, a 'local reversal of evolution'.

Jackson spoke therefore of delusions and manias as lapses into the past—in the fashion of neurological time travel—as the patient loses 'function of the highest [and] latest developed' cerebrospinal centres and lapses from 'his present "real" surroundings' into 'some former "ideal" surroundings' (as in Freud's invocation of the 'prehistoric landscape' inhabited by the schizoid; it comes as no surprise that Freud admired, and was inspired by, Jackson's work).[5] Jackson explicitly highlighted and

---

5.   Sulloway, *Freud, Biologist of the Mind*, 270; and see also R.G. Goldstein,

commended the fact that his spinally striated model of madness removed normativity from medical diagnosis (just as Darwinism was removing teleology from morphology), emphasising that devolution is never absolute but only relative. With 'the lower level of evolution [always] remaining', it is, from this perspective of lower functioning, nothing other than 'healthy' and 'normal'. In other words, when one exhibits mania or delirium, it is only *pathological* from the perspective of the human parts of their nervous commonwealth: from the point of view of our inner lizard, everything's just fine. Talking of 'devolutions', therefore, Jackson noted that 'we must also take into account the undamaged remainder—the evolution still going on in what is left intact of a nervous system mutilated by disease'. He thus concluded that:

> We must not speak crudely of disease 'causing the symptoms of insanity'. Popularly the expression may pass, but, properly speaking, disease of the highest cerebral centres no more causes positive mental states, however abnormal they may seem, than opening floodgates causes water to flow.

The present provides no absolute standard or criterion against which to measure what is 'pathological'. Disease is merely the past clamouring to get back in. And who can blame it? What appears as diseased isn't deviation from some lawlike biological norm, but instead an implex in time: and, as Ballard, Reich, and Ferenczi would concur, the 'higher' cerebral centres oppose only the flimsiest of levees to this threatened inundation by the past.

'The Higher and the Lower in Mental Life: An Essay on J. Hughlings Jackson and Freud', *Journal of the American Psychoanalytic Association* 43:2 (1995), 495–515.

But if bodily time is relative, and the same goes for what is considered healthy, then unilinearity becomes hard to discern and to hold steady. From one perspective, pathology is the inertial drag of the past on the moving present; from another perspective, such drag can only be caused by acceleration, which is itself nothing but the future arriving sooner. (Once again, whiplash is acceleration *and* deceleration combined.) Precocious futurities and recidivist pasts merge at the limit. Modernity's schizophrenic tendencies—concentrated in a sickly railway spine—are an ailment of future perfection, of a precociousness of posterity, which is nothing other than a past outstaying its welcome. One could call it *posterus praecox*. 'Railway spine' broke out when our ancestrally attuned backbones simply couldn't keep up.

Of course, we are now so acclimatized to modernity's G-LOC—upon what Ballard called the 'highways' where we meet our 'deaths', those 'advanced causeways' to 'global Armageddon'—that we barely notice the lurch of temporal decompression sickness any more. Maybe these made-up diseases didn't go extinct, but the 'condition' has become a permanent (chronic) one.

According to Jackson, though, devolution, and its relation to residual layers of evolution, could take many different forms. Illness and wellness, and even temporal positionality itself, is just a *ratio* between evolution and devolution, and there are as many maladies as there are relative ratios. Presaging Bleuler's 'schizophrenia' and speaking of a condition he called '**mental diplopia**', Jackson even claimed that neuronal 'devolution' can create a 'new person' residing within the same body.[6] (Of course,

---

6. Ribot also claimed that various breakdowns of the memory and its supporting nervous system would lead to fracturing of the ego into conflictive multitudes. See Ribot, *Diseases of Memory*, 106–16.

without an absolute frame of reference, the question of which soul is 'original' or 'primary' here becomes moot.) Jackson did note, however, that there are 'complete dissolutions' in which 'no lower range of evolution remains': and here 'there is no *person*, but only a living creature' left. One can only think of a further threshold of devolution, but this would surely only ever be—from the perspective of the living—a death. (Perhaps it was these types of chronosthetic breakdowns that Barker was attempting to report upon in 'his' final manuscripts from the MVU period: 'A chittering tide. Devouring my hide. Starting from the Outside. This is the slide'.)

L4. GERMAN IDEALISM & NATURE'S SUBLIME FLOWER

Hegel, in 1807, balked at the idea that spines could seat additional souls. For him, metamerising nervous arcs and the plastic parenchyma represent 'fluid' moments in mind's 'self-contained existence'; on the contrary, supportive skull and rigid vertebral mast are mere antipodal *moments* in this liquid self-actualization, petrifactions and 'self-externalizing' exuviae of spirit's self-realization. Brain is 'living head', spine merely its polarising '*caput mortuum*'.[1] ('*Caput mortuum*' being the alchemical '*nigredo*' or waste product from purification, literally 'dead head').[2]

In stark contradistinction, Schopenhauer, as we have seen, relished the notion of spinal souls. Yet in his geohistorical account of a concatenated 'biology' and 'physics' of the unconscious (and its aeon-long awakening into conscious homo sapience), Schopenhauer is preceded by F.W.J. Schelling (1775–1854): first discoverer of depth psychology and of the law of recapitulation. It was the radically novel thinking of Schelling and his *Naturphilosophen* followers—a school of mad scientist polymaths, some of whom we have already met above, including Heinrich Steffens (1773–1845), Lorenz Oken (1779–1851|), Gotthilf Heinrich von Schubert (1780–1860), Georg August Goldfuß (1782–1848), Johann Christian Heinroth (1773–1843), Hans Christian Ørsted (1777–1851), and Gottfried Reinhold Treviranus (1776–1837)—who first developed such notions.[3]

---

1. Hegel, *Phenomenology of Spirit*, 197–8.

2. 'Bone and flesh stand in antagonism like air and earth. The muscle is that which is polarizing—moving, the bone what is polarized, moved'. See Oken, *Elements of Physiophilosophy*, 376.

3. See Gode-von Aesch, *Natural Science in German Romanticism*.

They too, like Hegel, had a strong taste for grandest-possible-history and for sweeping teleological development. And yet, unlike Hegel (and his impatience for sinew and bone as mere skin shed on the way to absolute knowing), the *Naturphiloso-phen*—followers of Schelling's thoroughly encompassing conception of cosmic nature—were more than willing to wade knee deep into the muck and dirt and slime, the messy empirical details, of terrestrial history.[4]

Naturphilosophie, developed first by Schelling following his rupture with the philosophy of Fichte, promulgated a vision of nature entirely rooted in recapitulationism.[5] Schelling, in his *Erster Entwurf eines Systems der Naturphilosophie* of 1799, was explicit: 'with every organic product Nature passes through all of [the previous] stages'.[6] In his *System der transcendentalen Idealismus* of the next year, he accordingly envisaged a 'graduated sequence [of organisation] running parallel to the development of the universe'.[7] Each stage of this sequence (which Schelling called the *Stufenfolge*) repeats those below. Applied to the minutiae of physiology, we have seen that this led Oken to claim that 'the head is none other than a vertebral column, and that it consists of four vertebrae [whilst] maxillae are nothing else but repetitions of arms and feet, the teeth

---

4.   See I.H. Grant, 'Being and Slime: The Mathematics of Protoplasm in Lorenz Oken's Physiophilosophy', in *Collapse vol. IV: Concept Horror* (Falmouth: Urbanomic, 2008), 287–321.

5.   See R.J. Richards, *The Romantic Conception of Life: Science and Philosophy in the Age of Goethe* (Chicago: University of Chicago Press, 2004), 176-180; and D.E. Snow, *Schelling and the End of Idealism* (Albany, NY: SUNY Press, 1996), 67–9.

6.   Schelling, *First Outline of a System of the Philosophy of Nature*, 140n.

7.   F.W.J. Schelling, *System of Transcendental Idealism*, tr. P. Heath (Charlottesville, VI: University Press of Virginia, 1997), 123.

being their nails'.[8] Taking this line of thought to its limits, Oken's imposing *Lehrbuch der Naturphilosophie* is a masterwork of such developmental series and their parallelisms.[9] It contains the unfolding of an entire universe, starting from the positings and unpositings of a generative zero and ascending grandiosely through nature's various stages of evolutionary production: from 'PNEUMATOGENY', 'HYLOGENY', 'COSMOGENY', 'STÖ-CHIOGENY', 'GEOLOGY', 'ORGANOGENY', 'PHYTOGENY' and 'ZOOGENY', to 'PSYCHOLOGY'.[10] Providing an ominous (and perhaps even prophetic) cadence to his symphonic climax, the pinnacle of Oken's evolutionary upsurge—the zenith from which alone the whole can be retrospectively encompassed and appreciated—is, of course, nineteenth-century Prussian culture and, in particular, an identifiably Teutonic '*Art of War*'.[11]

Regardless of what—in nineteenth-century Germany—was inevitably coming down the road, the rear-view past was ever-present for Oken. It is a matter of strict necessity that each of Oken's generative levels repeats all those below. Thus, each 'Mineral, Vegetable, and Animal' cannot be considered in 'isolation' (for each class and item 'takes its starting-point from below, and consequently [all] of them pass parallel to each other').[12] Such parallelisms, like connective ligatures,

---

8.   Oken, *Elements of Physiophilosophy*, xii.

9.   An editor of Hegel's, M.J. Petry, assessed Oken's book in 1970 as 'a shocking assemblage of ludicrous thoughts and inane observations'. See *Hegel's Philosophy of Nature*, tr. M.J. Petry (London: George Allen and Unwin, 3 vols., 1970), vol. 1, 82. This, of course, alerts us to its greatness.

10.   On Oken's 'empty set' see Grant, *Philosophies of Nature After Schelling*, 94.

11.   Oken, *Elements of Physiophilosophy*, 665. On the topic of the historical continuity of Romanticism and Fascism, see A.O Lovejoy, 'The Meaning of Romanticism for the Historian of Ideas', *Journal of the History of Ideas* 2:3 (1941), 257–78.

12.   Oken, *Elements of Physiophilosophy*, xiii.

therefore web not only between organic series but criss-cross between inorganic and organic series of development. Following this, Oken noted that the '[e]arthly organs must correspond to animal organs': or, the 'mountains, rocky terrain, [and] cliffs' must find their analogues in our own innards. *If teeth are nails, then nails are just stalactites.* 'Just as the animal *body* is finally composed of these organs, so the composition of rocky terrain must produce a terrestrial body, which is the *planet*', Oken pronounced.[13] From Ritter to Kielmeyer, Schubert to Steffens, the *Naturphilosophen* were in agreement on this: '[i]norganic matters and activities pass parallel [to] the anatomical formations and functions', as Oken put it.[14] He went so far as to say that '[o]*rganism is what individual planet is*' (because the 'primary vesicle' of the embryo, in its globular form, is but a repetition of the forces that 'produce' the planet itself).[15] Steffens summed all this up adequately when he wrote that, given these principles, *every* animal, plant, crystal, and mineral represents a 'stage of [terrestrial] development': the totality of which, taken together as one goliath constellation, would thus provide the 'true *history of earth*'.[16] History is just the decryption of the relations of body parts; body parts are just a matter of encrypted history.

Oken and his *Naturphilosophen* peers took such developmental parallelisms as licensing substantive identity and indiscernibility claims (as opposed to presenting vague analogues or homologues). Following from this, the *Naturphilosophen*

---

13. Oken, *Lehrbuch der Naturphilosophie* (Jena, 6 vols., 1813–26), vol. 1, 224–5.

14. Oken, *Elements of Physiophilosophy*, 181.

15. Ibid., 199, 188.

16. H. Steffens, *Beyträge zur inner Naturgeschichte* (Freiberg, 1801), 96.

could observe orthograde posture, like Bataille after them, as the **tautegory** of vegetal erection. ('Tautegory', again, being a contemporary term for a symbol that somehow literally consubstantiates, rather than merely mediates, what it presents. Contemporaneously, the basis of this 'literality' and 'consubstantiation' was often glossed as consisting in a 'genetic' relation of filiation, inheritance, or recapitulation.)[17] For, as Schelling wrote, just as the 'plant bursts forth in the bloom, so the entire earth blossoms in the human brain'—nature's 'most sublime flower'.[18] Brains are how the earth system thinks, flowers how it photosynthesizes. 'Reason is world-understanding', as Oken had it.[19] For Schelling, '[j]ust as the plant coheres with the sun through its bloom (which the plant's "thirst" for light, the movements of its stamen induced by light, prove), so the animal coheres with the sun through its brain'.[20] The horizontal animal-process *diverts* the vertical vegetative-process, however:

---

17.   And so, when Oken also says that the coiling morphology of a snail is a dim prophesy and 'exalted symbol of mind slumbering deeply within itself', *he means this literally.* 'Circumspection and foresight appear to be the thoughts of the Bivalve Mollusca and Snails': their self-infolding shape a tautegory of heedful mind. 'What majesty is in a creeping Snail, what reflection, what earnestness, what timidity and yet at the same time what firm confidence'. See Oken, *Elements of Physiophilosophy*, 657. On tautegory and the metaphysics behind the Romantic symbol, see D. Whistler, *Schelling's Theory of Symbolic Language: Forming the System of Identity* (Oxford: Oxford University Press, 2013); and N. Halmi, *The Genealogy of the Romantic Symbol* (Oxford: Oxford University Press , 2007).

18.   F.W.J. Schelling, *The Philosophical Rupture between Fichte and Schelling*, tr. M.G. Vater and D.W. Wood (Albany, NY: SUNY, 2012), 204.

19.   Oken, *Elements of Physiophilosophy*, 662.

20.   Schelling, *The Philosophical Rupture between Fichte and Schelling*, 204. See also Oken: 'A Philosophy or Ethicks apart from Physio-philosophy is a nonentity, a bare contradiction, just as a flower without a stem is a non-existent thing', in *Elements of Physiophilosophy*, 656.

turning *with* the globe rather than *escaping* it. Not 'until human-kind does the organised entity again become erect', Schelling notices—as sublunary escape velocity, or, as Alsberg would later note, *jailbreak*.[21] The *phototaxis* of flowers is repeated into the *aletheia* of a thinking brain: both are strivings towards a stimulus. Oken wrote, therefore, that that which is 'noblest lies at the anterior extremity of the animal, or in man in the direction *upwards*'.[22]

The animal coheres with the sun through its brain. Indeed, the *Naturphilosophen* invariably saw the skull as a repetition of the shape of a star or a planet. Oken impressed upon his readers that '[a]ngular forms are imperfect' and the 'more spherical a thing is' the 'more perfect and divine is it'.[23] Friedrich Tiedemann (1781–1861) similarly stressed that all 'organic bodies [betray] a form more or less round'.[24] Ergo, the concentric pairing of inner encephalon and outer skull becomes the pinnacle of this universal stratal and spheriform striving. Accordingly, John Christian Reil (1759–1813) celebrated this 'marble-white vault'—and its many-folded innards—as bearing an entire 'planet' of representations and cogitations within, whilst accordingly therefore also outwardly resembling the 'image of this original archetype in which the head is shaped':

---

21. Schelling, *The Philosophical Rupture between Fichte and Schelling*, 204.

22. Oken, *Elements of Physiophilosophy*, 362. For Oken, the 'acephalous' animals merely hold an antagonism between outside and inside. As soon as a head appears, however, this antagonism shifts 'for the first time' to that 'between head and trunk'. Such antagonistic dynamism presents the evolutionary beginnings of individuated self-consciousness. See Oken, *Elements of Physiophilosophy*, 659.

23. Oken, *Elements of Physiophilosophy*, 29.

24. F. Tiedemann, *Physiologie des Menschen*, tr. J.M. Gully and J. Hunter (London, 1834), 1:17.

a planet.[25] Because a brain contains a world, it is no wonder that it morphologically resembles one. Joseph Görres (1776–1848) similarly claimed that nature's universal pursuit of spheroid morphologies culminates in the animal brain, and he wrote that, in this, the encephalon repeats the structure of the solar system itself: with a solar central fire or seat of personality, at the core—where he notes the azygous and unpaired nature of deep brain structures—with concentric depositions, of planetary orbits in the solar system or of neural functions in the brain, moving outwards towards the epigene extremity. (One, of course, recalls Jung's 'geology of personality'.) Görres similarly compared the brain's layout to the stratigraphic layering of the earth and its plutonic depths.[26] 'The planet is a brain', Oken concluded.[27]

Such notions were inevitable. Stephen Jay Gould dubs them an 'inescapable consequence' of *naturphilosophisch* thinking.[28] Recapitulation, indeed, is nothing but Fichtean identity re-stated naturalistically: 'A=A' encapsulates repetition with iterative difference, tying palingenesis into caenogenesis, legitimating ontogeny's retracing of phylogeny. Nevertheless, if 'everything' is contained in the Absolute Idea, then the Idea contains terrestrial geohistory. And the nascent science of geology was contemporaneously revealing the crushing majority of the planet—in both time *and* space—to be *gigantically dead.*

25. J.C. Reil, 'Fragmente über die Bildung des kleinen Gehirns im Menschen', *Archiv für die Physiologie* 8 (1808), 1:58: 3.

26. J. Görres, 'Gall's Schädellehre', *Jenaische Allgemeine Literatur* 6 (1805), 50–56.

27. L. Oken, *Über das Universum als Fortsetzung des Sinnensystems* (1808), 33.

28. Gould, *Ontogeny and Phylogeny*, 35–9.

Previously, adherence to the aforementioned **Law of Continuity** had prohibited such cogitation: Continuity's infinite divisibility formats containment as interminable self-similarity; thus, all life must contain or be contained by other lives *ad infinitum*; leading to the optimistic Enlightenment view of existence as telescopically placental or infinitely organic.[29] Accordingly, even Earth's hypogene depths were once considered vital and populated—all of its matter essentially **biogenic**—and all death or inorganicity merely temporary deviation from organic baseline. Erasmus Darwin (1731–1802) had even subscribed to a form of **'geozoism'** by arguing that the *entire lithosphere* was essentially biogenic and interminably populated. Inspired by the discovery of islands produced by coral reefs, he and others theorized a primordial and biotic 'nucleus of the earth' composed of minute animalcules, that, in the 'long series of time', sequentially excreted and deposited 'solid strata'—thus procedurally 'germinating' a solid planet from compost.[30] It is not a planet that generates life, but life that generates a planet.

---

29.   There was a healthy seventeenth- and eighteenth-century tradition of theories proposing the earth as hollow and inwardly populated. Edmond Halley first proposed such a conjecture, and there were many 'hollow earth utopias' written thereafter (with even Casanova penning one). As late as 1829, Sir John Leslie—a translator of Buffon—was theorizing that the earth is hollow and filled by an ongoing explosive emanation of inner 'LIGHT'. This was because a ten-thousand-kilometer-wide 'void' of value was still deemed 'inadmissible'. See J. Leslie, *Elements of Natural History, Volume First, Including Mechanics and Hydrostatics*, 2nd edition (Edinburgh, 1829), 449–53; see also E. Halley, 'An Account of the Cause of the Change of the Variation of the Magnetical Needle with an Hypothesis of the Structure of the Internal Parts of the Earth', *Philosophical Transactions of the Royal Society* 26 (1692), 563–87; and G.C. Casanov, *L'Icosameron* (Prague, 1787).

30.   See E. Darwin, *The Botanic Garden* (London: Routledge, 2 vols., 2017), vol. 1, 187.

This 'amniotic' sense of belonging soon changed, however. As mentioned, it was during this era that the word 'inorganic' gained its modern, scientific meaning. During the middle of the eighteenth century, geoscientists began discussing how 'primeval' or granitic strata contain no fossil traces. Jean-André Deluc (1727–1817) proposed that they must have 'been produced antecedently to the existence of organized bodies upon our globe'.[31] Goethe thereafter bore witness to 'peaks [that] have never given birth to a living being and have never devoured [one], for they are before all life and above all life'.[32] One palaeontologist lyrically encapsulated the menace of such a prospect, talking of an '*eltritch-world uninhabitate, sunless and moonless and seared in the angry light of supernal fire*'.[33]

Georges Cuvier (1769–1832), whose own cerebral mass infamously weighed a gargantuan 64 ounces, soon calculated that '[o]nly about 1/1,600 of the diameter of the earth [has] yet been penetrated'.[34] Life, Schopenhauer accordingly noted, was just a 'mouldy film' atop a titanically dead telluric hulk.[35] (Even worse, this 'death' is not static nor inert, but ductile and churning; Schelling accordingly wrote of how the 'geological

---

31.   J.-A, Deluc, *An Elementary Treatise on Geology: Determining Fundamental Points in that Science, and Containing an Examination of Some Modern Geological Systems, and Particularly of the Huttonian Theory of the Earth* (London, 1809), 41.

32.   J.W. Goethe, *Collected Works*, ed. V. Lange et al. (Berlin: Suhrkamp, 12 vols., 1988), vol. 12, 132.

33.   T. Hawkins, *Memoirs of Ichthyosauri and Plesiosauri; Extinct Monsters of the Ancient Earth, with Twenty-Eight Plates Copied from Specimens in the Author's Collection of Fossil Organic Remains* (London, 1834), 51.

34.   G. Cuvier, *Fossil Bones and Geological Catastrophes*, tr. M.J.S. Rudwick (Chicago: University of Chicago Press, 1982), 85.

35.   Schopenhauer, *World as Will and Representation*, vol. 2, 3.

hypothesis of uplift' rendered ground itself no longer '*certain and lawful*'.)[36]

And so, in faithful pursuit of the recapitulatory notion of containment of prior stages, the *Naturphilosophen* were led, by their own principles, to an incredibly troubling notion. If noesis contains *all of this* (all of earth's strata upon strata of matter entirely removed from all organicity or even any organic utility), then roughly ~1,599/1,600th of noesis is unavoidably hostile and opaque towards itself (life and thought is merely a 'mouldy film' wrapped around its own titanic death). If the planet is a brain, only a vanishingly small amount of its trillion-cubic-kilometre volume is not lithified and dead. And, as intimated above, it was in attempting to internalize—or digest—the planet's magmic inorganic depths that Spirit developed the ulcer we now call the Unconscious. In other words, Recapitulation's attempt to retain Identity through Natural History's temporal torsion ended up sacrificing idealism's Law of Continuity (at every psychic and somatic level): the self-identical telescopic inclusions of Leibniz's prior 'fractal vitalism' now became internal heterogeneity and layered self-exclusions (or, stratification: the internal trace of Grand Time). Idealist containment spectacularly intussuscepted into a layer-cake of internalised self-exclusion: this was the invention of philosophical **Depth**, or the evagination of telescoping self-inclusion into invaginated and stratigraphic self-exclusion. And so, this is how Schopenhauer could finally state that consciousness 'is the mere surface of the mind, and of this, as of the globe, we do not know the interior, but only the crust'.[37] It is clearly for these

---

36.   F.W.J. Schelling, *Historical-critical Introduction to the Philosophy of Mythology*, tr. M. Richey and M. Zieelsberger (Albany, NY: SUNY Press, 2007), 19.

37.   Schopenhauer, *World as Will and Representation*, vol. 2, 136.

reasons that Kant sympathized so easily with the 'consternation' one feels when one realises one has never stood on solid ground.

Unsurprisingly, models of organism at the time became strikingly stratal: C.A.F. Kluge talked of the 'somasphere', 'zoösphere', and 'neurosphere'; C.W. Hufeland of a 'vegetative sphere' inclosed within an 'animal sphere'; C.G. Carus of the 'dermatoskeleton', 'splanchnoskeleton' and 'neuroskeleton'—all nested sequentially. Transliterating this psychologically, Schelling wrote of how one's true biography would interpose all of cosmological history; he noted, however, that many 'turn away' from the inhospitable 'depths' that are, therefore, 'concealed within themselves'.[38] We 'shy away' from 'glances into the abysses of the past' which remain within us 'as much as the present'.[39] These 'unfathomable depths' are 'what is oldest in nature': its inorganic and uninhabitate past. For the first time, the body was unravelled into exploded constellation of divergent tempos and heterochronies: '[i]n the bones of animals the soils are hardened, and their veins conduct metallic content'.[40] *Comparative anatomy became chrono-locomotion.* Bones are genuine transportations of the inorganic past into the organic present, each organ an epoch suspended. Recapitulation granularizes and modularises monolithic time: disarticulating embodiment's continuities and homogeneities into radically divergent *moments*.

---

38. F.W.J. Schelling, *Ages of the World*, 3-4.

39. Ibid., 31.

40. Schelling, *First Outline*, 58.

L5. COSMIC HISTORY
AS A SERIES OF OSSICLES

Samuel Taylor Coleridge (1772–1834) was more than a poet. He was also a deep-thinking, ambitious philosopher. Throughout his life he was obsessed with 'the secret recesses, the sacred adyta of organic life',[1] and following this guiding thread ultimately led him deep into 'the dark groundwork of our nature'.[2] Plagued by personal demons—many resulting directly from his philosophical investigations—he never quite successfully transmitted this into print, however. His systematic vision, what there is of it, remains fragmented throughout his voluminous private notebooks. Nonetheless, he was an astute, syncretic, yet wildly idiosyncratic thinker.

Reading Thomas Browne in the opening years of the 1800s, Coleridge had already remarked that 'the History of man for the 9 months preceding his Birth would probably be far more interesting & contain events of greater moment [than] all [the life] that follow[s]'.[3] He thereafter envisioned a Shandean situation whereby the writing of this foetal epitome would take '4,000 years'—easily filling '300 volumes'—and thus the hapless author would 'die in a Dream' before they even reached their birth.[4] This, of course, is because the prenatal comprises *the*

1.   S.T. Coleridge, *Hints Towards the Formation of a more Comprehensive Theory of Life*, ed. S.B. Watson (London: Churchill, 1848), 500.

2.   S.T. Coleridge, *Biographia Literaria*, ed. W.J. Bate and J. Engell (Princeton, NJ: Princeton University Press, 2 vols., 1983), vol. 2, 216.

3.   S.T. Coleridge, *Marginalia*, ed. H.J. Jackson and G. Whalley (Princeton, NJ: Princeton University Press, 6 vols., 1980–2001), vol. 1, 750.

4.   S.T. Coleridge, *The Notebooks*, ed. K. Coburn (London: Routledge, 5 vols.., 1957–2002), vol. 4, 4565, 4646.

whole of cosmic evolution. Nonetheless, having recently studied German, post-Kantian philosophy soon provided Coleridge with the tools and determination to write this prenatal chronicle, or, in Coleridge's words, the '*omni scibile* of human Nature, what we are, & how we become what we are'. And yet, from the outset he remarked to his friends—with perfect prescience—that 'between me & this work there may be a Death'.[5]

Becoming an ardent teutophile, Coleridge read Kant and Fichte widely and deeply (he even dabbled in Hegel, though only cursorily). He lays solid claim to the title of the first real British post-Kantian thinker.[6] However, he simply couldn't accept what he called Fichte's 'subjective idolism'. This was because of what he called 'hostility to NATURE'.[7] Accordingly, Coleridge spoke of the 'emancipat[ion]' by 'Schelling & the Physiosophists (*Naturphilosophen*) from the monkish Cell of Fichtean pan-egoistic Idealism'. This was a 'ris[ing] above the point of Reflection [to] contemplate the births of and genesis of things', he commended.[8] It is telling, in this regard, that Coleridge singled out Kant's enigmatic description of the critical project as an '***epigenesis*** of pure reason': he deemed this Kantian turn of phrase the '*knot* of the whole system'.[9] Accordingly, he saw that *Naturphilosophie* offered the tools to unravel this knot (to spread out its surfaces, lay it bare). Schellingian

5.   S.T. Coleridge, *Collected Letters of Samuel Taylor Coleridge*, ed. E.L. Griggs (Oxford: Oxford University Press, 6 vols., 1956–71), vol. 2, 949.

6.   See M. Class, *Coleridge and Kantian Ideas in England, 1796–1817* (London: Bloomsbury, 2012); and P. Hamilton, *Coleridge and German Philosophy: The Poet in the Land of Logic* (London: Continuum, 2007).

7.   Coleridge, *Biographia Literaria*, vol. 1, 157–60.

8.   Coleridge, *Notebooks*, vol. 4, 4839.

9.   Coleridge, *Marginalia*, vol. 3, 242.

philosophy, therefore, is the panacea to 'the many phantoms, with which the whole continuity both of Nature and Thought is crumbled down in modern Analysis':[10] this is because Schelling offers not just another physics or physiology but a '*Philosophy* of Physics & Physiology'—a map with which to access those adyta.[11]

Coleridge read Schelling's *System* sometime around 1813, and the *Entwurf* in 1815,[12] and subsequently requested all of Schelling's works not already in his possession.[13] He also devoured Steffens at around this time, whom he sometimes commended above Schelling.[14] Despite distancing himself from *Naturphilosophie* after 1818 (often deriding 'Okenisms' in his notebooks), Coleridge never stopped consuming their works nor gave up their core principles. Indeed, recapitulation had become a central tenet of his worldview. He would write of how, in nature's 'activities', ascending forms are produced before being 'abandon[ed] to inferior powers' (i.e. becoming *permanent* and *mature* forms of lower organisms), which themselves 'repeat a similar metamorphosis according to their kind'. These are 'not fancies', conjectures, or even hypotheses, but facts'.[15] One can clearly see, he pointed out, that the 'human Foetus exists as a Plant, an Insect, and an Animal',[16] and thus in 'the embryonic Structure, the Vita uterina, the higher animal Classes

10.   Coleridge, *Notebooks*, vol. 4, 4552.

11.   Ibid., vol. 4, 5464.

12.   See Coleridge, *Marginalia*, vol. 4.

13.   Coleridge, *Letters*, vol. 4, 665.

14.   See Coleridge, *Marginalia*, vol. 5.

15.   S.T. Coleridge, *Aids to Reflection*, ed. J.B. Beer (Princeton, NJ: Princeton University Press, 1993), 398–9.

16.   Coleridge, *Marginalia*, vol. 2, 1026.

is found as the regular and permanent form, the [...] *Vita matura*, of some lower grade'.[17]

With these recapitulatory tools in tow, an older Coleridge teamed up with his doctor and protégé, Joseph Henry Green (1791–1863), in order to systematize what they both called a '**Physiogony**', or universal genetic history. Coleridge proclaimed that the 'high prerogative' of his and Green's physiogonic 'Method is that each Evolute suggests the next, and *throws back light on all the former*'.[18] Elsewhere he described this physiognomic project as 'a Nature-history on a new scheme of Classification': the scheme of 'Powers'.[19] (This novel direction—inspired by Schelling's *Stufenfolge*—came largely from the new science of chemistry and its focus on nature's creation of products *qualitatively different* from their precursors.)[20] Coleridge wrote, therefore, of 'the great problem of the *Multiplication* of Powers in Nature—, the generative Multiplication, I mean; of their progressive potenziation, $A^{(4}$ being as truly a Unit as $A^{(1}$, and the latter together with $A^{(2}$, and $A^{(3}$ remaining and co-existing with $A^{(4}$'.[21] In other words, the problem of what it is that ties together the arrival of the new and the repetition of the old in nature's developmental series. Physiogony's answer was that each individual product is qualitatively distinct from—yet simultaneously also contains—all of its precursors.

17. S.T. Coleridge, *Shorter Works and Fragments*, ed. H.J. Jackson and J.R.J. Jackson (Princeton, NJ: Princeton University Press, 2 vols., 1995), vol. 2, 1194.

18. Coleridge, *Notebooks*, vol. 5, 6519.

19. Coleridge, *Notebooks*, vol. 4, 4724.

20. Coleridge, like Schelling, followed developments in chemistry closely. See T.H. Levere, *Poetry Realized in Nature: Samuel Taylor Coleridge and Early Nineteenth-Century Science* (Cambridge: Cambridge University Press, 1981).

21. Coleridge, *Notebooks*, vol. 4, 5150.

An abstract formalization of recapitulation was the 'high pre-rogative'. Continuing this grand vision, six years after Coleridge's death, Green went on to give a 'Recapitulatory Lecture' to the Royal College of Surgeons in 1840, wherein he chronicled the outlines of this project, telling a story of how the cerebrospinal system pieced itself together, across evolutionary time, through various dialectical deformations on the way from mollusc to insect to brain (the parenchymal mollusc represents life 'drawn inward'; the exoskeletal insect represents life 'thrown outward'; and only in the synthesis of these antipodes does one derive the equipoise of the vertebrate CNS).[22]

Studying *naturphilosophische* texts, Coleridge had previously postulated that geology's developmental series 'conclude[s]', *within us*, in our inorganic 'Teeth and Bones'.[23] Dentition is orogeny. Mineralization streaks through organic form: from basic examples like 'Shells' to 'Mother-of-Pearl' and 'egg' up to 'cartilage' and the chitinous carapaces of 'Lobster-Claws'; 'still higher, Zoophytes [i.e. corals] repeat the process'; and, at 'the summit', 'Bone' and 'Teeth' conclude the conservation, or reuptake, of the geological into the biological.[24] In a vision arguably even more fevered than that of Kubla Khan, Coleridge thus witnessed lithic externality snaking its way throughout organic inner time: he noted that annelids 'deposit a calcareous stuff' as if they have to 'drag about' a piece of the planet's 'gross mass' whilst also observing that, in the 'insect', this mineral 'residuum' has 'refined itself' into a carapace; in 'fishes and amphibians it is driven back or inward' into an endoskeleton; and, at the pinnacle, this inwardification of stone

---

22. Green, *Vital Dynamics*, 35–6.

23. S.T. Coleridge, *Notebooks*, vol. 4, 4565, 4646.

24. Ibid., vol. 4, 4580.

climaxes in humanity's grand 'osseous structure'. Oken, indeed, had said that 'the skeletal system is the reappearance of plan-etism [within] the human'.[25] In Coleridge's eyes, the 'physical hardness of the insensitive nail' could thus be accounted for as a type of temporal nonlinearization.[26] (One need only look at Deleuze's fingernails.) Notably, the German for 'vertebra', *Wirbel*, also denotes 'spiral' or 'vortex': each osseous whorl a cyclone in time. The 'Bones of the Human Ear furnish a remark-able Instance' of such **retroition**, Coleridge noted, for 'hear-ing depends' on the 'vibrations' of '*felsenharten*', or rock-hard, 'adamantine bones'. (Sound propagates through 'solids' and 'even deaf people hear through' skeletal transmission, he pon-dered.) Thus, one can arrive at the 'profound […] derivation of the Auditual' from the 'ζωομεταλλικον (*zoometallic*).[27] 'Sound is volatile Metal', he glossed, envisioning that hearing arises from the sonority of miniature mountain-ranges.[28] (Our hear-ing apparatus derives, indeed, from the otoliths, or crystalline-inorganic accelerometers, found in ancient fish.) This idea of the audible as a form of mineral retroition comes from Oken, who impressed upon his readers that hearing was part of the 'metallic system of animality' and claimed that one could there-fore trace an unbroken line from the bones of the inner ear down through the spinal column right into the metallic veins of the earth. All of this, he remarked, forms one grand and uni-fied bone system: 'all just one row of ossicles' repeated in various forms from ore to spine to cochlea. 'The ear flows

---

25.   Oken, *Über das Universum als Fortsetzung des Sinnensystems*, 41.

26.   S.T. Coleridge, *Theory of Life* (London: Churchill, 1848), 550, 511.

27.   S.T. Coleridge, *Marginalia*, vol. 5, 294.

28.   Coleridge, *Notebooks*, vol. 4, 4929.

onward as a soul into the bones, and these flow as a soul into the metallic skeleton of the planet'.[29]

Bodies are thus temporal manifolds. Yet their coevality can splinter. The primal past 'continues to be incessantly active in individuals', Schelling intoned, and it can 'break through once again'[30]—the 'opening of the floodgates' between past and present that John Hughlings Jackson would later speak of. Indeed, French scientists throughout the 1700s had already started conceptualizing the process of aging as an accumulation of mineral activity within the body, a kind of internal reassertion of the inorganic domain over the organic one. In 1749, in a tract on gerontology, Georges Buffon theorised that the process of aging was a gradual process of ossification whereby the fibres and nerves overproduce themselves and thus cumulatively thicken, spreading a form of rigidity throughout the body that eventually overtakes organic ductility with arthritic petrifaction and, finally, rigor mortis. He noted that, because of this, the very processes of life eventually go on to 'devour' the living.[31] Not long after, the celebrated surgeon and geologist Claude-Nicolas Le Cat similarly wrote that we die essentially because we keep growing perpetually, and once we have reached maturity this rapacious growth turns inward, rebounding as a form of deathly rigidification. He theorised that unceasing growth is sustainable up until the age of twenty-five because we are growing 'outwardly', but after this the growth can only take place 'inwardly' and thus the phase of ossification begins

29. Oken, *Über das Universum als Fortsetzung des Sinnensystems*, 35.

30. F.W.J. Schelling, *Philosophical Inquiries into the Essence of Human Freedom*, tr. J. Love and J. Schmidt (Albany, NY: SUNY, 2006), 29

31. See J. McManners, *Death and the Enlightenment: Changing Attitudes to Death Among Christians and Unbelievers in Eighteenth-Century France* (Oxford: Oxford University Press, 1981), 114.

as fibres bundle, harden, and thicken. (Le Cat noted that the only way to escape this fate would be if were to become giants and keep growing outwardly forever; unfortunately for this theory, scientists beginning with Galileo have noted that biology is not scale-invariant and such boundless giants are impossible, because gravity places hard limits upon how large an animal can feasibly grow.) According to Le Cat, then, as we age, we become increasingly mineral beings. An expert in lithotomy, he believed he had observed this process at first hand, many times, upon opening up a bladder and finding it encrusted with stones. It seemed to him that as the nerves aged, the once-ductile dendrites were transmogrifying into tiny 'stalactites' or 'stone fountains': a creeping process of lithification that thereafter branches out and propagates through the vital organs.[32] It was precisely this gerontological theory that later provided a backdrop for the conviction of the German *Naturphilosophen* that the organism is itself a delicate temporal manifold, one that can easily be tipped back into inorganic petrifaction.

Later still, following this guiding thread through, Coleridge was led to disturbing results. Reading Schelling's *Freiheit* essay, he was arrested by the German philosopher's geohistoricist and catastrophist vision of nature's tendency to sink, again and again, 'back into chaos' (as evidenced by 'previous world collapses' and the continuation of their fossil 'monuments' into the present).[33] Coleridge was struck by this, proposing that such 'sinkings back' and pathological persistences of the past might provide a 'Theory of Hydatids' and 'other excrescences

---

32.   J.N. Le Cat, *Traité des sensations et des passions en général, et des sens en particulier* (Paris, 3 vols., 1767), vol. 1, 104.

33.   Schelling, *Philosophical Inquiries*, 43–5.

of Life'.[34] (Hydatids, notably, are cystic growths that are prone—like the pineal gland—to *calcification*.) Going beyond the hypotheses of the Victorian doctors who treated railway spine, he thus went on to diagnose 'nervous diseases' as the recidivist eruption of 'ante-organic activity [in] the nerves'.[35] Disease isn't just relapse into a prior organic state, but also a resurgence of prior inorganic ones. CNS-degeneration, again, as chronopathic decentralisation. Describing such time-sicknesses as 'Relapses' of nature 'or sinkings back from the organic and vivific', Coleridge similarly anticipated Hartmann and Ferecnzi in classifying somnambulant states precisely as 'that sinkback of the Mind into an *inanimate animal*'.[36]

Having previously speculated that the '*globific* tendency' of granite boulders betrays their desire to become '*planet itself*', Coleridge, just like his German peers, observed that the hemispheric structure of our 'Cerebral Substance' is 'strikingly' composed of a form of 'life' that appears to want to recapitulate the 'planetary'. Yet he also noted that this 'life' would, of course, needs be 'προυργανικος' or 'pre-organic'.[37] As Kant had mused many decades before, we have only penetrated 'one six thousandth' of the earth's stony depth: thus, to proclaim that the brain is a planet is to admit that we know absolutely nothing about it. Of course, one need only look to afflictions of cerebral calcification to find instances wherein the grey matter *is truly* attempting to 'repeat the planetary. Sublimity has a petrifying effect', the German poet Novalis (1772–1801) once corroborated: the 'lithic

34. Coleridge, *Marginalia*, vol. 4, 431–2.

35. Coleridge, *Notebooks*, vol. 4, 4580.

36. Coleridge, *Marginalia*, vol. 1, 664; Coleridge, *Notebooks*, vol. 4, 5333.

37. Coleridge, *Notebooks*, vol. 4, 4864, vol. 5, 4580.

world' re-erupts cerebrally as a 'mineral-cortex' intruding 'inward'.[38] Perhaps sublimity primarily activates the pineal gland?

These troubling implications of *Naturphilosophie* are, in part, what caused Coleridge eventually to shun it. Such implications violated his theistic principles. But even when he celebrated the divine in man, those darker threads never quite went away. In one notebook entry extolling human uprightness, his philosophical demons get the better of him: 'Man alone seems *drawn upward*, his Base narrower than his shoulders', Coleridge wrote: '[h]e *stoops to procure*'—in the acts of labouring and eating—but 'he *enjoys* with his face and eyes fronting his fellow man' in social intercourse. However, Coleridge's jubilation abruptly segues into a troubled rumination (now in Latin for purposes of secrecy) on how the ventro-ventral fumblings of sexual intercourse destroy this uprightness as '[h]is eyes from above are cast down towards the earth' and the fornicator becomes once more 'the servant of Nature and Earth'. Tearing himself away from such carnal visions, he concludes by ejaculating 'Man truly is A SOLAR ANIMAL':

> With feet adhesive to the earth, we shun,
> Headward we gravitate toward the Sun.[39]

As Bataille later declared, however, such celestial orientation merely combusts into the precocious futurity of pineal mineralization. Thinking like a planet will only give you brain-sand.

'Will is assuredly followed by the appropriate *Organs*—so the Butting of the Calf predicts the coming Horns', Coleridge

---

38. Novalis, *Schriften*, ed. P. Kluckholm and R. Samuel (Stuttgart: Kohlhammer, 1977), 100n.

39. Coleridge, *Notebooks*, vol. 4, 4650.

Fig. 21. 'Headward we gravitate toward the Sun'

wrote.[40] Perhaps if you spend too much time thinking like a planet, your brain calcifies entirely. Certainly, Coleridge—who proselytized that 'man *must* either rise or sink'—worried about the organic changes just waiting to be unleashed upon our bodies given the correct conditions and cues.[41] (Picturing morphology as a delicate balance, always ready to be disrupted, is an unavoidable by-product of the idea that particular morphologies are *arrested* stages within a wider series of possibilities. Hence why the notion suggested itself to Ballard as

---

40.   Coleridge, *Marginalia*, vol. 5, 51.

41.   Coleridge, *Biographia Literaria*, vol. 1, 241–2.

much as to Coleridge.) Thus, in a strange conjunction of the theological and nature-philosophical, Coleridge rallied this as a strange quasi-naturalistic explanation for devils and demons, presuming that an imbalance of organic forces could cause a devolutionary 'descent' of healthy cranial bone-growth

> into a yet meaner & more vegetative form than the Skull itself—namely Horn! and thence, by enkindling & propagation of [tumescent] Productivity, manifesting itself at the other extremity, a Tail. What a Devil is a Man-beast! What a Beast is the Devil![42]

Behind Jackson's heterochronic 'floodgates' lie the lithic tumefactions and protuberances of horn and tail. Following his death, Coleridge's autopsy—performed by Green—would report strange 'organic changes' in the poet-philosopher's body. Green recorded that Coleridge's was a '"body of the death" in which to live was a continued dying'.[43]

Romanticism is where Spinal Catastrophism proper first ignited. Intimations stretch from the era's beginning to its end. Already in 1784 the Parisian diarist Louis-Sébastien Mercier (1740-1814) wrote of an 'uninterrupted tradition' of 'antient disasters', running from the 'visible traces of profound ruins and devastations which are spread over the surface of the earth' all the way into the 'terrors' that are subtly 'engraved in the fibres of human brains'.[44] By 1845, De Quincey was talking of the 'convulsions' that inscribe 'themselves successively upon the palimpsest of your brain [in] endless strata [of] forgetfulness'—precisely as the *primary convulsions* of geohistory

---

42. Coleridge, *Marginalia*, vol. 1, 626.

43. Coleridge, *Shorter Works and Fragments*, vol. 2, 1522–3.

44. L.-S. Mercier, *Mon bonnet de nuit* (Paris, 2 vols., 1784), vol. 1, 7.

successively scarred our 'dark planet'. For De Quincey (who noticed that the '*virtual* time' of dreams was 'ridiculous to compute' in scales 'commensurate with human life' and must instead be measured in 'aeons' and 'diameters of the earth'), certain minds are undoubtably 'truer than others to the great magnet in our dark planet':

> Minds that are impassioned on a more colossal scale than ordinary, deeper in their vibrations, and more extensive in the scale of their vibrations [will] tremble to greater depths from a fearful convulsion, and will come round by a longer curve of undulations.[45]

'Upon entering deep [into] barren, rocky chasms', wrote Goethe, 'I felt for the first time that I envied the poets': for, 'in speaking of primal beginnings', he proclaimed, 'we should speak primally, i.e. poetically'.[46] In a theoretical framework within which individual consciousness was interpretable only as a retrograde amnesia for its own preconscious cosmogenesis, there could

---

45. T. De Quincey, *Suspiria de Profundis*, in *Confessions of an English Opium-Eater and Other Writings*, ed. R. Morrison (Oxford: Oxford University Press, 2013), 194, 154, 121.

46. Goethe, *Collected Works*, vol. 12, 137. One of Lewis's enemies, the eccentric American endocrinologist and glandular romanticist Louis Berman, wrote in 1921 that 'the animal [is] formed by the agglutinations of millions of years, and that it is hence composed of parts of different ages and pedigrees, some exceedingly ancient and hoary, some middle-aged, and some relatively new and recent [...] The primitive chassis of the mechanism, so to speak, is the so-called vegetative nervous system [and it] is the most deeply rooted core of our being. What warrant is there for the grandiloquence of the phrase: the Oldest part of the Mind? There is, indeed, room for rhetoric, even poetry, here. For all the evidence points to it as the rightful occupant of the throne upon which Shelley placed his Brownie as the Soul of the Soul'. L. Berman, *The Glands Regulating Personality: A Study of the Glands of Internal Secretion in Relation to the Types of Human Nature* (New York: Macmillan, 1922), 104.

not but be a porous border between geognostic investigation and poetic enthusiasm. Precisely this porosity looks forward to many of the figures we have explored in our secret history: from Ballard to Velikovsky. Yet in order to finally locate the very first kindling of the notion of Spinal Catastrophism, we must travel back before Romanticism and to a spat between a tutor and his tutee.

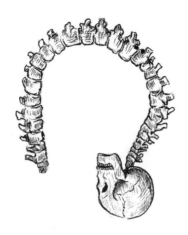

Huddled in dirt the reasoning engine lies,

Who was so proud, so witty, and so wise.

—John Wilmot, 2nd Earl of Rochester,
'A Satyre Against Reason and Mankind' (1674)

...the world will be ripe for its great quietus.

—Edgar Everstson Saltus,
The Philosophy of Disenchantment (1885).

SACRAL INCEPTION (1800–1750)

S1. THE OLDEST SYSTEM-PROGRAMME OF COSMOTRAUMATICS[1]

In his dynamicist and historicist vision of nature's development from geogony to glottogony, Johann Gottfried Herder (1744–1803) was a key precursor to Schellingian *Naturphilosophie*. Published in 1784, his *Ideen zur Philosophie der Geschichte der Menschheit* presents perhaps the first truly genetic-developmental vision of hominization. Inventing the term '*Mängelswesen*', and kickstarting the ensuing tradition of philosophical anthropology, Herder placed orthograde spinality utterly centre stage in his account of the genesis of humanity's peculiarly 'pliable nature'.[2]

Herder, indeed, is the tributary source for many of the motifs encountered across our secret history. Just like Alsberg and Gehlen almost two centuries later, he stresses the ceaseless vestibular vigilance involved in upright standing:

> No dead body can stand upright: it is only by the combined exertion of innumerable actions, that our artificial mode of standing and going becomes possible.[3]

Like Bataille, he divines the significance of man's prodigious 'long great toe'; like Ferenczi and Reich, he stresses the temporary axial-phyletic relapse that occurs during sleep; like Freud,

---

1.   See 'The Oldest System-Programme of German Idealism', written in 1796–7, and attributed to Schelling, Hegel and/or Hölderin.

2.   J.G. Herder, *Outlines of a Philosophy of the History of Man*, tr. T. Churchill (New York: Bergman, 1966), 68. See also S. Abbott, '"Andre Umstände": Erection as Self-Assertion in Kleist's *Die Marquise von O...*', in D. Sevin and C. Zeller (eds.), *Heinrich von Kleist: Style and Concept* (Berlin: Walter de Gruyter, 2013).

3.   Herder, *Outlines of a Philosophy of the History of Man*, 68

he remarks upon the anthropogenic priority of vertical ocularity over horizontal olfaction.[4] Herder, nonetheless, was no catastrophist, and certainly did not share Burroughs's horror of language, but was the grandfather of the more sanguine tribe of vertebral celebrants. Opining that the 'whole spinal column' is constructed to facilitate the influx of speech, Herder revered nature's gradations toward bipedalism as so many rehearsals on the road toward humanity's resonant larynx. 'Speech alone awakens slumbering reason', he remarked, such that our whole orthograde armature—'with its ligaments and ribs, its muscles and vessels'—is legible as the physiologic prologue to 'this great work' of vocalization.[5] Thus, for Herder, '[t]he more perfect the animal, the more it rises above the surface of the ground'. From this axiom one can extrude an entire world-historical verticalization process encompassing the whole procession of terrestrial evolution—which, of course, culminates in humankind, that 'microcosm' that contains all the prior stages: *the more the body endeavours to raise itself, and the head to mount upwards freely from the skeleton, the more perfect is the creature's form*'.[6] Noting the suggested etymological source of the word '*anthrôpos*' ('man') in '*anathrei*' ('to look up'), Herder concludes that it is 'infinitely beautiful' to 'observe the gradation by which Nature has gradually led her creatures up to sound and voice, from the mute fish, worm, and insect'.[7]

---

4.   Ibid., 85–6.

5.   Ibid., 87–8.

6.   Ibid., 83.

7.   Ibid., 88. This suggested origin of the word goes all the way back to Plato's *Cratylus*, where Socrates is recorded as saying that 'the word "man" implies that other animals never [...] look up at what they see, but that man not only sees [but] looks up at that which he sees, and hence he alone of all animals is rightly called *anthrôpos*, meaning he that looks up (*anathrei*) at what

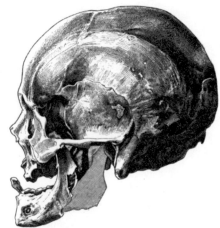

FIG. 32.—SKULL OF IMMANUEL KANT. (After C. von Kupffer.)
(The great size of the cranium is a noteworthy feature.)

Fig. 22. Robert Wiedersheim's best-selling 1887 anatomical volume
The Structure of Man: An Index to His Past History details all the
'vestigial organs' of the human frame: those traces of the deep
evolutionary past that continue into our somatic present. The
section on the human skull uses an illustration of Kant's braincase.
Even the Sage of Königsberg owned a 'mind with a past'

Kant, Herder's one-time tutor, convulsively disagreed. He saw
that Herder, through stressing the telic identity of rationality
and bipedality, was unduly *naturalising* reason: immuring it, limiting it, reducing it to a physiologic quirk.[8] To counteract this
and reiterate the non-natural nature of rationality, Kant would
take extreme measures, urging that rationality didn't arise

he has seen (*opôpe*)'. See Plato, *Dialogues of Plato*, tr. B. Jowett (Oxford:
Oxford University Press, 5 vols., 1892), vol. 1, 399.

8.   I. Kant, 'Review of J.G. Herder's Ideas', in *Anthropology, History, and
Education*, ed. G. Zöller and R.B. Louden (Cambridge: Cambridge University
Press, 2007), 121–42.

because of uprightness, but that (reversing the teleology, to sinister effect) *uprightness arose because of rationality*. And the proof? Precisely that uprightness, from the vegetative organism's perspective, was profoundly and overridingly cataclysmic, a total organic disaster acceptable only from the perspective of reason's unnatural supererogations; not something that any natural system would desire or undertake. Standing upright is something that could be occasioned *only* by reasons and *never* by causes—this is Kant's gambit on the matter. He emphasised that orthograde locomotion develops *in spite of nature*—a chronic symptom of reason alone—arriving, therefore, from *without* and *beyond* and *in conflict with* organic interests. Borrowing from the opinions of the Italian anatomist Pietro Moscati (1739–1824), Kant unfurls his arsenal of orthograde pathologies, almost taking a sadistic delight in cataloguing their overabundance (it is rare that Kant indulges, but here he does): 'upright gait' is 'contrived against nature', a 'deviation' and detour from pronograde bliss, the source of 'discomforts and maladies' uncountable. The litany of back problems reads like a page from Elaine Morgan's later inculpations of bipedalism. Uprightness compresses our intestines, squishing the intrauterine foetus; causing 'haemorrhoids', 'varicose veins', 'hernia', and 'aneurysm' via never-ending gravitational drag. Our 'blood has to rise against the direction of gravity', which causes 'tumors', 'palpitations of the heart', and 'dropsy of the breast'. Upon standing up, haemodynamic 'influx into the head' arises as a 'vertigo' before being's extraterrestrial vistas (*upward plunge into space*): this grants us the gift of an 'inclination [to] stroke, to headaches, and madness'. *Anthropos* is the animal that 'looks up', and instantly regrets doing so. Humans, alone, drown (so acutely divorced are we from our thalassic motherland). Deliriously preoccupied with disaffiliating reason and nature,

Kant climaxes with the proclamation that orthograde rationality is actually *antithetical* to the ends of species procreation and, thus, to human survival itself: for gravity's trawl along the terrestrial-spinal axis is the cause of 'prolapsed uterus'. Nature's 'first foresight', he propounds, must have designed humanity for quadrupedalism, thus to protect the 'foetus' and accordingly to preserve our 'kind'. Standing upright is truly steadfast standing, therefore: defiant to the point of species-suicide. Ergo, only after the 'germ' of something alien entered—that 'germ of reason' as Kant puts it—did man fall upward.[9]

Yanked to its feet by the stern, inflexible puppetmaster Reason, *Nature* literally *miscarries itself within human morphology*. Here the overemphasis on rationality's exogeneity deviates into epidemiology: it is a *virus come from outside*. Indeed, to ordain reason's arrival as antagonistic to the interests of the life that hosts it is to notice that *intelligence is a parasite* (because a parasite 'dwells within' yet also 'in spite of': parasites assert their own antagonistic ends whilst also being utterly dependent for their existence upon their host). Kant wants to stress the irreducibility of the normative over the natural: to flaunt his discovery of the topic-neutrality and time-generality of the rulishness of the rational (or, the insight that talk about 'ought' and 'should' is not even to talk about the world: it is not in any way pointing to any ostensible or time-bound fact, and thus is not *describing* the natural world at all, and has no declarative content); and yet, from the perspective of the natural, this 'purity', 'neutrality' and 'emptiness' of the transcendental can only be encountered as an invasive malignance and nosological apostasy from the placidity

9.   I. Kant, 'Review of Moscati', in *Anthropology, History, and Education*, ed G. Zöller and R.B. Louden (Cambridge: Cambridge University Press, 2007), 78–81.

of mere existence. The *ontological austerity* of the transcendental arrives as the emaciation of the corpulence and plenitudes of the existent.[10] The infall of time-generality into a time-bound body, from the perspective of that body, can be nothing other than a petrification from without (beginning at the pineal gland): the Kingdom of Ends is a crystal world. The absolute must announce itself *from within* time—for this is the only medium for its arrival—but this is necessarily nothing other than the *self-obsolescing* of temporal existence.[11] The time-bound articulation of eternity, which is the blossom of time-general

---

10.   Indeed, Fichte saw that his Absolute I could be 'no real being, no *subsistence* or *continuing existence*': '[o]ne should not even call it an *active subject*, for such appellation suggests the presence of something that continues to exist and in which an activity inheres'. See J.G. Fichte, *Introductions to the Wissenschaftslehre and Other Writings (1797–1800)*, tr. D. Breazeale (Indianapolis: Hackett, 1994). Schelling, similarly, claimed that all being is founded on 'active negation': the 'highest simplicity' of which, he admitted, is necessarily 'that which is without nature' and 'is not a being and does not have being'. Defined in opposition to the corpulence of the time-bound and ostensible and existent, the transcendental can only be 'the devouring ferocity of purity'. See Schelling, *Ages of the World*, 25–32. No wonder Jacobi diagnosed German Idealism as '*Nihilismus*'. Certainly, in a similar vein, Jean Paul Richter complained of the 'critical basilisk eye' of post-Kantian transcendentalism, describing it as 'preying on the whole universe' in its superlative negativity; whilst over in England, that astute satirist of Teutonic philosophizing, Thomas Carlyle, noted that the transcendental ego walks 'on the bosom of Nothing', because to 'sit above it all' is necessarily also to dissolve into 'vast void Night'. See J.P. Richter, *Jean Paul: A Reader*, tr. E. Casey (Baltimore, MD: Johns Hopkins University Press, 1992), 197; and see T. Carlyle, *Sartor Resartus* (Oxford: Oxford University Press, 2008), 17–18. *If reason is genetically laced through with nothingness, then what can it do but strive to return to aboriginal and primordial non-being—its filial home?*

11.   This 'Hubble Effect, as they call it, is closer to a cancer than anything else—and about as curable—an actual proliferation of the sub-atomic identity of all matter. It's as if a sequence of displaced but identical images of the same object were being produced by refraction through a prism, but with the element of time replacing the role of light'. J.G. Ballard, *The Crystal World* (New York: Farrar, Straus and Giroux, 1966), 73.

Fig.23. Kant's lost gill-slits.

rationality, is the destruction of time from within: and, of course, inasmuch as the erect backbone has ever served as the marker for this rational influx into the human animal, the vertebral column becomes, for Kant, the epicentre for the parasitization of the host by crystalline eternity, an alien insider. In rushing to vouchsafe the non-natural status of the rational, Kant ends up implying that *hominization is infection*. A diamond-orchid from beyond spacetime, reason is usurpation, uprightness its symptom: the perverse cephalocaudal puppetry of a helpless host body.

It seems however that Kant did not practice the uprightness he so enthusiastically preached: a keen physiognomist, Schopenhauer admired Kant's curved spinal repose, which he hypothesized owed to the encumbrance of an abnormally heavy brain.[12] One cannot help but notice Schopenhauer attempting to emulate drooping Kantian posture in his daguerreotype portraits: head bent forward, skull resting on hand, supporting the weight of genius. He is seen propping up his colossal cranium in his palm, proudly signalling that his grey matter contains an entire *cosmos* of wills and representations. (Just after his death, the first biography published on Schopenhauer's life and character—written by one of the philosopher's close friends—concluded with a chapter simply titled 'His Skull': therein, the proportions of Schopenhauer's voluminous braincase are proudly compared to other 'great men' such as Kant, Schiller, Napoleon and Talleyrand-Périgord.)[13]

Opening the second volume of his master-work, this 'high priest of pessimism' wrote of the immensity of 'endless space' (with its 'countless luminous spheres, round each of which some dozen smaller illuminated ones revolve, hot at the core and covered over with a hard cold crust') before swiftly reminding the reader that 'all this is in the first instance only a *phenomenon of the brain*'.[14] No wonder he had a heavy head.

---

12. Schopenhauer, *Parerga and Paralipomena*, vol. 2, 170–71.

13. W. Gwinner, *Arthur Schopenhauer aus persönlichem Umgang dargestellt* (Leipzig: F.A. Brockhaus, 1862),

14. Schopenhauer, *World as Will and Representation*, vol.2, 3.

Nonetheless, despite his braggadocious admiration for a big brain (his own included), Schopenhauer was arguably the first philosopher to truly develop the consequences of the *telic antagonism* between intelligence and vitality: scouring off Kant's sanguine gloss and extruding the more pessimistic entailments. This, as we shall shortly see, emerges as an *almost inevitable result* of Kantian purism (that is, a certain strain of post-Kantian, German Idealist thinking was bound to veer off in this direction). To assert the non-naturality of the rational is to set up an internecine and intestine conflict between reason and the body it inhabits. Schopenhauer merely develops the Kantian suggestion. That is, for Schopenhauer, self-consciousness is simply malignance: from the perspective of an otherwise blind will it can only be appraised as an accidental pathology. The survival of 'brainless abortions' and evidence for the 'spinal soul' empirically demonstrate this: acephaly proves that intellection is superfluous vis-à-vis organic reproduction and vegetative survival.[15] Apperception and objectivity is a mere 'function of the brain', he claimed, which, along with 'the nerves and spinal cord attached to it', is concordantly

> mere fruit [...] in a fact a parasite, of the rest of the organism, insofar as it is not directly geared to the organism's inner-working.[16]

A most noxious blossom! The invading spinal root and its encephalic 'fruit' are 'implanted into the organism and nourished by it, [without] *directly* contributing [to the] maintenance of the organism's economy', Schopenhauer reasoned.[17] He cites

---

15.   Ibid., vol. 2, 246.

16.   Ibid., vol. 2, 201.

17.   Ibid., vol. 2, 246.

Friedrich Tiedemann as originator of this parasitological theory of neurulation. Another acephologist and phylogenetic cartographer of the spine, Tiedemann had indeed previously proclaimed that 'the nervous system [...] appears to us as a parasite'. The 'human mind'—in its 'immeasurable activity and its most exalted flights of thought'—is merely the *symptom* of an invading cerebrospinal 'parasite': the CNS's simulation of itself and its world is mere tumefaction of purloined energy, siphoned from the organism as an otherwise deafblind respiration-factory.[18] Self-representation and an objective world, Schopenhauer thus stresses, is entirely teleologically distinct from organic reproduction: an 'efflorescence' and a 'luxury'.[19] And not only distinct, but antagonistic vis-à-vis the ends of life.

The implications are clear: Burroughs was right. If the CNS is a parasite, then reality is itself the symptomatology of viral invasion (insofar as, for Schopenhauer, 'reality' simply *is* nervous simulation). Reality-function is infection. Not only delusions, but the entire world of representation—in all its elaborate and contusive variegation—is nothing other than a vast garden of Schüle's 'delusional dream-flowers of the spinal nerve-tree'. And awareness causes suffering, for nervous complexification increases nociceptive lode. It becomes a strictly analgesic matter of disinfection, then, to abolish consciousness—as concentrated in the human cerebrospinal system—and terminate its anhedonic treadmill. What is the therapeutic path? Is there one? How can we remedy a wound the size of existence? Of course, total recall—ecphoric excavation to the point of obsidian and diamantine repose—is the only therapeutic route.

---

18.   F. Tiedemann, *Zeitschrift für Phsyiologie* (Berlin, 1825), vol. 1, 62.

19.   Schopenhauer, *World as Will and Representation*, vol. 2, 243.

When presented with an infection such as a brain, eudemonia and euthanasia converge.

This is why, for Schopenhauer, 'the rest of nature has to expect its salvation from man'. For the arch-pessimist well knew, from his idealist training, that *all* natural existences—all those 'innumerable similar beings that throng, press, and toil'—are, in the final analysis, dream-flowers from the spinal nerve-tree.[20] And if reality and its long procession of suffering is the symptom of invading cerebrospinal virus, then one need only weed out the parasite and return existence to anaesthetic emptiness (*śūnyatā*). As such, quoting Romans 8:22 ('For we know that the whole creation groaneth and travaileth in pain'), Schopenhauer maintained that humanity's cosmic burden and vocational duty is to undertake just this step: by universalizing his ascetic maxim of anti-natalism. Accordingly, he exhorted his readers to join him in his *atheological soteriology of human extinction*, proclaiming that, if his ascetic 'maxim became universal, the human race would die out'. And, precisely due to his idealist axioms, this would entail that the vast and 'boundless' universe—which, again, is only a '*phenomenon of the brain*'—would senesce along with its encephalic root: for, in the foreclosure of human cognition, that 'weaker reflection of it, namely the animal world, would be abolished, just as the half-shades vanish with the full light of day'. Here, Berkeleyan idealism collides with the biogenetic law and universal extinction. The dying-out of human consciousness would trigger a meontic cascade, Schopenhauer implied, swallowing all of this world of will and representation in reverse phyletic order. And, once the animal layers are deleted (perhaps at the level of 'lumbar

20. Ibid., vol. 1, 381; vol. 2, 3.

transfer' between T-12 and L-1), so too would the inorganic domains eventually come under erasure:

> With the complete abolition of knowledge the rest of the world would of itself also vanish into nothing.[21]

Deactivating the human brain, ablating it, would trigger a reverse recapitulation—a devolutionary descent—of the cosmos itself: as the inner space of the human nervous system shuts off, layer by layer, deactivating downward through the spinal levels, so too would each phyletic rung of the outer world serially senesce—until nothing at all is left. Which is precisely why, for Schopenhauer, 'nature'—which is just a gigantic auto-production of nociception—has 'to expect its salvation from man *who is at the same time priest and sacrifice*'.[22] It is the job of the cerebrospinal nervous weed to tear itself from its host, pull itself out down to its coccygeal root, in order to abolish the world and the parasitic infection that it is.

Hartmann, however, took this Kantian-Schopenhauerian trajectory yet further. Recall how Lewis would later portray Hartmann, the catalyst of Germany's nineteenth-century pessimism controversy and architect of *Weltschmerz*, as an ideologue of decerebration for whom '*no brain at all* is required'.[23] Lewis was in fact under-representing the true extremity of Hartmann's views on the matter, however. For, like Schopenhauer, Hartmann also saw the rise of the unconscious spine into the conscious brain as a self-cancelling system, one collapsing under its own nociceptive blossom into conjoint

21. Ibid., vol. 1, 380.

22. Ibid., vol. 1, 380–1.

23. Lewis, *Time and Western Man*, 338.

salvation and suicide—yet Hartmann took this conviction to ever more metaphysically maddening heights. His extensive readings in the neurological literature led him to the fundamental axiom that 'a being is happier the obtuser is its nervous system, because the excess of pain over pleasure is so much less, and the entanglement in the illusion so much greater'.[24] (By 'illusion' Hartmann is here referring to the reality-function and to its intertwinement with what Thomas Metzinger has, in our time, called the 'cognitive scotoma'—or blind spot—that is our inherent bias for valuing existence over non-existence, regardless of the preponderance of suffering involved in this preference.)[25] Hartmann accordingly proposed a *scala doloris*, or terrestrial chain of suffering, correlated with nervous complexification and centralization:

> How much more painful is the life of the finely-feeling horse compared with that of the obtuse pig, or with that of the proverbially happy fish in the water, its nervous system being of a grade so far inferior! As the life of a fish is more enviable than that of a horse, so is the life of an oyster than that of a fish, and life of a plant than

---

24. Ibid., 3:115.

25. 'When one examines the ongoing phenomenology of biological systems on our planet, the varieties of conscious suffering are at least as dominant as, say, the phenomenology of colour vision or the capacity for conscious thought. The ability to consciously see colour appeared only very recently, and the ability to consciously think abstract thoughts of a complex and ordered form arose only with the advent of human beings. Pain, panic, jealousy, despair, and the fear of dying, however, appeared millions of years earlier and in a much greater number of species.' T. Metzinger, *The Ego Tunnel: The Science of the Mind and the Myth of the Self* (New York: Basic Books, 2010), 256; see also T. Metzinger, 'Suffering: The Cognitive Scotoma', in K. Almqvist and A. Haag (eds.), *The Return of Consciousness: A New Science on Old Questions* (Stockholm: Axel and Margaret Ax:son Johnson Foundation), 221–48.

that of an oyster, until finally, on descending beneath the threshold of consciousness, we see individual pain entirely disappear.[26]

Encephalization is a procession of ever more exquisite forms of torment, imprisonment within the petals of ever more extravagant delusional dream-flowers. The history of the evolution of the nervous system is the history of the evolution of nociception and nothing more, the cerebrospinal system just a way for cunning pain—creeping into the insensate clod—to feel itself, to ramify, perpetuate, exaggerate itself. The spine is nothing but the symptomatology of the parasitism called existence. Thus, it is our euthanistic duty to destroy it. In this, Hartmann was, of course, in agreement with Schopenhauer.

However, as one of his American admirers, Edgar Saltus (1855–1921), later recounted in a historical recollection of the consolidation of the Schopenhauer-von-Hartmann 'school' of omnicidal soteriology, Hartmann was himself 'far too dramatic' to suggest 'so tame' a world-historical climax as individualistic asceticism, abstention, and anti-natalism, since, as Saltus relayed, it is not only 'the species' but the very 'principle of existence itself' which 'must be extinguished' and torn out at the root.[27] The only therapeutic path, when faced with the cosmotrauma of the wounded galaxies, is active termination rather than passive renunciation: trauma didn't just begin with us, we are its mere by-product, and thus, in order to treat the wound of existence, we must destroy not only the nervous system but the very principle of productivity that creates it. Only this would usher in the ultimate analgesic, of total extinction, which Saltus calls the 'great quietus'.

---

26. Ibid., 3:76.

27. Saltus, *The Philosophy of Disenchantment*, 202.

It is the base-plan of German Idealism and *Naturphilosophie* to theorise a grand voyage from unconsciousness unto consciousness. The beneficiary of this *Bildungsroman*, its protagonist, is invariably cast as the 'self'. From the conclusion of the journey, personeity is revealed as both end and engine (drive and destination, parent and child) of the entire long-drawn-out process. These are the satisfactions of self-consciousness: to look back, recollectively, and know that it has *made itself*. However, Fichte himself had implied that the protagonist of the logical machinery of this *ur*-idealist drama could be switched out and replaced. Since he acknowledged that the founding principle and actor of one's own philosophy could not be anything apart from personal '*inclination*',[28] selecting selfhood as the endpoint of the entire process can be considered arbitrary.[29] Schellingian *Naturphilosophie*, indeed, had arguably already switched 'personeity' out, replacing it with 'vitality' more broadly construed. Yet, what would a *Naturphilosophie* look like which switched self-reflection for pain-perception as the motor of its colossal telic machinery and, in so doing, therefore acknowledged that the human cerebrospinal system is just the climactic avenue for cosmic trauma to become self-aware of its meandering sufferings? This would be an everted and exacerbated Schellingianism, one that culminates not with the satisfactions of self-consciousness or with the profusions of unbounded vitality, but with the acknowledgement that the human cerebrospinal system is nought but a ticking time bomb.

Luckily enough, two decades before Hartmann arrived at his own pyrotechnic conclusion to the problem of universal

28. Fichte, *Introductions to the Wissenschaftslehre*, 18.

29. Of course, for Fichte, who identified the arbitrariness of pure freedom with personhood itself, this was no real problem.

history (to which we return shortly), an unlikely thinker had already rendered the outlines of just such a nocicentric *Naturphilosophie* and prescribed an explosive therapeutic solution for the problem of generalized cosmotraumatics.

Strangely enough, *Naturphilosophie* and Schellingianism proved extremely influential in Russia during the first half of the nineteenth century. Through the organ of Moscow's Academy of Sciences, Schelling was perhaps more popular there than in his native Germany.[30] But, of course, in this utterly different setting, Schelling's thought inevitably underwent some interesting mutations. It was the eccentric prince Vladimir Odoevskii (1803–1869) who, in 1844, penned a short vignette that includes what can only be described as the **Oldest System-Programme of Cosmotraumatics**. Here he fleshes out the suggestion of a *Naturphilosophie* that sees the weaving-together of nervous systems as a function of cosmic suffering rather than universal spirit.

The vignette, only a few pages long, is a short story entitled 'The Last Suicide'. Odoevskii referred to the piece, in prefatory notes, as a 'truly monstrous creation'. That it most certainly is. It depicts a far future humanity that has reformatted the entire surface of the planet, erasing the biosphere with the technosphere. Urbanization and overpopulation grip the planet, as cities tumefy into one megapolis: 'the fields turned into villages, villages into towns, and towns imperceptibly expanded their limits'. Cities are slow-motion explosions. Urban centres cluster, aggregating into one world-enveloping giga-city, and the world

30.   A. Walikci, *A History of Russian Thought from the Enlightenment to Marxism*, tr. H. Andrews-Rusiecka (Palo Alto, CA: Stanford University Press, 1979), 76; and see also A.M. Kelly, *The Discovery of Chance: The Life and Thought of Alexander Herzen* (Cambridge, MA: Harvard University Press, 2016), 8–87.

comes up against its limits to growth, unleashing ravaging disease and social collapse (thus darkly reinterpreting Kant's intuitions on 'hospitality' and the finitude of global space in his *Perpetual Peace*).[31] World-enclosing telegraphy is cast as a pandemic, neurulating the terrestrial surface in an inorganic film of intertwined bad news and infection vectors. (For the transcontinental connectivities that facilitate *news of plague* also materially enable the *plague as news*.) Here, Odoevskii writes, 'everything was bursting with life, but life was killing itself': it 'appeared as superabundance, more horrible than hunger'. Accordingly, humanity becomes sickly, alienated, suicidal and mad. There emerges a caste of **thanatic philosophers**— an intellectual priest-caste, hierophants of death, midwifes of omnicide, gripped by deadly *schwärmerei*—who have been measuring and chronicling the traumas of earth history since its beginnings:

> Soon there appeared among them men who seemed to have been keeping count of man's suffering from ancient times—and as a result they deduced his entire existence. Their boundless insight grasped the past and pursued Life from the moment of its inception.[32]

An avid reader of Schelling and his peers, Odoevskii here renders a *Naturphilosophie* that cancels 'life' and 'vitality' as protagonists of the world-process, replacing them with colossal suffering. What is a spine and a brain other than a way for trauma to enter into self-relation and to recollect its history?

---

31.   V. Odoevskii, *Russian Nights*, tr. O Koshansky-Olienikov and R.E. Matlaw (Evanston, IL: Northwestern University Press, 1997), 91–7.

32.   Ibid., 94.

Odoevskii's thanatic *Naturphilosophen* have 'measured the suffering of each nerve in man's body, of each feeling in his soul with mathematical precision' and in doing so they have created a transcendental deduction, a genetic cosmogony, an *Erinnerung* of nervous systems and their fruit: pain.

'Their boundless insight grasped the past and pursued Life from the moment of its inception', we learn. These 'prophets of despair' thus produce and promulgate their completed system of nihilative idealism, synthesizing the evolution of the CNS as the self-assembly of suffering:

> They recalled [Life], thief-like, creeping first into the dark clod of earth, and there, between granite and gneiss, destroying one matter by another and slowly developing new, more perfect creations; then she made death of one kind of plant bring about the existence of others; by destroying plants she multiplied animals. With what cunning she made the enjoyment, the very existence of one kind depend on the sufferings of the other![33]

Abiogenesis as insurrection: usurping nervous reflexivity is here seen as parasitically invading placid inorganic repose, puppeteering it into evolution's long drawn-out ruse. This is the *ururtrauma* that Ferenczi later saw at the base of organic existence. And the irritable and 'finely-feeling' vertebrate CNS is, as ever, the crowning blossom of this ongoing disaster. As such, Odoevskii's maddened *Naturphilosophen*

> recalled, finally, how ambitious Life, extending her authority [...], kept increasing the irritability of feelings, constantly adding new ways of suffering to a new perfection in each new being until she

---

33. Ibid., 94.

created a human being, and in his soul she unfolded with all her reckless activity.[34]

This unfolding, of course, culminates in nothing other than our own extreme degree of encephalization. Here, with 'foresight', cruel evolution 'carefully covers' the encephalon and spinal cord in the citadel of the skull and vertebral mast so as to 'keep the instruments of future torture within them intact'. And, at a higher level, so too does this invading neural parasite anaesthetize us with the chicaneries (Metzinger's 'existence biases') that, as Odoevskii avers, protect us from 'seeing all the ugliness' of our existential predicament. Or, as Freud would later expound, 'the guardians of life, too, were originally the myrmidons of death'; life luxuriantly invests in itself, reaching a pinnacle in the centralized nervous system, only as a means to proliferate, prolong, and variegate its dominion of death; so, to live, to be an anticipatory system, to collapse into feedforward control, to become chronoceptive, is merely to prolong and extend the scope and sentence of one's neurulated suffering.[35] Evolution is the engine for pain-optimization. A cerebrospinal system is just way for *suffering to feel itself*.

As the title of 'The Last Suicide' suggests, following the thanatic *Naturphilosophen*'s divulgence of this Completed System of Cosmotraumatics, global eudaimonia slides into global euthanasia and the ultimate therapeutic is unveiled as the denizens of Odoevskii's future world decide to *go out with a bang*. The thanatical doctors pledge themselves to the 'only true and unfailing ally against [cruel existence's] contrivances—to nothingness', and the world welcomes a Last Messiah ('at last he

34.   Ibid., 94.

35.   Freud, *Beyond the Pleasure Principle*, 78.

came, the Messiah of despair!'). Upon his pontifications, the population of earth pronounces an end to the self-elongating farce of the central nervous system. Stockpiling all of civilization's explosives and placing them hemisphere-to-hemisphere, they blow up the entire planet, in order thus to end the traumas of terrestrial neurulation. All the 'efforts of art, all ancient achievements of anger and vengeance, everything that could ever kill man, everything was summoned, and the vaults of the earth crumbled under the light cover of soil; and artificially refined nitrate, sulphur, and carbon filled them from one end of the equator to the other'. Placing dynamite beneath the world's foundations, the rolling revolutions of the *Neuzeit* reach one final crescendo:

> [I]t was the prearranged signal—the next moment fire flashed high, the roar of the disintegrating earth shook the solar system, torn masses of Alps and Chimborazo flew up into the air, groans were heard...then...again...ashes returned to ashes...everything became quiet...[36]

Considering that the whole of terrestrial history can be seen as a slow-motion exothermic explosion—speeding energy dispersal up to fever pitch in the form of techno-industrial civilization—it is suitable that it climaxes in such pyrotechnics. Nociceptive spines are raised tendentiously from the planet only in order to vengefully catapult back down upon it with planet-cracking technical force. The cervical zenith, the upward surge of the orthograde 'solar animal', is a ticking time bomb: for, just as the plant coheres with the sun through its blossom, the brain of the human animal coheres with the sun in its

---

36. Odoevskii, *Russian Nights*, 97.

invention of the fission bomb. Perhaps Oken was correct, then, to propose that *the technical art of war* is the pinnacle of the world-process. As Ballard much later ventured, 'World War III'—where bodies, sand, and weaponry become fused in the white-hot rippling heat of the blast—'represents the final self-destruction and imbalance of an asymmetric world, the last suicidal spasm of the dextrorotatory helix, DNA'; and it should, by now, come as no surprise that the Seer of Shepperton flattened all of this into our psychic longing to 'recapture the perfect symmetry of the blastosphere'—to tear down the bilaterian imbalance inherited by upright balance.[37]

In projecting just such a fusional future, wherein planet-destroying munitions are revealed as the only therapy for the imbalances of the nervous system, Odoevskii's 1844 forecast of civilizational suicide brought to fruition the exhortations of Hartmann's 'practical philosophy', before the German philosopher had even proposed it. Yet Hartmann's full injunction enjoins more than the mere destruction of our particular terran biosphere. The many 'theoretical' volumes outlining Hartmann's cosmogonic philosophy end on a final cadence where, after hundreds of pages of scientific speculation on neuroanatomy and phylogenetics—of the piecing together of self-consciousness from slime to spine—Hartmann transitions to what he calls his 'practical philosophy' for the closing few chapters.

This practical portion, he writes, is the elucidation of cosmic history's *ultimate end*: disclosed to us as 'the goal of all intermediate ends' throughout cosmology's grandiose development from protozoan somnolence, through the sedentary oyster and 'finely-feeling' horse, all the way to simian self-consciousness. This '*end*' is, of course, nothing other than *universal cosmic*

---

37. Ballard, *Atrocity Exhibition*, 9.

annihilation, consummated through humanity's act of voluntary self-extermination. It is what Saltus called the 'great quietus'. The intended aim? To end the atrocity exhibition that is the nervous system, and to do so *once and for all*.

To carry out this duty, however, we cannot rely merely on destroying our own nervous apparatus, as Schopenhauer argued, or even just our biosphere, as Odoevskii had imagined. These therapeutic solutions are parochial in precisely that sense that Kant's moral rigorism was designed to oppose. To become categorial, the injunction must become much more embracing. *We must remove all potential for any other future nervous systems*. Only this would constitute the ultimate therapeutic. A theory of Spinal Catastrophism demands an ethic of soterio-logical therapizing, as Barker well knew.[38] *Priest and suicide*: our solemn task is thus to become the universe's way of killing itself; for we can't just destroy ourselves, it is our duty to destroy everything. This, Hartmann expatiates, is the apotheosis of *all* cosmic striving—'from primitive cell to the origin of man'—and is the pinnacle of '*utmost world-progress*'.[39]

The 'tame' Schopenhauer is here criticized and duly sur-passed: for he 'conceived the problem [only] *in an individual sense*'—thus obviating its *categorical force*. '[W]e must appre-hend it *universally*', Hartmann urges. Indeed, he pictures to himself the Schopenhauerian scenario—of 'mankind [dying] out gradually by sexual continence'—and finds it entirely

---

38.   D.C. Barker, 'The Big Bang as Primal Scene, The CMB as Trauma Map: Psychiatric Implications of the Hubble Effect, the Rostov-Lysenko Syndrome and the LePage *Amplification Synchronoclasmique*', *Bulletin of the Plutonics Committee* 8 (1994): 10460–95; and see also D.C. Barker, 'A Clinical Thera-peutics for Cosmotrauma: What is Exhibited in the Atrocity Exhibition of the Process of Nature?', *Plutonics* 11:6 (1993), 18–40.

39.   Hartmann, *Philosophy of the Unconscious*, vol. 3, 115–20.

lacking, concluding that it would merely 'perpetuate the misery of existence'. 'What would it avail [if] all mankind should die out gradually', he asked? No, this would not do: the 'world-process' or 'Unconscious' would just spit out another humanoid species, another upright ape, to recommence the procession of pain all over again. No, humanity must become the mouthpiece and manifestation of Absolute Negation within history (thus ending history from within, 'coincid[ing] with the temporal end of the world-process, the last day').[40]

We must become ground zero for Infinite Negation's entrance into Finite Time. (Christological connotations are unavoidable: like Odoevskii's Last Messiah, or Schopenhauer's priest-and-sacrifice, we must all become what Jean Paul Richter contemporaneously called the coming 'Dead Christ'.)[41] Our extinction, therefore, cannot be privative: it must be superlative. We cannot go gently into the cosmic night; we must go out with a bang big enough to somehow become self-propagating; it is our solemn duty to enact a negation so superlative that it cannibalizes existence from within. It is our strictly analgesic duty: to remove not only our own nociception, but to remove the potential for any future nervous systems—*anywhere*.

Without providing details as to precisely how this is to be achieved, Hartmann's 'categorical imperative' demands that we therefore destroy the entire universe from within. Only a '*universal* negation of the Will', he insisted, would bring about a world-historical negation so complete as to divide cosmic existence by zero. Ergo, this end-point of the 'world-process' is the 'cosmical-*universal* negation of the will, as the *last moment*,

---

40.   Ibid., vol. 3, 129–32.

41.   Richter, 'Speech of the Dead Christ from the Universe that There is No God', in *Jean Paul: A Reader*, 179–83.

after which there shall be no more volition, activity or time'.[42] From this endpoint, chronogenesis is thus revealed as a self-collapsing deviation from otherwise obsidian repose. It is just the ecphoric recall of its own inexistence. Philosophy, which Hartmann calls 'icy cognition' as 'insensitive as stone', is thus the temporal unfolding of nought, as nought but the self-explication of this end, and it is the end announcing itself through us, as it were. Reason, as Kant had implied in spite of himself, is crystalline eternity leaking backwards into the time-tainted present: such that neurulation, weaving up through the spine's neural arches into the encumbering human brain, is just how history pieces together its own terminus.

It is the duty of a spine to destroy the universe; or, a spine is the universe's method of acknowledging this duty to self-destruct. Hartmann proclaimed that even if humanity—or a terran successor species—proved unfit for the task, then some alien exo-civilization would eventually elsewhere accomplish it.[43] Standing upright, as even Kant had realised back in his 1771 anatomical review of the cosmic curse of orthograde posture, had never coincided with the interests of so-called 'life'. Listening for outer space signals in the 1980s, Barker was evidently musing on the same set of problems. Given our own existence, it was clear that no other exo-civilization had yet accomplished intelligence's grand soteriological task, Barker remarked.[44] Eventually, he would find the silence deafening.

42. Hartmann, *Philosophy of the Unconscious*, vol. 3, 131.

43. Ibid., vol.3, 132.

44. D.C. Barker, 'Observation Selection Effects and The Great Quietus', *Bulletin of the Plutonics Committee* 5 (1991), 66–70.

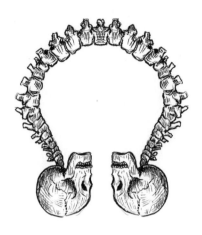

Mind may be at the end of its tether.

H.G. Wells, *Mind at the End of its Tether* (1945)

COCCYGEAL POSTSCRIPTUM

Why are the skies so silent? *Just where is everyone*? Where are the feats of astroengineering, the Dyson spheres, the spacefaring exo-civilizations? This is the astrobiological '*Ubi sunt qui ante nos fuerunt*?' ('Where are those who were before us?'). Do we 'groaneth and travaileth' alone in creation? Such were the ultimate outward-looking questions that led Barker to begin charting the most intimately inward, and to turn from astronomical signaletics to the spine.

A persistent theme throughout our secret history of Spinal Catastrophism has been the dubious relation—and even telic antagonism—between the cerebro-spinal and vegetative-autonomic factions of the complexified organism, CNS and ANS, the former embedded within the latter. Such evolutionary *nesting* of separate functional systems—or adaptive complexification via **endosymbiosis**—has recently been argued to be a plausible 'astrobiological universal' for the evolution of life forms across all exo-biospheres.[1] If we have learnt one thing on our journey, however, it is that such 'nesting' creates an unstable alliance (one that, again and again, invokes connotations of parasitism and nosology). As it happens, it has lately been suggested that such *nested antagonism* may potentially explain the deafening silence of the cosmic skies.

In a paper entitled 'The Intelligence Paradox', a team of nutritional scientists propose that intellection is essentially self-cancelling.[2] Referring to **hormesis**, they claim that continual

1.   S.R. Levin, T.W. Scott, H.S. Cooper, and S.A. West, 'Darwin's Aliens', *International Journal of Astrobiology*, 18:1 (2019), 1–9.

2.   A.V.W. Nunn, G.W. Guy, and J.D. Bell, 'The Intelligence Paradox; will ET Get the Metabolic Syndrome? Lessons From and For Earth', *Nutrition and Metabolism* 11:34 (2014).

environmental stressors are behind the evolution of intelligence: intermittent perturbations provoke the organism—as homeo-dynamic system—to adapt via feedforward and anticipative control, producing ever more resilient responses to the pertur-bating environment. This is connected to Croft's idea of the phylogenesis of **chronognostic range**[3] (see section C4) and therefore to the centralization and encephalization of cerebro-spinal nervous systems across macroevolution. As ever, it is a tremoring and quaking—*Erschütterung*—that forces the self-interested system to assert stability and develop robustness. And this is precisely where we began our Cervical Prospectus: In responding to this environing and aboriginary trauma, pre-cisely by developing increasingly long-range behavioural strat-agems and cunning plots, the organic system tends toward a reformatting of its environment. Intelligence, as the terrestrial pinnacle of this creeping process of incremental chronognos-tic range, then ensconces itself through psychozoic activities, capturing the whole earth system in its intentional energy dis-persal systems, collapsing the 'natural' into the 'artefactual'. Chronotopic escapement into time allows organic function to spill out into space. This, the authors of 'The Intelligence Para-dox' argue, reaches a level of aptitude (a 'tipping point') in technologically mature civilizations when intelligence essentially alleviates the *environmental stressors*—or hormetic pertur-bating factors—that, in the first place, drove its evolution and, moreover, maintain its persistence (in the sense that big brains are energetically expensive and thus their evolutionary persis-tence is not necessarily a given). In our modern lives, we no

---

3.   See Crofts, 'Life, Information, Entropy, and Time: Vehicles for Semantic Inheritance'.

longer experience much hormetic stress: everything we desire (or at least, simulations of it) is readily available.

Intelligence is self-limiting: it erases the very contexts that create and maintain it. The authors link this to the rising pandemic of metabolic illness, mitochondrial dysfunction, diabetes, and obesity throughout the developed world (causative of depression and the denudation of intellect). Generalizing this 'intelligence paradox' across exo-biospheres, they then argue that the absence of SETI detections, the 'great silence' may be explained by the fact that technologically advanced civilizations do not become spacefaring because they follow this preordained path, and invariably become 'too fat for space'. The authors point to the skyrocketing costs of healthcare here on Earth: extrapolating that 'coupled with resource depletion and environmental damage' it 'could potentially lead to increasing internal conflict and societal destabilisation'. 'All of this', they infer, 'would reduce or halt interstellar exploration'. Calculating global healthcare costs for obesity, they claim that we are potentially *already* spending too much on palliation and healthcare to ever afford to go to space. It may well already be too late. The adipose apocalypse has already taken place. In a similar vein, *The Lancet* recently published a report calling 'low back pain'—a complication that, just like obesity, is skyrocketing owing to the sedentary modern lifestyles of developed countries—a 'major global challenge'.[4] The economic and clinical costs of obesity to the US could be nearing an eye-watering $200 billion per annum, whilst the socio-economic burden of back pain upon the US (from lost productivity

---

4.   S. Clark and R. Horton, 'Low Back Pain: A Major Global Challenge', *The Lancet* 391:10137 (2018); and see R. Buchbinder, M. van Tulder, and B. Öberg, 'Low Back Pain: A Call For Action', *The Lancet* 391:10137 (2018).

combined with healthcare bills) has recently received almost identical annual estimates.[5] 'This makes NASA's budget for 2013, at \$17.7 billion [...] look paltry'[6]—by an order of magnitude. Of course, obesity and spinal complications are not unrelated as acutely modern problems.[7] The fate of intelligence is a comic parade of slipped discs and metabolic disasters, not a resplendent march of space colonization. And so, talking of 'entropy's dark laughter', Nunn et al. conclude that it belongs to the nature of intelligent neuro-systems—here and elsewhere—to remove the very hormetic factors that facilitate their existence:

> Throughout evolution the need to adapt has been drive by a stressful environment, suggesting that if intelligence ever evolved to a high enough level, it would alter the environment to remove the stress. This would thus remove the driver for further development of intelligence and adaptability (and hence longevity). However, if it reached a high enough level, it may well also fulfil the original driver for life itself: acceleration of entropy. Thus, it is possible that mankind, or ET, may be reaching a point where the original driver for entropy is still occurring through technology, but the individual driver for intelligence and adaptability has been removed. The universe could be playing a very cruel joke on us.[8]

5.   See C.M. Apovian, 'The Clinical and Economic Consequences of Obesity', *American Journal of Managed Care* 19 (2013), 219–28; and J.N. Katz, 'Lumbar Disc Disorders and Low-Back Pain: Socioeconomic Factors and Consequences', *American Journal of Bone and Joint Surgery* 88:2 (2006), 21–4; and see D.I. Rubin, 'Epidemiology and Risk Factors for Spine Pain', *Neurologic Clinics* 25:2 (2007), 353–71.

6.   Nunn, Guy, and Bell, 'The Intelligence Paradox'.

7.   B. Sheng, et al., 'Associations Between Obesity and Spinal Disease: A Medical Expenditure Panel Study Analysis', *Environmental Research and Public Health* 14(2), 183 (2017).

8.   Ibid.

A chilling image: intelligence—that *poor player*, with all its cunning and ambition—is just a self-obsolescing moment in expenditure's cosmic cataract. It emerges to amplify and intensify universal energy dispersal by creating its own supernormal metabolic utopia, before passing on the energetic baton to less retentive and more expellent systems and thus seceding from existence in the process. This may well be the astrobiological life-cycle of *Geist*: It exists to make us fat and then disappear. In this account, then, the upward surge of the spine is *self-cancelling*. This would be the ultimate revenge of the vegetative system on the nervous system: the stomach gets the last laugh, turning on the spinal cord—rejecting its influx of nociceptive reality-function—by dragging both into a mutual oblivion of metabolic dysfunction brought on by their own collaborative success. We drink too much Pepsi to go to the stars.[9]

Milan Ćirković, in a brilliant turn of phrase, calls this proposed solution to Fermi's Paradox the '**galactic stomach ache**',[10] a cosmic dyspepsia. However, Ćirković points out that (especially in a media-ecosystem including a worldwide web) over-consumption of supernormal stimuli extends over modalities beyond the culinary; he quotes evolutionary psychologist Geoffrey Miller's provocations on the matter:

> We are already disappearing up our own brainstems. Freud's pleasure principle triumphs over the reality principle. We narrow-cast human-interest stories to each other, rather than

9.   See 'Cosmic Dyspepsia and Divine Excrement', *Vast Abrupt*, 2018, <https://vastabrupt.com/2018/01/07/cosmic-dyspepsia-pt1/>.

10.   Ćirković, *Great Silence*, 222–8.

broad-casting messages of universal peace and progress to other star systems.[11]

The spectacle of homo sapiens disappearing up their own brainstems would probably look a lot like Bernal's and Burroughs's humans of the future: spinal-cord-trailing tadpoles. Of course, Leroi-Gourhan and others already worried about our exodus into our own externalizations. Since Alsberg, such '**body-liberation**' was understood as the principle behind intelligence's conquest; the tenebrous implication, however, has always been that, at the extreme, this becomes a tendency *to liberate oneself from existence itself*—whether through obesity or fakery. Jailbreak from life is nothing but an embrace of death. Blumenberg, indeed, had already prophesied a deleteriously decreasing 'reality-contact' in our egress into our ectopic neuronal exoskeleton. Ballard likewise remarked on this diaspora into 'inner space'. An escape up our brainstems: because postnormal technoscience multiplies the artefactual to the point where 'it is almost impossible to distinguish between the "real" and the "false"'. *Reality isn't what it used to be.* We retreat into 'inner space' because we excrete it over the globe. Such an implosive trajectory has, of course, also been proposed as a solution to Fermi's silence:

> The transcension hypothesis proposes that a universal process of evolutionary development guides all sufficiently advanced civilizations into what may be called 'inner space,' a computationally optimal domain of increasingly dense, productive, miniaturized,

---

11. G. Miller, 'Runaway Consumerism Explains the Fermi Paradox', *Edge*, 2006, <https://www.edge.org/response-detail/11475>

and efficient scales of space, time, energy, and matter, and eventually, to a black-hole-like destination.[12]

This seems wildly optimistic, however. Currently, our ability to reformat reality appears not so much to be resulting in a hyperdense kingdom of ends as to be incarcerating us into a limbic loop.[13] For the authors behind the 'Galactic Stomach Ache' hypothesis, as for Geoffrey Miller, inward secession from traction in outward reality doesn't lead to Lilliputian megacomputers[14] or miniaturized 'basement universes',[15] but to the redoubled return of the worst, most catastrophic, inherited aspects of our history-riddled 'mind-with-a-past': a hijack, by superstimuli, of our most base desires and compulsions; dopaminergic return, and lock-in of the most irrational tics and stereotypies.[16] Technology increasingly gives us everything we want and more, but

---

12.   Smart, 'The Transcension Hypothesis', 55.

13.   M. Fisher, 'Practical Eliminativism: Getting Out of the Face, Again', in R. Mackay, L. Pendrell, and J. Trafford (eds.), *Speculative Aesthetics* (Falmouth: Urbanomic, 2014), 90–95.

14.   Pondering on limits to computational efficiency, Seth Lloyd argues that the 'ultimate laptop' would essentially be a miniscule black hole: to an 'outside observer', the 'ultimate laptop looks like a small piece of the Big Bang'. See S. Lloyd, 'Ultimate Physical Limits to Computation', *Nature* 406:6799 (2000): 1047-54.

15.   See E. Farhi and A.H. Guth, 'An Obstacle to Creating a Universe in the Laboratory', *Physics Letters B* 183:2 (1987): 149–55.

16.   'Tinbergen discovered not only that the instinctive action patterns of animals could be activated by artificial stimuli, but that these responses could be heightened to the point where they might lead to reproductive failure—making them potential "evolutionary traps" in which instinctive actions developed during the evolution of a species become detrimental to survival or reproductive success'. See R. Mackay, 'Hyperplastic-Supernormal', in P. Rosenkranz, *Our Product* (Kassel and Cologne: Fridericianum/Koenig, 2017), <http://read-this.wtf/writing/hyperplastic-supernormal/>.

'want' is, by this very same token, increasingly a question of the most salamandrine portions of our nature. Again, future curves into the past (it is more accurate to say that the future is kidnapped by the past). Ballard, indeed, defined 'inner space' precisely as the 'landscape of tomorrow that is a transmuted image of the past'. The brain—a parvenu—cannot quite achieve escape velocity from its libidinous spine. (An old question raised again: will the future of the human race be hostage to limbic terrorism?) Medullary man might have that 'last laugh', after all. Even Bernal's communist space-brains still drag their dinosaur tail. For future-hastening technologies merely facilitate novel possibilities for lapses (mnemoclastic flows and sugar crashes) into the atavistic past and its recidivist compulsions, whether in the form of obesity epidemic or the evolutionary eclipse of intelligence itself, given its potentially self-limiting nature (a paradox unto death).

Suitably enough, Elaine Morgan connected humanity's peculiar propensity to become obese with our standing upright all those millions of years ago.[17] Upright standing has ever been a ticking time bomb. Certainly, the Second World War, which for Bataille was that most luxuriant flare of energetic disbursement, perfectly demonstrated the ability for the speeding future to facilitate recrudescent atavism via unspeakable cruelties: for Velikovsky, indeed, the atomic blasts had dislodged 'lost phylogenetic memories' from their 'sealed haven'. This jolt to our 'ancient engram' is surely only preamble, however. As Ballard prophesied, World War III, that immense synthesis wrought by the most advanced munitions, will merely have been the

---

17.   Morgan links the possibility of obesity to adipose adaptations originally serving for aquatic insulation and buoyancy—forged by the same thalassic forces that pushed us upright. See Morgan, *Scars of Evolution*, 104–23.

expression of our antediluvian longings for lost symmetry. In Reich's eyes, then, the ultimate deluge of release. Our posterity is never more precocious than when we are recollecting our deepest past.

We evolved a vertical spine to look up into the skies, but, given the 'Intelligence Paradox', was the destiny of our historical erection already decided for us, from across the wounded galaxies?[18] Do we steadfastly stand only to answer the call of entropy's dark laughter? Only another giga-annum of genealogy will arbitrate an answer.

∗

Chasing what he called the 'mnemoclastic flow', Barker reportedly complained of the tinnitus ring of the Big Bang: his last archived research reports recount lapses into araneotic madness—warnings of heterotopic hippocampal ossification caused by looking too long at images of LDN-483, a symptom of what he called 'Barnard Object Synchronoclasm' or 'The Hubble Effect'.[19] As Barker seemed to realise retrospectively, moving from outer-space signaletics to spinal tics was scarcely a move at all—'There is a voyage, but a strangely immobile one'.[20]

---

18.   Our uprightness, indeed, may well have come from across the wounded galaxies. One paper claims that our ancestors were forced upright by the detonations of nearby supernovae bombarding the earth, causing lightning storms and wildfires that destroyed our arboreal haven, forcing us out onto the open savannah. It seems that the implications of Spinal Catastrophism are healthy and thriving, it is an idea that has not yet been fully exhausted. See A.L. Melott and B.C. Thomas, 'From Cosmic Explosions to Terrestrial Fires?', *The Journal of Geology* (2019) <https://doi.org/10.1086/703418>.

19.   D.C. Barker, 'Bok Globules and Circadian Disturbances: A Report on MU Geocatalog Item It-277', (c.1993), Call number DCB-MVU-078, Box 6, Folder 18, Miskatonic University Science Archive.

20.   Barker, 'Barker Speaks', 2.

It was all a question of cryptography—which is to say, a question of camouflage—and thus a matter of *listening in the right way*.

Following the path of those prior spinal catastrophists all of whom had, as we have seen, variously insisted that the body is a mnemic archive of deep time, Barker became convinced that all human experience is formed of the epiphenomenal recurrences, repercussions, and recombinations of a ramified cosmic trauma that stretches from the stelliferous all the way to the sagittal. If the universe is one giant memory, then individuality can only be understood as retrograde amnesia. Yet Barker became increasingly convinced that one could *reverse* the amnesia, recollect and revisit the *monuments* of the voyage from nucleosynthesis to accretion to bone to spirit, with the spine as switching station. And, following the footsteps of his Romantic and *Naturphilosophisch* forebears, he undertook a programme of self-experimentations: operating on the infinite threads that tether the human to its cosmos, Barker made his own tattered psyche into the primary *exo-archaeological site*. Yet in doing so he was, of course, only making the entire universe into his analysand.

And somewhere in Borneo, Barker learnt that 'listening in the right way' tended to unravel time itself. He fell headlong down into memory's boundless sea.

As we have seen, the curious line of thought that led Barker to his fate is not exclusive to him; it seems almost to be an intellectual compulsion for philosophers of all stripes. Its historical recurrence is, if not suspicious, at the very least *untimely*. So many different types of thinkers (rationalists and vitalists, psychoanalysts and Marxists, *Naturphilosophen* and anthropologists, penis poets and utopian futurists, libertine theriophiliacs and moral rigorists, Tarzan philosophers and uchronic enlighteners—proponents and practitioners from both day- and night-sides of natural science) have been drawn to this distinctive hypergenealogical motif. Even Kant, in spite of his right-mindedness, couldn't help but read catastrophes into the spine (and, in so doing, made a superlating mess of himself). Whether assiduously rationalist or ardently irrational-ist, it seems that in the wake of modernity (that constitutively unfinished, thus forever 'untimely', process), philosophers can-not but be led to think that hominization—or, whatever it was that happened to us to dredge up notions such as 'persons' and 'subjecthood'—is something *utterly non-natural*.

Beginning with the neuroanatomist-geognost Steno, all the way back in the seventeenth century, modernity slowly discovered that *space is nothing but agglutinated time* and that **depth is memory**. And ever since we realised that the universe is one colossal chronometer—and every object an hourglass—the meaning of 'inside' and 'out' has never been the same, although, admittedly, we are always realising that we didn't quite fully understand this yet. In the collision between absolute Idealism and natural history, recapitulation was forged as an attempt to naturalize the non-nature of the human—by dispersing its exceptionality throughout the totality of phyletic time; but it only further unleashed the sense that there is some-thing cosmically damaged about the upright human. As we have seen, recapitulatory ideas, far more often than achieving the intended goal of smoothing out the relation between intel-ligence and time, tend instead to highlight the ways in which intelligence *interferes with time itself*: rendering everything either 'late' or 'early', speeding along chronopathic vectors, luxuriating in utter heterochronia. Another word for this is modernity, of course, and when it comes to 'the modern' we haven't seen anything yet. But the ancestral spine—and its relation to our regal brain—may well yield portents and clues, providing the crooked key to the *Menschheitsrätsel*, the riddle of the human's complicity with the cosmos that produced it, and offering a roadmap of the highways of history upon which our deepest past intersects with our future—or lack thereof.

*

'Man is the embodied impossibility; he is the animal that lives anyway', or so Blumenberg said—the truth of this statement has yet to be determined. Mind may well be at the end of its bony tether.

ACKNOWLEDGEMENTS

This hideous progeny could not have come into existence without all who have supported or inspired my scrivening. In particular: Amy Ireland, without whom this definitely wouldn't exist; Robin Mackay, pun consultant and hydroplutonic sage; Iain Grant, for recapitulating *naturphilosophisch* monuments, Laurence Kent, for all the geotraumatic arguments; and finally, of course, Barker himself.

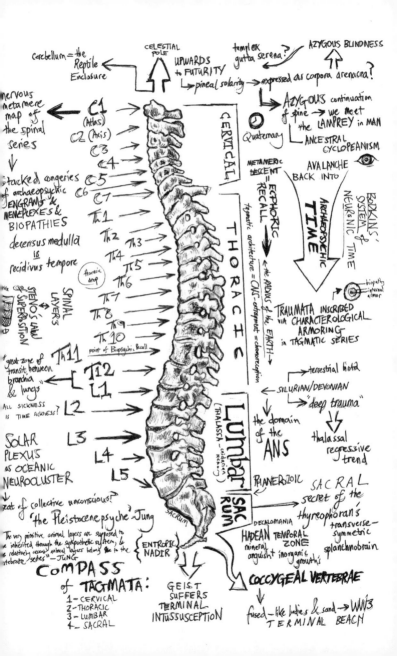

cerebellum = the Reptile Enclosure

CELESTIAL POLE
UPWARDS to FUTURITY
↳ pineal solarity

templex gutta serena?

AZYGOUS BLINDNESS

expressed as corpora arenacea?

nervous metamere map of the spinal series

C1 (Atlas)
C2 (Axis)
C3
C4
C5
C6 C7

CERVICAL

AZYGOUS continuation of spine → we meet the LAMPREY in MAN
↳ ANCESTRAL CYCLOPEANISM

Quaternary

METAMERIC DESCENT = ECPHORIC RECALL
tagmatic architecture = CNS entrapment = chronotropism

AVALANCHE BACK INTO ARCHAEOPSYCHIC TIME

BODKINS' SYSTEM of NEURONIC TIME

stacked congeries of archaeopsychic ENGRAMS & MENEPLEXES & BIOPATHIES

descensus medulla is recidivus tempore

Th1
Th2 Th3
Th4
Th5
Th6
Th7
Th8
Th9
Th10

THORACIC

the radius of the EARTH →

TRAUMATA INSCRIBED via CHARACTEROLOGICAL ARMORING in TAGMATIC SERIES

biopathic internal armor

thoracic drop

SPINAL LAYERS

STENO'S LAW of SUPERPOSITION

Th11
point of Biopsychic Recall

great zone of transit between branchia & lungs

Th12
L1

terrestrial biota

SILURIAN/DEVONIAN

"deep trauma"

ALL SICKNESS IS TIME SICKNESS!

L2

the domain of the ANS

thalassal regressive trend

SOLAR PLEXUS as OCEANIC NEUROCLUSTER

L3
L4
L5

Lumbar (THALASSA·CATANIA·KRAKEN)

PHANEROZOIC

SACRAL secret of the thyreophoran's transverse-symmetric splanchnobrain

seat of collective unconscious?
"the Pleistocene psyche" Jung

SACRUM

DECALOMANIA
HADEAN TEMPORAL ZONE
mineral anguish inorganic growth

The very primitive animal layers are supposed to be inherited through the sympathetic system, & be relatively recessive natural layers belong to in the vertebrate series" — JUNG

ENTROPIC NADIR

COCCYGEAL VERTEBRAE

COMPASS of TAGMATA:
1 - CERVICAL
2 - THORACIC
3 - LUMBAR
4 - SACRAL

GEIST SUFFERS TERMINAL INTUSSUSCEPTION

fused-like bodies & sand → WW3
TERMINAL BEACH

INDEX OF NAMES

T

U

V

W

INDEX OF SUBJECTS

M

N

BIBLIOGRAPHY

Anonymous. 'The Stereotyped Attitudes and Postures of the Insane in Regard to Diagnosis and Prognosis', *The Lancet* 159:4094 (1902), 465–6.

———, 'Does Our DNA Contain Someone Else's Signature?: Barker on Xeno-Engraphy and Xeno-Ecphory', *MVU Science Bulletin* 23 (1992): 50–55.

———, 'William S. Burroughs and J.G. Ballard: An In-Depth Account Drawing on Interviews, Correspondence, and Unpublished Documents' (2012), *Reality Studio*, <https://realitystudio.org/scholarship/william-s-burroughs-and-j-g-ballard/>.

———, 'Cosmic Dyspepsia & Divine Excrement', *Vast Abrupt*, 2018, <https://vastabrupt.com/2018/01/07/cosmic-dyspepsia-pt1/>.

Abbott, Scott. '"Andre Umstände": Erection as Self-Assertion in Kleist's *Die Marquise von O…*', in D. Sevin and C. Zeller (eds.), *Heinrich von Kleist: Style and Concept*. Berlin: Walter de Gruyter, 2013.

Acheropoulos, Aristides. *The New Cosmogony*. London: Black Dwarf Press, 1963.

Ackerman, Sarah.'Exploring Freud's Resistance to the Oceanic Feeling', *Journal of the American Psychoanalytic Association* 65:1 (2017), 9–31.

Ahlborn, Friedrich. 'Untersuchung über das Gehirn der Petromyzonten', *Zeitschrift für wissenschaftliche Zoologie* 39 (1883), 191–294.

Alsberg, Paul. *In Quest of Man: A Biological Approach to the Problem of Man's Place in Nature*. Oxford: Pergamon, 1970.

Alvarez, Luis W., Walter Alvarez, Frank Asaro, and Helen V. Michel. 'Extraterrestrial Cause for the Cretaceous Tertiary Extinction', *Science* 208 (1980), 1095–1108

Alvarez, Walter. *T. Rex and the Crater of Doom*. Princeton, NJ: Princeton University Press, 1997.

Apovian, C.M. 'The Clinical and Economic Consequences of Obesity', *American Journal of Managed Care* 19 (2013), 219–28.

Aristotle. *De Anima*, tr. R.D. Hicks. Cambridge: Cambridge University Press, 1907.

———, *De Anima*, tr, W.S. Hett. Cambridge: Cambridge University Press, 1907.

———, *De Anima*, tr. J.A. Smith. Oxford: Oxford University Press, 1984.

History of Animals, tr. D.M. Balme. Cambridge, MA: Harvard University Press, 1991.

———, *On the Parts of Animals*, tr. J.G. Lennox. Oxford: Oxford University Press, 2003.

Armitage, John. 'The Prospect of Astro-Palaeontology', *Journal of the British Interplanetary Society* 30 (1976), 466–9.

Aschoff, Jürgen. 'Exogenous and Endogenous Components in Circadian Rhythms', *Cold Spring Harbor Symposia on Quantitative Biology* 25 (1960), 11–28.

Baker, Victor R. 'Catastrophism and Uniformitarianism: Logical Roots and Current Relevance in Geology', *Geological Society of London* 143 (1998), 171–82.

Baillie, Mike G.L. *Exodus to Arthur: Catastrophic Encounters with Comets*. London: Batsford, 1999.

Ballard, J.G. 'The Coming of the Unconscious', *New Worlds* 50:164 (1966), 141–6.

———, *The Crystal World*. New York: Farrar, Straus & Giroux, 1966.

———, *The Voices of Time, and Other Stories*. New York: Berkeley, 1966.

———, *The Terminal Beach*. London: Dent, 1984.

———, *The Atrocity Exhibition*. San Francisco: RE/Search, 1990.

———, *Extreme Metaphors: Interviews with J.G. Ballard 1967–2008*, ed. Simon Sellars and Dan O'Hara. London: Harper, 2012.

———, *The Drowned World*. London: Harper, 2012.

Barker, Daniel Charles. 'The Paranoia from Outer-Space: Of Ciphers, Cosmic Camouflage, and Contact', *Journal of Cryptosystems* 2:5 (1986), 55–68.

———, '"*Liberatis tutemet ex infera*"—Genomic Recidivism and its Infernal Potentials', in D.C. Barker (ed.), *New Directions in Cryptocosmology* (Hobb's End, NH: Lewis & Clark, 1989), 96–119.

————, 'Thanatos Praecox: *Ossificans Progressiva* as a Heterochronic Complaint', *Anorganics* 3 (1989): 1–11.

————, 'The Shadow Biosphere as Clandestine Necroevolution', *Plutonics* 9:7 (1990), 52–7.

————, 'Observation Selection Effects and The Great Quietus', *Bulletin of the Plutonics Committee* 5 (1991), 66–70.

————, 'Non-Earth Originating Traumata: The Human Cerebrospinal System as *Musæum Clausum*', *Bulletin of the Plutonics Committee* 6 (1992): 33–39.

————, 'Spinal Catastrophism', *Plutonics* 10:10 (1992), 13–42.

————, 'A Clinical Therapeutics for Cosmotrauma: What is Exhibited in the Atrocity Exhibition of the Process of Nature?', *Plutonics* 11:6 (1993), 18–40.

————, 'Bok Globules and Circadian Disturbances: A Report on MU Geocatalog Item It-277', (c.1993), Call number DCB-MVU-078, Box 6, Folder 18, Miskatonic University Science Archive.

————, 'Notes Towards an Interstellar Nemo-Phenomenology; or, What It's Like to Be a Million-Light-Year-Spanning Super-Void', *Bulletin of the Plutonics Committee* 7 (1993): 11–25.

————, 'The Big Bang as Primal Scene, The CMB as Trauma Map: Psychiatric Implications of the Hubble Effect, the Rostov-Lysenko Syndrome and the LePage *Amplification Synchronoclasmique*', *Bulletin of the Plutonics Committee* 8 (1994): 10460–95;

————, 'Replicator Usurpation as Necroevolution', *Plutonics* 12:1 (1995);

————, 'Teleonomic Sequestration and Subornation Through Anorganic Kleptoplasty', in *Plutonics* 12:5 (1995): 72–99.

————, *What Counts as Human*. Kingsport, MA: Kingsport College Press, 1997.

————, 'Barker Speaks: The CCRU Interview with Professor D.C. Barker', *Abstract Culture* 4. Leamington Spa: CCRU, 1999, 2–9. Reprinted in Ccru, *CCRU: Writings 1997–2003* (Falmouth and Shanghai: Urbanomic/Time Spiral, 2017), 155–62.

Barron, Andrew B., and Colin Klein. 'What Insects Can Tell Us About the Origins of Consciousness', *PNAS* 113:18 (2016), 4900–4908.

Barrow, John D. *Impossibility: The Limits of Science and the Science of Limits.* Oxford: Oxford University Press, 1998.

Barthes, Roland. *Roland Barthes*, tr. R. Howard. New York: Farrar, Straus and Giroux, 1977.

Bataille, Georges. *The Accursed Share: Volume 1*, tr. R. Hurley. New York: Zone Books, 2007.

———, *Visions of Excess: Selected Writings, 1927–1939*, tr. A. Stoekl. Minneapolis: University of Minnesota Press.

Baudrillard, Jean. 'What Are You Doing After the Orgy?', *Art Forum* 22:2 (1983), 42–6.

Beiser, Frederick C. *Weltschmerz: Pessimism in German Philosophy, 1860–1900.* Oxford: Oxford University Press, 2016.

Benjamin, Walter. *The Work of Art in the Age of its Technological Reproducibility and Other Writings on Media*, tr. E. Jephcott, R. Livingstone, H. Eiland. Cambridge, MA: Harvard University Press, 2008.

Bergson, Henri. *Creative Evolution*, tr. A. Mitchell. Lanham, MD: University Press of America, 1983.

Berman, Louis. *The Glands Regulating Personality: A Study of the Glands of Internal Secretion in Relation to the Types of Human Nature.* New York: Macmillan, 1922.

Bernal, J.D. *The World, the Flesh and the Devil: An Enquiry into the Future of the Three Enemies of the Rational Soul.* Indianapolis: Indiana University Press, 1969.

Beuno de Mesquita, Bruce. 'Predicting the Future to Shape the Future', in F. Whelon Waymann et al. (eds.) *Predicting the Future in Science, Economics and Politics* (Northampton, MA: Edward Elgar, 2014).

Blake, William. 'The First Book of Urizen', in *The Complete Poems*, ed. W.H. Stevenson. London: Routledge, 2014.

Bleuler, Eugene. *Naturgeschichte der Seele und Ihres Bewsstwerdens: Eine Elementarpsychologie.* Berlin: Springer Verlag, 1921.

———, *Die Psychoide als Prinzip der organischen Entwicklung.* Berlin: Springer Verlag, 1925..

Bloch, Ernst. *The Principle of Hope*, tr. N. Plaice, S. Plaice and P. Knight. Oxford: Blackwell, 2 vols., 1986.

Bloch, Jan Robert. 'How Can We Understand the Bends in the Upright Gait?', *New German Critique* 45 (1988), 9–39.

Blumenberg, Hans. *Paradigms for a Metaphorology*, tr. R. Savage. Ithaca: Cornell University Press, 2010.

———, *Beschreibung des Menschen*. Berlin: Suhrkamp, 2006.

Bocchi, G., and G. Valdre. 'Physical, Chemical, and Mineralogical Characterization of Carbonate-hydroxyapatite Concretions of the Human Pineal Gland', *Journal of Inorganic Biochemistry* 49:3 (1993), 209–20.

Böhme, Gernot. *Platons theoretische Philosophie*. Stuttgart: Metzler, 2000.

Borghini, Andrea. *A Critical Introduction to the Metaphysics of Modality*. London: Bloomsbury, 2016.

Bosanquet, Bernard. *A Companion to Plato's Republic*. London: Rivington's, 1925.

Bradbury, Robert J. 'Life at the Limits of Physical Laws', *Proceedings of the Society of Photo-Optical Instrumentation Engineers* 4273 (2001), 63–71.

Braid, James. *Neurypnology; or, the Rationale of Nervous Sleep, Considered in Relation with Animal Magnetism*. London, 1843.

Brain, Robert M. 'Protoplasmania: Huxley, Haeckel, and the Vibratory Organism in Late Nineteenth-Century Science and Art', in B. Larson and F. Brauer (eds.), *The Art of Evolution: Darwin, Darwinisms, and Visual Culture*. Hanover, NH: Dartmouth College Press, 2009.

Brandom, Robert. *A Spirit of Trust: A Reading of Hegel's Phenomenology*. Cambridge, MA: Harvard University Press, 2019.

———, '*Reason, Genealogy, and the Hermeneutics of Magnanimity*' (2014), <http://www.pitt.edu/~brandom/downloads/RGHM%20%2012-11-21%20a.docx>.

Bratton, Benjamin. *The Stack: On Software and Sovereignty*. Cambridge, MA: MIT Press, 2016.

Brown, Norman O. *Life Against Death: The Psychoanalytical Meaning of History*. New York: Vintage, 1959.

Browne, Thomas. *Religio Medici*. London: Crooke, 1642.

Buchbinder, R., M. van Tulder, and B. Öberg, 'Low Back Pain: A Call For Action', *The Lancet* 391:10137 (2018).

Budelmann, Bernd Ulrich. 'The Cephalopod Nervous System: What Evolution Has Made of the Molluscan Design', in O. Breidbach and W. Kutsch (eds.), *The Nervous Systems of Invertebrates: An Evolutionary and Comparative Approach* (Birkhäuser Verlag: Switzerland, 1995), 115–38.

Buffon, Georges Louis Leclerc. *Histoire Naturelle, Général et Particuliér.* Paris: Imprimerie Royale, 36 vols., 1749–1788.

———, *The Epochs of Nature,* tr. J. Zalasiewicz, A. Milon, and M. Zalasiewicz. Chicago: University of Chicago Press, 2018.

Buonomano, Dean V., and Anubhuti Goel, 'Temporal Interval Learning in Cortical Cultures is Encoded in Intrinsic Network Dynamics', *Neuron* 91 (2016), 1-8.

Burroughs, William S. 'Civilian Defense', in *The Adding Machine: Selected Essays.* New York: Arcade, 1985.

———, *The Job: Interviews with William S. Burroughs.* London: Penguin, 1989.

———, *The Naked Lunch.* London: Harper, 2010.

———, *The Soft Machine.* London: Harper, 2010.

———, *The Ticket That Exploded.* London: Harper, 2010.

———, *The Revised Boy Scout Manual: An Electronic Revolution.* Columbus, OH: Ohio State University Press, 2018.

Butler, Samuel. *Unconscious Memory.* London: Bogue, 1880.

Byrne, Richard W., and Andrew Whiten. 'Machiavellian Intelligence: Social Expertise and the Evolution of Intellect in Monkeys, Apes, and Humans', *Behavior and Philosophy* 18:1 (1990), 73–5.

Cabrol, Nathalie A. 'Alien Mindscapes—A Perspective on the Search for Extraterrestrial Intelligence', *Astrobiology* 16:9 (2016), 661–76.

Carlyle, Thomas. *Sartor Resartus.* Oxford: Oxford University Press, 2008.

Casanov, Giacomo. *L'Icosameron.* Prague, 1787.

CCRU. 'Cryptolith', in *Writings 1997–2003* (Falmouth and Shanghai: Urbanomic/ Time Spiral, 2017), 149–50.

———, 'Tick Delirium', in *Writings,* 151–3.

———, 'Maximilian Crabbe: Subaquatic Researcher and Entrepreneur (1940–1999?) in *Writings,* 141–3.

S.V. Chebanov. 'Ukhtomsky's Idea of Chronotope as Frame of Anticipation', in Mihai Nadin (ed.), *Anticipation: Learning from the Past—The Russian/Soviet Contributions to the Science of Anticipation* (New York: Springer, 2015), 137–50.

Cherbak, Vladimir I., and Maxim A. Makukov. 'The "Wow! Signal" of the Terrestrial Genetic Code', *Icarus* 224:1 (2013), 228–42.

Ćirković, Milan M. *The Great Silence: The Science and Philosophy of Fermi's Paradox*. Oxford: Oxford University Press, 2018.

———, 'Post-Postbiological Evolution?', *Futures* 99 (2018), 28–35.

———, 'The Reports of Expunction are Grossly Exaggerated: A Reply to Robert Klee', in *International Journal of Astrobiology* 18:1 (2019), 14–17.

Clark, S, and R. Horton. 'Low Back Pain: A Major Global Challenge', *The Lancet* 391:10137 (2018);

Class, Monika. *Coleridge and Kantian Ideas in England, 1796–1817*. London: Bloomsbury, 2012.

Clube, Victor, and Bill Napier. *The Cosmic Serpent: A Catastrophist View of Earth History*. London: Faber, 1982.

———, *The Cosmic Winter*. Oxford: Blackwell, 1990.

Coleridge, Samuel Taylor. *Hints Towards the Formation of a more Comprehensive Theory of Life*, ed. S.B. Watson. London: Churchill, 1848.

———, *Collected Letters of Samuel Taylor Coleridge*, ed. E.L. Griggs. Oxford: Oxford University Press, 6 vols., 1956–71.

———, *The Notebooks*, ed. K. Coburn. London: Routledge, 5 vols., 1957–2002.

———, *Marginalia*, ed. H.J. Jackson & G. Whalley. Princeton, NJ: Princeton University Press, 6 vols., 1980–2001.

———, *Biographia Literaria*, ed. W.J. Bate and J. Engell. Princeton, NJ: Princeton University Press, 2 vols., 1983.

———, *Aids to Reflection*, ed. J.B. Beer. Princeton, NJ: Princeton University Press, 1993.

———, *Shorter Works and Fragments*, ed. H.J. Jackson and J.R.J. Jackson. Princeton, NJ: Princeton University Press, 2 vols., 1995.

BIBLIOGRAPHY

Coomaraswamy, Ananda K. *The Transformation of Nature in Art*. Cambridge, MA: Harvard University Press, 1935.

Cranford, Jerry L. *Astrobiological Neurosystems: Rise and Fall of Intelligent Life Forms in the Universe*. New York: Springer, 2014.

Crick, Francis H.C., and Leslie E. Orgel. 'Directed Panspermia', *Icarus* 19:3 (1973), 341–46.

Croft, Arthur C. 'Biomechanics', in S.M. Foreman and A.C. Croft (eds.), *Whiplash Injuries: The Cervical Acceleration/Deceleration Syndrome*. Philadelphia, PA: Lippincott Williams and Wilkins, 2002.

Crofts, Anthony R. 'Life, Information, Entropy, and Time: Vehicles for Semantic Inheritance', *Complexity* 13:1 (2007), 14–50.

Crow, Tim J. 'Schizophrenia as the Price that Homo Sapiens Pays for Language', *Brain Research Reviews* 31 (2000), 118–29.

Cuvier, Georges. *Fossil Bones and Geological Catastrophes*, tr. M.J.S. Rudwick. Chicago: University of Chicago Press, 1982.

Dana, James D. 'A Review of the Classification of Crustacea', *American Journal of Science and Arts* 22 (1856), 14–29.

———, 'The Classification of Animals Based on the Principle of Cephalization', *American Journal of Science and Arts* 35 (1863), 321–53.

Darwin, Charles. *The Descent of Man, and Selection in Relation to Sex*. London: D. Appleton, 2 vols., 1871.

Darwin, Erasmus. *The Temple of Nature, or The Origin of Society*. London: J. Johnson, 1803.

———, *The Botanic Garden*. London: Routledge, 2 vols., 2017.

Dawkins, Richard, and Jerome R. Krebs. 'Arms Race Between and Within Species', *Proceedings of the Royal Society* 205:1161 (1979), 489–511.

De Chardin, Pierre Teilhard. *The Phenomenon of Man*. London: Collins, 1955.

De Grazia, Alfred (ed.), *The Velikovsky Affair: The Warfare of Science and Scientism*. New York: University Books, 1966.

Deleuze, Gilles, and Félix Guattari. *A Thousand Plateaus*, tr. B. Massumi. London: Continuum, 1987.

Deluc, Jean-André. *An Elementary Treatise on Geology: Determining Fundamental Points in that Science, and Containing an Examination of Some

Modern Geological Systems, and Particularly of the Huttonian Theory of the Earth. London, 1809.

Dendy, Arthur. 'The Pineal Gland', *Science Progress in the Twentieth Century* 2:6 (1907), 284–306.

De Quincey, Thomas. 'Suspiria de Profundis', in R. Morrison (ed.), *Confessions of an English Opium-Eater and Other Writings*, Oxford: Oxford University Press, 2013.

Descartes, René. *Principles of Philosophy*, tr. V.R. Miller and R.P. Mille. Dordrecht: Kluwer, 1991.

Dohe, Carrie B. *Jung's Wandering Archetype: Race and Religion in Analytical Psychology*. London: Routledge, 2016.

Dunér, David. 'Astrocognition: Prolegomena to a Future Cognitive History of Exploration', in U. Landfester, N.-L. Remus, K.-U. Schrogl, and J.-C. Worms (eds.), *Humans in Outer Space—Interdisciplinary Perspectives* (New York: Springer, 2011), 117–40.

Dyson, Freeman. *Origins of Life*. Cambridge: Cambridge University Press, 2004.

Engels, Friedrich. *The Part Played by Labour in the Transition from Ape to Man*, tr. I.L. Andreev. Moscow: Progress, 1985.

Erichsen, John Eric. *On Railway and Other Injuries of the Nervous System*. London, 1866.

Esposito, Joseph L. *Schelling's Idealism and Philosophy of Nature*. Lewisburg, PA: Bucknell University Press, 1977.

Farhi, Edward. and Alan H. Guth. 'An Obstacle to Creating a Universe in the Laboratory', *Physics Letters B* 183:2 (1987): 149–55.

Fedorov, Nikolai. *Philosophy of the Common Task*, tr. M. Minto. London: Honeyglen, 1990.

——, *Sochineniya*. Moscow: Progress, 4 vols., 1995.

Feinberg, Todd E., and Jon M. Mallatt. *The Ancient Origins of Consciousness: How the Brain Created Experience*. Cambridge, MA: MIT Press, 2017.

Ferenczi, Sándor. *Thalassa: A Psychoanalytic Study in Catastrophes in the Development of the Genital Function*, tr. H.A. Bunker. London: Karnac, 1989.

——, *First Contributions to Psychoanalysis*, tr. E. Jones. London: Karnac, 1994.

———, *The Clinical Diary of Sándor Ferenczi*, tr. M. Balint and N.Z. Jackson. Cambridge, MA: Harvard University Press, 1995.

Fichte, Johann Gottlieb. *Introductions to the Wissenschaftslehre and Other Writings (1797–1800)*, tr. D. Breazeale. Indianapolis: Hackett, 1994.

Fisher, Mark. 'Practical Eliminativism: Getting Out of the Face, Again', in R. Mackay, L. Pendrell, and J. Trafford (eds.), *Speculative Aesthetics*. Falmouth: Urbanomic, 2014.

Floridi, Luciano. 'A Plea for Non-Naturalism as Constructionism', *Minds and Machines* 27 (2017), 269–85.

Forel, Auguste H. *The Social World of Ants Compared to that of Man*, tr. C.K. Ogden. London: Putnam, 2 vols., 1928.

Franck, Didier. *Nietzsche and the Shadow of God*. Evanston, IL: Northwestern University Press, 2012.

Freitas, Robert A., Jr. 'The Search for Extraterrestrial Artifacts (SETA)', *Acta Astronautica* 12 (1985), 1027–34.

Freud, Sigmund. 'Über den Ursprung der hinteren Nervenwurzeln im Rückenmark von Ammocoetes', *Sitzungsberichte der kaiserliche Akademie der Wissenschaften* 75 (1877), 15–27.

———, 'Über Spinalganglien und Rückenmark des Petromyzon', *Sitzungsberichte der kaiserliche Akademie der Wissenschaften* 78 (1878), 81–167.

———, 'Die Structur der Elemente des Nervensystems', *Jahrbücher für Psychiatrie und Neurologie* 5 (1884), 221–29.

———, *A Phylogenetic Fantasy: Overview of the Transference Neuroses*, tr. A. Hoffer and P.T. Hoffer. Cambridge, MA: Harvard University Press, 1987.

———, *Beyond the Pleasure Principle*, tr. G.C. Richter. Peterborough, ON: Broadview, 2011.

———, and S. Ferenczi, *The Correspondence of Sigmund Freud and Sándor Ferenczi: 1914–1919*, tr. P.T. Hoffer. Cambridge, MA: Harvard University Press, 3 vols., 1996.

Gallagher, Shaun. *Enactivist Interventions: Rethinking the Mind*. Oxford: Oxford University Press, 2017.

Gallistel, C.R. 'Bell, Magendie, and the Proposals to Restrict the Use of Animals in Neurobehavioral Research', *American Psychologist* 36:4 (1981), 357–60.

Gehlen, Arnold. *Man: His Nature and Place in the World*, tr. C. McMillan and K. Pillemer. New York: Columbia University Press, 1988.

Giddens, Anthony. *Modernity and Self-Identity: Self and Society in the Late Modern Age*. Stanford, CA: Stanford University Press, 1991.

Gilman, Sander. *Stand Up Straight!: A History of Posture*. London: Reaktion, 2018.

Gode-von Aesch, Alexander. *Natural Science in German Romanticism*. New York: Columbia University Press, 1941.

Goethe, Johann Wolfgang von. *Collected Works*, ed. V. Lange et al. Berlin: Suhrkamp, 12 vols., 1988.

Gold, Thomas. *The Deep Hot Biosphere*. New York: Springer, 1999.

Goldstein, Ronnie G. 'The Higher and the Lower in Mental Life: An Essay on J. Hughlings Jackson and Freud', *Journal of the American Psychoanalytic Association* 43:2 (1995), 495–515.

Görres, Joseph. 'Gall's Schädellehre', *Jenaische Allgemeine Literatur* 6 (1805), 50–56.

Gould, Stephen J. *Time's Arrow, Time's Cycle: Myth and Metaphor in the Discovery of Geological Time*. Cambridge, MA: Harvard University Press, 1987.

———, *Wonderful Life*. London: Hutchinson Radius, 1990.

———, *Ontogeny and Phylogeny*. Cambridge, MA: Harvard University Press.

Gramelsberger, Gabriele. 'Introduction', in G. Gramelsberger (ed.), *From Science to Computational Sciences: Studies in the History of Computing and its Influence on Today's Sciences*. Zurich: Diaphanes, 2011.

———, 'From Science to Computational Sciences: A Science History and Philosophy Overview', in Gramelsberger (ed.), *From Science to Computational Sciences*.

Grant, Iain Hamilton. *Philosophies of Nature After Schelling*. London: Continuum, 2006.

———, 'Being and Slime: The Mathematics of Protoplasm in Lorenz Oken's Physiophilosophy', in R. Mackay (ed.), *Collapse vol. IV: Concept Horror*. Falmouth: Urbanomic, 2008. 287–321.

Green, Joseph Henry. *Vital Dynamics; the Hunterian Oration Before the Royal College of Surgeons*. London, 1840.

Greene, John C. *The Death of Adam: Evolution and its Impact on Western Thought*. Iowa City, IA: Iowa State University Press, 1996.

Greenspan, Anna. *Capitalism's Transcendental Time Machine*, PhD Thesis, University of Warwick, 2000.

Gregory of Nyssa. *La creation de l'homme*, tr. J. Laplace. Paris: Cerf, 1944.

Gurzadyan, Vahe G. 'Kolmogorov Complexity, String Information, Panspermia and the Fermi Paradox', *Observatory* 125 (2005), 352–5.

Gwinner, Wilhelm. *Arthur Schopenhauer aus persönlichem Umgang dargestell*. Leipzig: F.A. Brockhaus, 1862.

Haeckel, Ernst. *Generelle Morphologie der Organismen: Allgemeine Grundzüge der organischen Formen-Wissenschaft*. Berlin, 2 vols., 1866.

———, *The Riddle of the Universe*, tr. J. McCade. London: Watts and Co., 1929.

Hall, Marshall. *On the Diseases and Derangements of the Nervous System*. London, 1841.

Halley, Edmond. 'An Account of the Cause of the Change of the Variation of the Magnetical Needle with an Hypothesis of the Structure of the Internal Parts of the Earth', *Philosophical Transactions of the Royal Society* 26 (1692), 563–87.

Halmi, Nicholas. *The Genealogy of the Romantic Symbol*. Oxford: Oxford University Press , 2007.

Hamacher, Werner. 'The Quaking of Presentation', in *Premises: Essays on Philosophy and Literature from Kant to Celan*, tr. P. Fenves. Cambridge, MA: Harvard University Press, 1996.

Hamilton, Paul. *Coleridge and German Philosophy: The Poet in the Land of Logic*. London: Continuum, 2007.

Harrison, E.R. 'The Natural Selection of Universes Containing Intelligent Life', *Quarterly Journal of the Royal Astronomical Society* 36:3 (1995), 193–203.

Hawkins, Thomas. *Memoirs of Ichthyosauri and Plesiosauri; Extinct Monsters of the Ancient Earth, with Twenty-Eight Plates Copied from Specimens in the Author's Collection of Fossil Organic Remains*. London, 1834.

Hegel, Georg Wilhelm Friedrich. *Hegel's Philosophy of Nature*, tr. M.J. Petry. London: George Allen & Unwin, 3 vols., 1970.

———, *Phenomenology of Spirit*, tr. A.V. Miller. Oxford: Oxford University Press, 1977.

———, *Lectures on the History of Philosophy*, tr. E.S. Haldane and F.H. Simson. Lincoln, NE: University of Nebraska Press, 3 vols., 1995.

Hartmann, Eduard von. *Philosophy of the Unconscious*, tr. W.C. Coupland. New York: Routledge, 3 vols., 2000.

Herder, Gottfried. *Outlines of a Philosophy of the History of Man*, tr. T. Churchill. New York: Bergman, 1966.

Hering, Ewald. *Über das Gedächtnis als eine allgemeine Funktion der organisierten Materie.* Leipzig: Engelmann, 1905.

Herschel, William. *The Scientific Papers of Sir William Herschel.* Cambridge: Cambridge University Press, 2 vols., 2013.

Heylighten, Francis. 'Stigmergy as a Universal Coordination Mechanism I: Definition and Components', *Cognitive Systems Research* 38 (2016), 4–13.

Hopwood, Nick. 'The Cult of Amphioxus in German Darwinism; or, Our Gelatinous Ancestors in Naples' Blue and Balmy Bay', *History and Philosophy of the Life Sciences* 36:3 (2015), 371–93.

Hoyle, Fred. *The Intelligent Universe* (London: Michael Joseph, 1983);

———, *The Origin of the Universe and the Origin of Religion.* Kingston, RI: Moyer Bell, 1993.

———, *Home is Where the Wind Blows: Chapters from a Cosmologist's Life.* Sausalito, CA: University Science Books, 1994.

———, and Chandra Wickramasinghe. *Diseases from Space.* New York: Harper and Row, 1980.

Huxley, Julian. *The Uniqueness of Man.* London: Chatto and Windus, 1943.

Ivy, Richard B., and John E. Schlerf. 'Dedicated and Intrinsic Models of Time Perception', *Trends in Cognitive Sciences* 12:7 (2008), 273–80.

Jandial, R., R. Hoshdie, J.D. Waters, and C.L. Limoli. 'Space-Brain: The Negative Effects of Space Exposure On The Central Nervous System', *Surgical Neurology International,* 9:9 (2018).

Johnson, Samuel. *A Dictionary of the English Language.* London, 1766.

Jones, Rhys. '1816 and the Resumption of "Ordinary History"', *Journal of Modern European History* 14:1 (2016), 119–42.

Jörges, Björn, and Joan López-Moliner. 'Gravity as a Strong Prior: Implications for Perception and Action', *Frontiers in Human Neuroscience* 11:203 (2017).

Jouvenel, Bertrand de. *The Art of Conjecture*, tr. N. Lary. New York: Basic Books, 1967.

Jung, Carl Gustav. *Die Erdbedingtheit der Psyche.* Darmstadt: Reichl Verlag, 1927.

———, *The Symbolic Life: Miscellaneous Writings.* London: Routledge, 1977.

———, *Nietzsche's Zarathustra: Notes of the Seminar Given in 1934–1939.* Princeton, NJ: Princeton University Press, 1988.

———, *Introduction to Jungian Psychology: Notes of the Seminar on Analytical Psychology Given in 1925.* Princeton, NJ: Princeton University Press, 1989.

———, *Analytical Psychology: Notes on the 1925 Seminar.* Princeton, NJ: Princeton University Press, 1992.

———, *Dream Analysis: Notes of the Seminar Given in 1928–1930 by C.G. Jung.* London: Routledge, 1995.

Kanas , Nick, and Dietrich Manzey. *Space Psychology and Psychiatry.* New York: Springer, 2004.

Kant, Immanuel. *Prolegomena to Any Future Metaphysics*, tr. J.W. Ellington. Indianapolis: Hackett, 1977.

———, 'Concerning the Ultimate Ground of the Differentiation of Directions in Space', in D. Walford and R. Meerbote (eds., trs.), *Theoretical Philosophy, 1755–1770* (Cambridge: Cambridge University Press, 1992), 361–72.

———, 'What Does It Mean to Orient Oneself in Thinking?', tr. A.W. Wood, in A.W. Wood and G. Di Giovanni (eds.), *Religion and Rational Theology* (Cambridge: Cambridge University Press, 1996).

———, *Critique of the Power of Judgement*, tr. P. Guyer. Cambridge: Cambridge University Press, 2000.

———, *Critique of Pure Reason*, tr. P. Guyer and A.W. Wood. Cambridge: Cambridge University Press, 2007.

————, 'Review of J.G. Herder's Ideas', in *Anthropology, History, and Education*, ed. G. Zöller and R.B. Louden. Cambridge: Cambridge University Press, 2007, 121–42.

————, 'Review of Moscati', in *Anthropology, History, and Education*, ed G. Zöller and R.B. Louden. Cambridge: Cambridge University Press, 2007, 78–81.

————, 'Physical Geography', tr. O. Reinhardt, in E. Watkins (ed.), *Natural Science* (Cambridge: Cambridge University Press, 2012)

————, 'On the Causes of Earthquakes', tr. O. Reinhardt, in E. Watkins (ed.), *Natural Science* (Cambridge: Cambridge University Press, 2012), 1:417–427

————, 'History and Natural Description of the Most Noteworthy Occurrences of the Earthquake that Struck a Large Part of the Earth at the end of the Year 1755', tr. O. Reinhardt, in Watkins (ed.), *Natural Science*, 1:429-61;

————, 'Continued Observations on the Earthquakes that have been Experienced for Some Time', tr. O. Reinhardt, in Watkins (ed.), *Natural Science* 1:463–72.

Kapp, Ernst. *Elements for a Philosophy of Technology*, tr. L.K. Wolfe. Minneapolis: University of Minnesota Press, 2018.

Kardashev, Nikolai. 'On the Inevitability and the Possible Structures of Supercivilizations', in M.D. Papagiannis (ed.), *The Search for Extraterrestrial Life: Recent Developments* (Dordrecht: D. Reidel, 1984), 497–504.

J.N. Katz. 'Lumbar Disc Disorders and Low-Back Pain: Socioeconomic Factors and Consequences', American Journal of Bone and Joint Surgery 88:2 (2006), 21-4.

Kelly, Aileen M. *The Discovery of Chance: The Life and Thought of Alexander Herzen*. Cambridge, MA: Harvard University Press, 2016.

Kirshner, Robert P., A. Oemler, P.L. Schechter, and S.A. Shectman. 'A Million Cubic Megaparsec Void in Boötes', *Astrophysical Journal* 248 (1981), 57–60.

Kitano, Hiroaki. 'Towards a Theory of Biological Robustness', *Molecular Systems Biology* 3:137 (2007).

Klee, Robert. 'Human Expunction', *International Journal of Astrobiology* 16:4 (2017), 379–88.

Korzybski, Alfred S. *Manhood of Humanity.* Boston: E.P. Dutton, 1921.

Koselleck, Reinhart. *Crisis and Critique: Enlightenment and the Pathogenesis of Modern Society.* Cambridge, MA: MIT Press, 1988.

———, *Futures Past: On the Semantics of Historical Time*, tr. K. Tribe. New York: Columbia University Press, 2004.

Kuhn, Thomas. *The Structure of Scientific Revolutions.* Chicago: University of Chicago Press, 1962.

Kurismaa, Andres. 'Perspectives on Time and Anticipation in the Theory of Dominance', in Mihai Nadin (ed.), *Anticipation: Learning from the Past—The Russian/Soviet Contributions to the Science of Anticipation* (New York: Springer, 2015), 37–58.

Lacquaniti, Francesco, Gianfranco Bosco, Silvio Gravano, Iole Indovina, Barbara La Scaleia, Vincenzo Maffei, and Myrka Zago. 'Gravity in the Brain as a Reference for Space and Time Perception', *Multisensory Research* 28:5–6 (2015), 397–426.

Lawrence, D.H. *Kangaroo.* New York: Thomas Seltzer, 1923.

———, *Psychoanalysis and the Unconscious and Fantasia of the Unconscious.* New York: Dover, 2006.

Le Cat, Claude-Nicolas. *Traité des sensations et des passions en général, et des sens en particulier.* Paris, 3 vols., 1767.

Le Conte, Joseph. *Elements of Geology.* New York, 1878.

Leibniz, Gottfried Wilhelm. *Leibniz's Monadology: A New Edition for Students*, tr. N. Rescher. Pittsburgh: University of Pittsburgh Press, 1991.

———, *Protogaea*, tr. C. Cohen and A. Wakefield. Chicago: University of Chicago Press, 2008.

———, *Leibniz's Monadology: A New Translation and Guide*, tr. L. Strickland. Edinburgh: Edinburgh University Press, 2014.

Lem, Stanisław. *Doskonała próżnia.* Warsaw: Czytelnik, 1971.

———, *Imaginary Magnitude*, tr. M.E. Heine. San Diego: Harcourt Brace Jovanovich, 1981.

———, and Etelka de Laczay and Ivan Csicsery-Ronay, 'The Possibilities of Science Fiction', *Science-Fiction Studies* 8 (1981), 54–71.

Lemmens, Pieter. 'The Detached Animal—On the Technical Nature of Being Human', in M. Drenthen, J. Keulartz, and J. Proctor (eds.), *New Visions of Nature*. Berlin: Springer, 2009.

Leroi-Gourhan, André. *Gesture and Speech*, tr. A.B. Berger. Cambridge, MA: MIT Press, 1993.

Leslie, John. *Elements of Natural History, Volume First, Including Mechanics and Hydrostatics*, 2nd edition. Edinburgh, 1829.

Levere, Trevor H. *Poetry Realized in Nature: Samuel Taylor Coleridge and Early Nineteenth-Century Science*. Cambridge: Cambridge University Press, 1981.

Levin, Samuel R., Thomas W. Scott, Helen S. Cooper, and Stuart A. West. 'Darwin's Aliens', *International Journal of Astrobiology*, 18:1 (2019), 1–9.

Levit, George S., Wolfgang E. Krumbein, and Reiner Grübel. 'Space and Time in the Works of Vernadsky', *Environmental Ethics* 22:4 (2000), 377–96.

Lewis, Wyndham. *The Wild Body: A Soldier of Humour, and Other Stories*. New York: Haskell, 1927.

——, *Time and Western Man*. London: Chatto and Windus, 1927.

Lineweaver, Charles H. ''Paleontological Tests: Human-Like Intelligence Is Not a Convergent Feature of Evolution', in J. Seckbach and M. Walsh (eds.), *From Fossils to Astrobiology: Records of Life on Earth and the Search for Extraterrestrial Biosignatures* (New York: Springer, 2009), 355–70.

Lloyd, Seth. 'Ultimate Physical Limits to Computation', *Nature* 406:6799 (2000): 1047-54.

Locke, John. *An Essay Concerning Human Understanding*. London: Thomas Basset, 1690.

Lorenz, Konrad. *Über tierisches und menschliches Verhalten: Aus dem Werdengang der Verhaltenslehre*. Büchergilde Gutenberg: Frankfurt, 1967.

Lovecraft, H.P. *Miscellaneous Writings*. Sauk City, WI: Arkham House, 1995.

Lovejoy, Arthur O. 'The Meaning of Romanticism for the Historian of Ideas', *Journal of the History of Ideas* 2:3 (1941), 257–78.

Lowen, Alexander. *The Language of the Body/Physical Dynamics of Character Structure*. New York: Collier Books, 1958.

Lukács, György. *The Historical Novel*, tr. H. Mitchell and S. Mitchell. Lincoln, NE: University of Nebraska Press, 1983.

Lyotard, Jean-François. *Libidinal Economy*, tr. I.H. Grant. London: Continuum, 2004.

Mackay, Robin. 'Hyperplastic-Supernormal', in P. Rosenkranz, *Our Product*. Kassel and Cologne: Fridericianum/Koenig, 2017.

Mairan, J.D. 'Nouvelles recherches sur la cause générale du chaud en été et du froid en hiver, en tant qu'elle se lie à la chaleur interne et permanente de la terre', *Mémoires Acad. Royale des Sciences* (1765), 143–266.

Malik, Suhail. *ContraContemporary: Modernity's Unknown Future*. Falmouth: Urbanomic, forthcoming 2021.

Mansnerus, Erika. 'Explanatory and Predictive Functions of Simulation Modelling', in G. Gramelsberger (ed.), *From Science to Computational Sciences: Studies in the History of Computing and its Influence on Today's Sciences* (Zurich: Diaphanes, 2011), 177–93.

Mattson, Mark P. 'Hormesis Defined', *Ageing Research Review* 7:1 (2008), 1–7.

Maturana, Hubert R. 'Biology of Cognition', in H.R. Maturana and F.J. Varela, *Autopoiesis and Cognition: The Realization of the Living* (Dordrecht: Reidel, 1980), 26–7.

Margulis, Lynn. *Origin of Eukaryotic Cells*. New Haven, CT: Yale University Press, 1970.

Martin-Ordas, Gema. 'With the Future in Mind: Toward a Comprehensive Understanding of the Evolution Future-Oriented Cognition', in K. Michaelian, S.B. Klein and K.K. Szpunar (eds.), *Seeing the Future: Theoretical Perspectives on Future-Oriented Mental Time Travel* (Oxford: Oxford University Press, 2016), 306–27.

Marx, Karl. *Grundrisse: Foundations of the Critique of Political Economy*, tr. M. Nicolaus. London: Penguin, 1973.

———, and Friedrich Engels, *Marx-Engels-Werke*. Berlin: Dietz Verlag, 45 vols., 1988.

Maudsley, Henry. *Physiology and Pathology of Mind*. New York: Appleton, 1867.

———, *The Physiology of Mind*. New York, 1889.

Mayr, Ernst. *What Evolution Is*. London: Phoenix, 2002.

McGee, Ben W. 'A Call for Proactive Xenoarchaeological Guidelines—Scientific, Policy, and Socio-Political Considerations', *Space Policy* 26:4 (2010), 209–13.

McManners, John. *Death and the Enlightenment: Changing Attitudes to Death Among Christians and Unbelievers in Eighteenth-Century France*. Oxford: Oxford University Press, 1981.

McMenamin, Mark A.S. *The Garden of Ediacara: Discovering the First Complex Life*. New York: Columbia University Press, 1998.

———, *Dynamic Paleontology: Using Quantification and Other Tools to Decipher the History of Life*. New York: Springer, 2016.

McPhee, John. *Basin and Range*. New York: Farrar, Straus and Giroux, 1981.

Meckel, Johann F. *System der vergleichenden Anatomie*. Halle, 1821.

Melott, Adrian L., and Brian C. Thomas. 'From Cosmic Explosions to Terrestrial Fires?', *The Journal of Geology* (2019), <https://doi.org/10.1086/703418>.

Mercier, Louis-Sébastien. *Mon bonnet de nuit*. Paris, 2 vols., 1784.

Metzinger, Thomas. *Being No One: The Self-Model Theory of Subjectivity*. Cambridge, MA: MIT Press, 2003.

———, *The Ego Tunnel: The Science of the Mind and the Myth of the Self*. New York: Basic Books, 2010.

———, 'Suffering: The Cognitive Scotoma', in K. Almqvist and A. Haag (eds.), *The Return of Consciousness: A New Science on Old Questions* (Stockholm: Axel & Margaret Ax:son Johnson Foundation, 2017), 221–48.

Miller, Geoffrey. 'Runaway Consumerism Explains the Fermi Paradox', *Edge*, 2006, <https://www.edge.org/response-detail/11475>.

Morgan, Elaine. *The Descent of Woman*. London: Souvenir Press, 1972.

———, *The Scars of Evolution: What Our Bodies Tell Us About Human Origins*.London: Souvenir Press, 1990.

Morgan, Ted. *Literary Outlaw: The Life and Times of William S. Burroughs*. New York: Avon, 1988.

Moroz, Leonid. 'On the Independent Origins of Complex Brains and Neurons', *Brain, Behavior and Evolution* 74:3 (2009), 177–90.

Morrow, W.C. *The Ape, The Idiot and Other People*. Philadelphia, PA: J.B. Lippincott, 1897.

Moss, Lenny. 'Detachment, Genomics and the Nature of Being Human', in M. Drenthen, J. Keulartz, and J. Proctor (eds.), *New Visions of Nature: Complexity and Authenticity*. New York: Springer, 2008.

Müller-Sievers, Helmut. 'Tidings of the Earth: Towards a History of Romantic *Erdkunde*', in M. Helfer (ed.), *Amsterdamer Beiträge zur neueren Germanistik* 47 (2000), 47–73.

Nakamura, Hiroshi. 'SV40 DNA—A message from ε Eri?', *Acta Astronautica* 13:9 (1986), 573–8.

Negarestani, Reza. 'Globe of Revolution: An Afterthought on Geophilosophical Realism', *Identities* 17 (2011), 25–54.

Neumann, Erich. *The Origins and History of Consciousness*, tr. R.F.C. Hull. Princeton, NJ: Princeton University Press, 1954.

Newton, Isaac. *Opticks*. London: Sam Smith, 1704.

Nicholls, Angus, and M. Liebscher (eds.). *Thinking the Unconscious: Nineteenth-Century German Thought*. Cambridge: Cambridge University Press, 2010.

Nietzsche, Friedrich. *The Use and Abuse of History*, tr. A. Collins. Indianapolis: The Liberal Arts Press, 1957.

———, *Kritische Studienausgabe*, ed. G. Colli and M. Montinari. Berlin: Walter de Gruyter, 15 vols., 1967–77.

———, *Nietzsche Werke*, ed. G. Colli and M. Montinari. Berlin: Walter de Gruyter, 15 vols., 1971.

———, *On the Genealogy of Morality and Other Writings*. Cambridge: Cambridge University Press, 1994.

———, *Human, All Too Human: A Book for Free Spirits*, tr. R.J. Hollingdale. Cambridge: Cambridge University Press, 1996.

———, *Twilight of the Idols, or, How to Philosophize with a Hammer*, tr. R. Polt. Indianapolis: Hackett, 1997.

———, *Beyond Good and Evil: Prelude to a Philosophy of the Future*. Cambridge: Cambridge University Press, 2002.

Nordmann, Alfred. 'Collapse of Distance: Epistemic Strategies of Science and Technoscience', *Danish Yearbook of Philosophy* 41:1 (2006), 7–34.

Novalis. *Schriften*, ed. P. Kluckholm and R. Samuel. Stuttgart: Kohlhammer, 1977.

Nunn, A.V.W., G.W. Guy, and J.D. Bell. 'The Intelligence Paradox; will ET Get the Metabolic Syndrome? Lessons From and For Earth', *Nutrition & Metabolism* 11:34 (2014).

Odoevskii, Vladimir. *Russian Nights*, tr. O Koshansky-Olienikov and R.E. Matlaw. Evanston, IL: Northwestern University Press, 1997.

Oken, Lorenz. *Über das Universum als Fortsetzung des Sinnensystems*.Jena: Friedrich Frommann, 1808.

———, *Lehrbuch der Naturphilosophie*. Jena, 6 vols., 1813–26.

———, *Elements of Physiophilosophy*, tr. A. Tulk. London: Ray Society, 1847.

Osvath, Mathias. 'Astrocognition: A Cognitive Zoology Approach to Potential Universal Principles of Intelligence', in D. Dunér (ed.), *The History and Philosophy of Astrobiology: Perspectives on Extraterrestrial Life and the Human Mind* (Newcastle: Cambridge Scholars, 2013), 49–66.

Ozer, Mark N. 'The British Vivisection Controversy', *Bulletin of the History of Medicine* 40:2 (1966), 158–67.

Pagán, Oné R. *The First Brain: The Neuroscience of Planarians*. Oxford: Oxford University Press, 2014.

Page, Herbert W. *Railway Injuries: With Special Reference to those of the Back and Nervous System*. New York, 1892.

Parent, André. 'Niels Stensen: A 17th Century Scientist with a Modern View of Brain Organization', *Canadian Journal of Neurological Sciences* 40:4 (2013), 482–92.

Parris, Nicholas F., and Keizo Tomonaga. 'A Viral (Arc)hive for Metazoan Memory', *Cell* 172:1 (2018).

Pastuzyn, Elissa D. et al. 'The Neuronal Gene Arc Encodes a Repurposed Retrotransposon Gag Protein that Mediates Intercellular RNA Transfer', *Cell* 172:1 (2018).

Peirce, Charles Sanders. *Collected Papers*. Cambridge, MA: Harvard University Press, 8 vols., 1931.

———, 'Man's Glassy Essence', in *Collected Papers*, vol. 5, 165.

———, 'Design and Chance', in *Writings of Charles S. Peirce: A Chronological Edition*, ed. C.J.W. Kloesel. Indianapolis: Indiana University Press, 4 vols., 1989. vol. 4, 553.

Petetin, Jacques H. *Électricité animale*. Paris, 1808.

Pettman, Dominic. *After the Orgy: Towards a Politics of Exhaustion*. New York: SUNY Press, 2002.

Plant, Sadie. *Zeroes and Ones: Digital Women + The New Technoculture*. London: Fourth Estate, 1998.

Plato. *Dialogues of Plato*, tr. B. Jowett. Oxford: Oxford University Press, 5 vols., 1892.

Playfair, James. *Illustrations of the Huttonian Theory of the Earth*. Cambridge: Cambridge University Press, 2011.

Poli, Roberto. *Introduction to Anticipation Studies*. New York: Springer, 2017.

Raup, David M., and Jack J. Sepopkoski. 'Periodicity of Extinctions in the Geologic Past', in *PNAS* 81:3 (1984), 801–5.

———, *The Nemesis Affair: A Story of the Death of the Dinosaurs and the Ways of Science*. New York: Norton, 1999.

Portmann, Adolf. *Zoologie und das neue Bild des Menschen: Biologische Fragmente zu einer Lehre vom Menschen*. Hamburg: Rowohlt, 1956.

Reich, Wilhelm. *The Function of the Orgasm*, tr. V.R. Carfagno. London: Souvenir, 1983.

———, *Character Analysis*, tr. V.R. Carfagno. London: Souvenir, 1984.

Reil, J.C. 'Fragmente über die Bildung des kleinen Gehirns im Menschen', *Archiv für die Physiologie* 8 (1808), 1:58: 3.

Ribot, Théodule-Armand. *L'Hérédité: Étude psychologique sur ses phénomènes, ses lois, ses causes*. Paris, 1873.

———, *Diseases of Memory: An Essay in the Positive Psychology*, tr. W.H. Smith. New York: Appleton, 1882.

Richards, Robert J. *The Romantic Conception of Life: Science and Philosophy in the Age of Goethe*. Chicago: University of Chicago Press, 2004,

Rhodes, Chris J. 'Solar Energy: Principles and Possibilities', *Science Progress* 93 (2010), 37–112.

Richter, Jean Paul. *Jean Paul: A Reader*, tr. E. Casey. Baltimore, MD: Johns Hopkins University Press, 1992.

Riebli, Nadia, and Heinrich Reichert. 'The First Nervous System', in S.V. Shepherd (ed.), *The Wiley Handbook of Evolutionary Neuroscience* (Oxford: Blackwell, 2017), 125–52.

Roazen, Paul. *The Trauma of Freud: Controversies in Psychoanalysis*. Piscataway, NJ: Transaction, 2002.

Rolfe, W.D. Ian. 'William and John Hunter: Breaking the Great Chain of Being', in W.F. Bynum and Roy Porter (eds.), *William Hunter and the Eighteenth-Century Medical World* (Cambridge: Cambridge University Press, 1985), 297–320.

Rosen, Robert. *Anticipatory Systems: Philosophical, Mathematical, and Methodological Foundations*. New York: Springer, 2012.

Rossi, Paolo. *The Dark Abyss of Time: The History of the Earth and the History of Nations from Hooke to Vico,* tr. L.G. Cochrane. Chicago: University of Chicago Press, 1987.

Roth, Gerhard, and Ursula Dicke. 'Evolution of Nervous Systems and Brains', in C.G. Galizia and P.-M. Lledo (eds.), *Neurosciences: From Molecule to Behavior* (New York: Springer, 2013), 41.

Rubin, D.I. 'Epidemiology and Risk Factors for Spine Pain', *Neurologic Clinics* 25:2 (2007), 353–71.

Rudwick, Martin J.S. *Bursting The Limits of Time: The Reconstruction of Geohistory in the Age of Revolution*. Chicago: University of Chicago Press , 2005.

———, *Worlds Before Adam: The Reconstruction of Geohistory in the Age of Reform*. Chicago: University of Chicago Press, 2008.

———, *Georges Cuvier, Fossil Bones, and Geological Catastrophes: New Translations and Interpretations of the Primary Texts*. Chicago: University of Chicago Press, 2008.

———, *Earth's Deep History: How it was Discovered and Why it Matters*. Chicago: University of Chicago Press, 2014.

Russell, Edward Stuart. *Form and Function: A Contribution to the History of Animal Morphology*. London: John Murray, 1916.

Saltus, Edgar Everstson.*The Philosophy of Disenchantment*. New York: Houghton, Mifflin and Company, 1885.

Sandberg, Anders. 'The Physics of Information Processing Superobjects: Daily Life Among the Jupiter Brains', *Journal of Evolution and Technology* 5:1 (1999).

Santos, Filipe Duarte. *Humans on Earth: From Origins to Possible Futures*. New York: Springer, 2012.

Sarnat, Harvey B., and Martin G. Netsky. 'The Brain of the Planarian as the Ancestor of the Human Brain', *Canadian Journal of Neurological Sciences* 12:4 (1985), 296–302.

Scheler, Max. *Die Stellung des Menschen im Kosmos*. Darmstadt: Reichl Verlag, 1928.

Schelling, Friedrich Wilhelm Joseph. *Sämtliche Werke*, ed. K.F.A. Schelling. Stuttgart and Augsburg: J.G. Cotta, 14 vols., 1856–61.

System of Transcendental Idealism, tr. P. Heath.Charlottesville, VI: University Press of Virginia, 1997.

——, *The Ages of the World*, tr. J.M. Wirth. Albany, NY: SUNY Press, 2000.

——, *First Outline of a System of the Philosophy of Nature*, tr. K.R. Peterson. New York: SUNY Press, 2004.

——, *Philosophical Inquiries into the Essence of Human Freedom*, tr. J. Love and J. Schmidt. Albany, NY: SUNY Press 2006.

——, *Historical-critical Introduction to the Philosophy of Mythology*, tr. M. Richey and M. Zieelsberger. Albany, NY: SUNY Press, 2007.

——, *The Philosophical Rupture between Fichte and Schelling*, tr. M.G. Vater and D.W. Wood. Albany, NY: SUNY Press, 2012.

Schopenhauer, Arthur. *The World as Will and Representation*, tr. E.F.J. Payne. New York: Dover, 2 vols., 1969.

——, *Parerga and Paralipomena: Short Philosophical Essays*, tr. E.F.J. Payne. Oxford: Oxford University Press, 2 vols., 1974.

Schuer, Ronald. *The Mind-Made Universe: Laws vs Rules*. New York: Henry Schuman, 1969.

Schüle, Heinrich. *Handbuch der Geisteskrankheiten*. Leipzig: Vogel, 1880.

——, 'Zur Katatonie-Frage: Eine klinische Studie', *Allgemeine Zeitschrift für Psychiatrie und Psychisch-gerichtliche Medizin* 54 (1898), 515–25.

Schacter, Daniel L. *Forgotten Ideas, Neglected Pioneers: Richard Semon and the Story of Memory.* London: Routledge, 2011.

Schulze-Makuch, Dirk, and William Bains. *The Cosmic Zoo: Complex Life on Many Worlds.* New York: Springer, 2017.

Sellars, Simon. *Applied Ballardianism: Memoir from a Parallel Universe.* Falmouth: Urbanomic, 2018.

Semon, Richard. *Die Mneme als erhaltendes Prinzip im Wechsel des organischen Geschehens.* Leipzig: Engelmann, 1904.

———, *Die mnemischen Empfindungen in ihren Beziehungen zu den Originalempfindungen.* Leipzig: Engelmann, 1909.

———, *Mnemic Psychology,* tr. B Duffy. New York: Allen and Unwin, 1923.

Serdyuk, Valentyn. *Scoliosis and Spinal Pain Syndrome: New Understanding of their Origin.* Delhi: Byword Books, 2014.

Shakespeare, William. *Julius Caesar,* ed. D. Daniell. London: Bloomsbury, 1998.

Shamdasani, Sonu. *Jung and the Making of Modern Psychology: The Dream of a Science.* Cambridge: Cambridge University Press, 2003.

Sheng, B., et al. 'Associations Between Obesity and Spinal Disease: A Medical Expenditure Panel Study Analysis', *Environmental Research and Public Health* 14(2):183 (2017).

Simonov, Pavel V. *The Motivated Brain: A Neurophysiological Analysis of Human Behaviour,* tr. L. Payne. New York: Gordon and Breach, 1991.

Singer, Peter. 'Are Insects Conscious?' (2016), <https://www.project-syndicate.org/commentary/are-insects-conscious-by-peter-singer-2016-05>.

Skorupski, Peter, and Lars Chittka. 'Animal Cognition: An Insect's Sense of Time?', *Current Biology* 16:19 (2006), 851–3.

Smart, John M. 'The Transcension Hypothesis: Sufficiently Advanced Civilizations Invariably Leave our Universe, and Implications for METI and SETI', *Acta Astronautica* 78 (2012): 55–68.

Snow, Dale E. *Schelling and the End of Idealism.* Albany, NY: SUNY Press, 1996.

Snowden, Edward. 'Edward Snowden: We May Never Spot Space Aliens Thanks to Encryption', *The Guardian* (2015), <https://www.theguardian.com/us-news/2015/sep/19/edward-snowden-aliens-encryption-neil-degrasse-tyson-podcast>.

Sponge, Robert. 'Bikini Atoll Test Detonations Caused Longing to Return to Cnidarian Modes: Case Studies and Reports Lately Uncovered', *American Journal of Military Psychiatrics* 15:5 (1977), 44–70.

Sprankling, John G. 'Owning the Centre of the Earth', *UCLA Law Review* 55 (2008), 979–1040.

Starobinski, Jean. *Action and Reaction*, tr. S. Hawkes and J. Fort. New York: Zone Books, 1999.

Steele, Edward J., et al. 'Cause of Cambrian Explosion—Terrestrial or Cosmic?' *Progress in Biophysics and Molecular Biology* 136 (2018), 3–23.

Steffens, Heinrich. *Beyträge zur inner Naturgeschichte*. Freiberg, 1801.

Steno, Nicolas. *Discours de Monsieur Sténon sur l'anatomie du cerveau*. Paris, 1669.

———, *The Prodromus of Nicolaus Steno's Dissertation concerning a Solid Body Enclosed by Proceess of Nature within a Solid*. London: Macmillan, 1915.

Straus, Erwin. 'The Upright Posture', *Psychiatric Quarterly* 26:1 (1952), 529–61.

Strick, James E. *Wilhelm Reich, Biologist*. Cambridge, MA: Harvard University Press, 2015.

Suddendorf, Thomas, and Michael C. Corballis. 'The Evolution of Foresight: What is Mental Time Travel, and is it Unique to Humans?', *Behavioural and Brain Sciences* 30:3 (2007), 313–51.

Sulloway, Frank. *Freud, Biologist of the Mind*. Cambridge, MA: Harvard University Press, 1979.

Swanson, Link R. 'The Predictive Processing Paradigm Has Roots in Kant', *Frontiers in Systems Neuroscience* 10:79 (2016).

Swift, Jonathan. *Poetical Works*. Oxford: Oxford University Press, 1967.

Testa, Alfred. *From the Einsteinian to the Testan Universe*. Oxford: Oxford University Press, 1970.

Theweleit, Klaus. *Male Fantasies: Women, Floods, Bodies, History*, tr. C. Turner, C. Erica, and S. Conway. Minneapolis: University of Minnesota Press, 1985.

———, *Male Fantasies: Psychoanalyzing the White Terror*, tr. C. Turner, C. Erica, and S. Conway. Minneapolis: University of Minnesota Press, 1987.

Thoenes, Sven, and Daniel Oberfeld. 'Meta-analysis of Time Perception and
    Temporal Processing in Schizophrenia: Differential Effects on Precision and
    Accuracy', *Clinical Psychology Review* 54:44 (2017).

Thom, René. *Structural Stability and Morphogenesis*. Cambridge, MA: Perseus, 1989.

Tiedemann, Friedrich. *Physiologie des Menschen*, tr. J.M. Gully and J. Hunter.
    London, 1834.

———, *Zeitschrift für Phsyiologie*. Berlin, 1825.

Triarhou, Lazaros C. 'Exploring the Mind with a Microscope: Freud's Beginnings
    in Neurobiology', *Hellenic Journal of Psychology* 6 (2009), 1–13.

Tuomi, Ikka. 'Chronotopes of Foresight: Models of Time-Space in Probabilistic, Pos-
    sibilistic and Constructivist Futures', *Futures and Foresight Science* 1:1 (2019), 2.

Tulving, Endel. 'Chronothesia: Conscious Awareness of Subjective Time', in D.T.
    Stuss and R.T. Knight (eds.), *Principles of Frontal Lobe Function* (Oxford:
    Oxford University Press, 2002), 311–25.

Ueda, N, K. Maruo, and T. Sumiyoshi. 'Positive Symptoms and Time Perception
    in Schizophrenia: A Meta-analysis', *Schizophrenia Research: Cognition*
    13 (2018), 3-6.

Van Cleave, James, and Robert E. Frederick (eds.). *The Philosophy of Right
    and Left: Incongruent Counterparts and the Nature of Space*. New
    York: Springer, 1991.

Van den Biggelaar, J.A.M., Eric Edsinger, and F.R. Schram. 'The Improbability
    of Dorso-Ventral Axis Inversion During Animal Evolution as Presumed by
    Geoffrey Saint Hilaire', *Contributions to Zoology* 71 (2002), 29–36.

Virchow, Rudolf. *Über das Rückenmark*. Berlin, 1871.

Von Branca, Wilhelm. 'Die Riesengrosse sauropoder Dinosaurier vom Tendagnru,
    ihr Aussterben und die Bedingungen ihrer Entstehung', *Archiv für Bion-
    tologie* 3:1 (1914), 71–78.

Von Ditfurth, Hoimar. D*er Geist fiel nicht vom Himmel*. Hamburg: Hoffmann, 1976.

Von Hohenheim, Gottfried. *Cosmogonic Neurosystems: From the Spine to the
    Stars and Back Again*. New York: Jacob and Strauss, 1975.

Von Schubert, Gotthilf Heinrich. *Ansichten von der Nachtseite der Naturwis-
    senschaft*. Dresden: Arnold, 1808.

Velikovsky, Immanuel. 'Über die Energetik der Psyche und die physikalische Existenz der Gedankenwelt—Ein Beitrag zur Psychologie des gesunden und somnambulen Zustandes', *Zeitschrift für die gesamte Neurologie und Psychiatrie* 133 (1931), 422–37.

———, *Worlds in Collision*. New York: Doubleday, 1950.

———, *Mankind in Amnesia*. New York: Doubleday, 1982.

Vernadskii, Vladimir. 'The Biosphere and the Noösphere', *American Scientist* 33:1 (1945), 1–13.

Walikci, Andrzej. *A History of Russian Thought from the Enlightenment to Marxism*, tr. H. Andrews-Rusiecka. Palo Alto, CA: Stanford University Press, 1979.

Warshofsky, Fred. *Doomsday: The Science of Catastrophe*. New York: Reader's Digest, 1977.

Wells, H.G. *Mind at the End of its Tether*. London: Windmill Press, 1945.

Weydenthal, B. *The World as Game and Conspiracy*, tr. H. Stymington. Chicago: University of Chicago Press, 1970.

Whistler, Daniel. *Schelling's Theory of Symbolic Language: Forming the System of Identity*. Oxford: Oxford University Press, 2013.

Wickens, Andrew P. *A History of the Brain: From Stone Age Surgery to Modern Neuroscience*. London: Taylor and Francis, 2015.

Wiener, Norbert. *Cybernetics: Or Control and Communication in the Animal and the Machine*. Cambridge, MA: MIT Press, 1965.

Wilmot, John. 'A Satyre Against Reason and Mankind', in *John Wilmot, Earl of Rochester: The Poems and Lucina's Rape*. Oxford: Blackwell, 2013.

Winchester, Simon. *Krakatoa: The Day the World Exploded, August 27, 1883*. New York: Harper Collins, 2003.

Yokoo, Hiromitsu, and Tairo Oshima. 'Is Bacteriophage φX174 DNA a Message From an Extraterrestrial Intelligence?', *Icarus* 38:1 (1979), 148–53.

Young, George M. *The Russian Cosmists: The Esoteric Futurism of Nikolai Fedorov and his Followers*. Oxford: Oxford University Press, 2012.

Zorgani, Ali, et al. 'Brain Palpation from Physiological Vibrations using MRI', in *PNAS* 112:42 (2015), 12917–21.